A

SHORT HISTORICAL

ENGLISH GRAMMAR

A

SHORT HISTORICAL
ENGLISH GRAMMAR

BY

HENRY SWEET

GYAN

Published by:

Gyan Publishing House
5, Ansari Road
Daryaganj, New Delhi-110002
Phone: 011-47034999, 9811692060
E-mail: books@gyanbooks.com

Distribution Network
gyanbooks.com
India, USA, Canada, UK, Australia

ISBN: 978-93-6433-337-5 (PB)
First Published, 1892

2nd Impression 2024

Printed at: Gyan Press, Delhi.

A SHORT HISTORICAL ENGLISH GRAMMAR
Author: HENRY SWEET

A

SHORT HISTORICAL ENGLISH GRAMMAR

SWEET

Clarendon Press Series

A SHORT HISTORICAL ENGLISH GRAMMAR

BY

HENRY SWEET, M.A., PH.D., LL.D.

Formerly President of the Philological Society
Editor of 'The Oldest English Texts,' Alfred's 'Cura Pastoralis' and 'Orosius'
Author of 'An Anglo-Saxon Reader'
'A First' and 'A Second Middle-English Primer'
'A Primer of Spoken English,' 'A History of English Sounds'
'A New English Grammar'
'A Primer of Phonetics,' 'Shelley's Nature-Poetry,' etc.

Oxford

AT THE CLARENDON PRESS

1892

PREFACE

For some years the want has been felt of a short historical English grammar up to date, especially as regards phonology, dialectology and chronology, the last implying careful discrimination between what is really in living use and what is obsolete. The present work is an attempt to supply this want. It is an abridgment of the historical portions of my *New English Grammar*. It does not include syntax, for the good reason that a grammar which attempted to deal—even if only superficially—with such a vast and difficult subject as historical English syntax could not possibly be designated as a 'short' grammar. But within the limits of phonology and accidence, including composition and derivation, it will, I hope, be found to contain all that is really essential to the beginner.

Some teachers will be disappointed at not finding here any exposition of that time-honoured generalization 'Grimm's Law,' and the still more popular 'Verner's Law.' I have for the present excluded them, because they do not belong to historical English grammar, but to comparative Arian philology; because, if studied adequately, they are too difficult for beginners; and because, without a detailed knowledge of

Sanskrit, &c., they are of little use for etymological purposes. But although most of those who have kept pace with the recent developments of Comparative Philology admit all this, some of them still plead for the retention of Grimm's Law on the ground of its being so interesting, and having such a stimulating effect on pupils. The answer to this is, By all means teach it then, but teach it as an extra, not as a part of English grammar, any more than you would include French, Latin, and Greek etymology in English grammar; although, of course, English grammar undoubtedly leads up to all these subjects, and is more or less directly connected with them, in the same way as it is connected with the political, social, and literary history of England.

The study of this grammar requires no preparation except a knowledge of the ordinary grammatical terms. It does not even postulate any practical knowledge of Old English, although I should advise every teacher of historical English grammar to let his pupils go through a preparatory course in Old English with the help of such a book as my *Anglo-Saxon Primer*.

Additional grammatical details and illustrations that may be required will easily be found in *The New English Grammar* and my *History of English Sounds*, in which latter will be found a concise statement not only of Grimm's and Verner's laws but also of all the other sound-laws by which English is connected with the older Arian languages.

HENRY SWEET.

SOUTH PARK, REIGATE,
7 *Sept.*, 1892.

CONTENTS

ACCIDENCE.

SHORT HISTORICAL ENGLISH GRAMMAR.

HISTORY OF ENGLISH.

Periods.

1. The name 'English language' in its widest sense comprehends the language of the English people from their first settlement in Britain to the present time. For the sake of convenience we distinguish three main stages in the history of the language, namely **Old English** (OE), **Middle English** (ME), and **Modern English** (MnE). OE may be defined as the period of *full* endings (*mōna, sunne, sunu, stānas*), ME as the period of *levelled* endings (*mōne, sunne, sune, stǭnes*), MnE as the period of *lost* endings (*moon, sun, son, stones* = stounz). We further distinguish periods of transition between these main stages, each of which latter is further divided into an **early** and a **late** period. The dates of these periods are, roughly, as follows :—

Early Old English (E. of Alfred)	700–900
Late Old English (E. of Ælfric)	900–1100
Transition Old English (E. of Layamon) . .	1100–1200
Early Middle English (E. of the Ancren Riwle) .	1200–1300
Late Middle English (E. of Chaucer) . . .	1300–1400
Transition Middle English (Caxton E.) . .	1400–1500
Early Modern English (Tudor E.; E. of Shakespere)	1500–1650
Late Modern English	1650–

to which may be added **Present English**, by which we understand the English of the present time as spoken, written, and understood by educated people, that is, roughly speaking, 19th-century English.

Cognate Languages.

2. English belongs to the **Arian** family of languages, descended from a hypothetical Parent Arian language, the chief of which are given in the following table, different periods of their development being separated by dashes:—

(A) **East-Arian**, or Asiatic:

(*a*) Sanskrit, the sacred language of India—Pali—Bengali and the other **Gaurian** languages of India.

(*b*) **Iranian** languages: Zend or Old Bactrian. Old Persian, which is the language of the Cuneiform inscriptions —Modern Persian.

(*c*) Armenian, which is really half-way between East- and West-Arian.

(B) **West-Arian** or European:

(*d*) Greek—Romaic or Modern Greek.

(*e*) Latin—the **Romance** languages: Italian, Provençal, French (Old French, Modern French), Spanish, Portuguese, Roumanian.

(*f*) **Celtic** languages. Gaulish. The **Goidelic** group: Irish, Manx, Gaelic. The **Cymric** group: Welsh, Cornish, Breton (introduced from Britain).

(*g*) **Slavonic** languages. Old Bulgarian — Russian, Polish, Bohemian, Servian, Bulgarian.

(*h*) **Baltic** languages. Lithuanian, Lettish.

(*i*) **Germanic** languages.

3. The Germanic group, to which English belongs, consists of the following languages:—

(A) **East-Germanic**:

(*a*) Gothic.

(*b*) **Scandinavian** languages. **West**-Scandinavian group: Norwegian, Icelandic. **East**-Scandinavian group: Danish, Swedish.

(B) **West-Germanic**:

(*c*) **Low German** languages. Old Saxon—Dutch, Flemish. **Anglo-Frisian** group: English, Frisian.

(*d*) High German, or German.

4. English is then a member of the Anglo-Frisian group of the Low German languages.

Old English.

5. In the fifth century—or perhaps earlier—Britain was partially conquered by a variety of Germanic tribes from the other side of the German Ocean, the chief of which were

(*a*) **Saxons**, from the country between the Elbe and the Rhine.

(*b*) **Angles**, from the district still called Angeln in the South of Schleswig.

(*c*) **Jutes**, from the North of Schleswig.

6. The first settlement is said to have been that of the Jutes, who took Kent and the Isle of Wight.

7. The Saxons occupied the country south of the Thames; except Cornwall, where the Britons still kept their nationality. Some of the Saxons settled in Sussex; some north of the Thames in Middlesex and Essex; the remaining portion of the tribe being called 'West-Saxons,' whence their state is called 'Wessex.'

8. The rest of England was occupied by the Angles. Suffolk and Norfolk were included under the name of

'East-Anglia.' Another tribe of Anglians occupied what are now the Midland Counties, between the Thames and the Humber. These were called **Mercians**, and their country is called 'Mercia.' The country north of the Humber was occupied by a variety of Anglian tribes included under the name of **Northumbrians.** Ancient Northumbria extended up to the Firth of Forth, and thus included the greater part of what is now the Lowlands of Scotland.

9. All these tribes spoke the same language with slight differences of dialect. These differences increased by degrees, so that already in the 8th century we can distinguish four main dialects: **Northumbrian** and **Mercian**, which together constitute the **Anglian** group; and **West-Saxon** and **Kentish**, which together constitute the **Southern** group.

10. All these tribes agreed in calling their common language **English**, that is, 'Anglish,' because the Angles were for a long time the dominant tribe. The supremacy afterwards passed to the West-Saxons, and their capital, Winchester, became the capital of England; and West-Saxon became the official and, to a great extent, the literary language all over England. The West-Saxons still continued to call their language English, the name 'Anglo-Saxon' being used only as a collective name for the people, not the language.

11. In this book OE words are always given—unless the contrary is stated—in their Early West-Saxon forms; that is, in the dialect of King Alfred.

Characteristics of Old English.

12. The characteristics of OE are those of the other Low German languages. It was, as compared with MnE, a highly inflected language, being in this respect intermediate between

Latin and Modern German. In its syntax it closely resembled Modern German. It also resembled Modern German in having an unlimited power of forming new words by derivation and composition, as when it made *Scribes and Pharisees* into 'bookers and separation-saints' (OE *bōceras and sundorhālgan*).

Latin Influence.

13. Nevertheless it adopted many Latin words, some of which it brought with it from the Continent, such as *strǣt* 'high road,' 'street,' *mīl* 'mile,' *cāsere* 'emperor' from Latin (*via*) *strāta*, *mīlia* (*passuum*), *Caesar*; while others were learnt from the Romanized Britons, such as *ceaster* 'city,' *læden* 'language' from *castra*, (*lingva*) *Latīna*. These are all popular words. There is another layer of learned words which came in after the introduction of Christianity in 597. Such words are *dēofol* 'devil,' *mynster* 'monastery,' *fers* 'verse,' from *diabolus*, *monasterium*, *versus*.

Celtic Influence.

14. Very few Celtic words came into OE, because the Britons themselves were to a great extent Romanized, especially the inhabitants of the cities, who were mainly the descendants of the Roman legionary soldiers. *drȳ* 'druid,' 'sorcerer' is an example of a Celtic word in OE.

Scandinavian Influence.

15. Towards the end of the 8th century Scandinavian pirates—chiefly from Norway, but also from Denmark, all being indiscriminately called 'Danes' by the Anglo-Saxons—began to harass the coasts of England. By the end of the next century they had conquered and settled East-Anglia (in

870), Mercia (in 874), and Northumbria (in 876); although in the next century they were forced to acknowledge the supremacy of the West-Saxon kings. In 1016 the whole of England was conquered by the Danes, and England was ruled by Danish kings till 1042, when the Anglo-Saxon royal line was restored in the person of Edward the Confessor.

16. It is not till the close of the OE period that Scandinavian words appear. Even Late Northumbrian (of about 970) is entirely free from Scandinavian influence.

French Influence.

17. With the accession of Edward the Confessor in 1042 Norman influence begins; and in 1066 the battle of Hastings made the Norman duke William king of England, although the actual conquest was not completed till 1071.

18. The Normans were Scandinavian by race, but their language was a dialect of Old French.

19. The influence of Norman French on OE was of course even slighter than that of Scandinavian, so that it does not become a factor of importance till the ME period. Nevertheless several French words passed into literary OE even before the Conquest, such as *castel* 'castle,' *capūn* 'fowl.'

Middle English.

20. In its Middle period English went through much the same changes as the other Germanic languages, though at a quicker rate. Many of the sounds were changed, most of the old inflections were lost, their place being supplied by form-words—prepositions, auxiliary verbs, etc.—and many words became obsolete.

Dialects of Middle English.

21. The Norman Conquest, by depriving the old West-Saxon of its literary and political supremacy, gave free play to the development of the dialects. Although the ME dialects are continuations of the OE ones, it is convenient to call most of them by different names. The main divisions are **Northern**, corresponding to the Old Northumbrian, **Midland**, corresponding to the Old Mercian, **Southern**, corresponding to the old West-Saxon, and **Kentish**. We include the first two under the term 'North-Thames English,' the last two under 'South-Thames English.'

22. Of these dialects the Midland was the predominating one. Its commanding position in the heart of England enabled it to exercise a direct influence on all the other dialects, while Southern and Northern were completely cut off from one another. Hence even the earliest Southern of about 1200 shows considerable influence of the Midland—or Old Mercian—dialect.

23. It is to be observed that the changes which distinguish one period of English from another went on much faster in the North of England than in the South. In fact, the Old Northumbrian dialect of the 10th century had already entered on its transition period—characterized by a general confusion in the use of inflections, and was thus almost on a level with the Early Southern Middle English of about 1200. Again, the Northern dialect in its Early Middle period had got rid of nearly all the inflections that are not preserved in MnE, being thus several centuries ahead of the South-Thames dialects. The Midland dialects were more conservative than the Northern, though less so than the South-Thames dialects. It will be seen, then, that the criteria of full, levelled, and lost endings by which we distinguish the periods of English (1) apply only to the South-Thames dialects.

Struggle between French and English.

24. For a long time the two languages, French and English, kept almost entirely apart. The English of 1200 is almost as free from French words as the English of 1050; and it was not till after 1300 that French words began to be adopted wholesale into English.

25. Meanwhile English was steadily gaining the upper hand. In 1258 we find it officially employed in the Proclamation of Henry III. In the next century French gradually fell into disuse even among the aristocracy. In 1362 English was introduced in the courts of law instead of French. About the same time English took the place of French as the vehicle of instruction in schools.

Rise of the London Dialect.

26. In the ME period the dialects had diverged so much that speakers of the extreme Northern and extreme Southern dialects were no longer able to understand one another, and the need of a common dialect became pressing. Such a common dialect can be formed only in a centre of intercourse where speakers from all parts of the country meet constantly. Such a centre was London, which now was not only the capital of England, but also a place of great and growing commercial importance.

27. The London dialect, as we find it in its earliest document, the Proclamation of Henry III, shows such a mixture of Midland and Southern forms as we might expect from its position on the border-line between these two dialects. The Midland dialect was intermediate between the two extremes, Northern and Southern, not only geographically but also linguistically; so that speakers of Midland could understand both Northern and Southern much better than Northerners and Southerners could understand one another. Hence the Midland element in the London dialect made the latter peculiarly fitted to serve as a means of general communication. Hence also the Midland element in the London dialect became stronger and stronger in the course of the ME period, till at last even Northern forms passed into it through the medium of the Midland dialect, while Southern influence became weaker and weaker.

Scandinavian Influence.

28. Although the Norwegians and Danes spoke different dialects, the difference between these dialects was very slight. The Scandinavian words imported into English seem to be mostly Danish. Although the Scandinavian dialects were not intelligible to the Anglo-Saxons, yet the cognate languages English and Scandinavian were so similar in structure and had so many words in common, that the languages blended together with the same facility as the races that spoke them. English got the upper hand, but Scandinavian nevertheless left its mark on every English dialect, especially the East-Midland and Northern dialects, where the population was half Scandinavian. *Ill*, *fro* in 'to and fro,' *bound* in 'bound for a place,' are examples of Scandinavian words in English (Icelandic *ill-r* 'bad,' *frā* 'from,' *būinn* 'ready').

French Influence.

29. The Norman French introduced into England was not a uniform dialect, but was itself split up into local varieties or sub-dialects, which in the Norman spoken in England—the 'Anglo-Norman' or 'Anglo-French' language—were mixed together indiscriminately. The loss of Normandy in 1204 put an end to the influence of Continental Norman; and henceforth Anglo-French was influenced only by the literary French of Paris, this Parisian French having the same predominance among the French dialects as London English had among the English dialects. At the time when the influence of Anglo-French on English begins to be important—that is, in the late ME period—it was, therefore, a mixture of Old French of different periods and different dialects, modified by changes of its own, and also by the influence of English itself, especially in its pronunciation.

30. French influence on English is most marked in the vocabulary. Soon after the Conquest English ceased for several centuries to be the language of the higher purposes of life, and sank almost to a mere peasant's dialect. So when English came again into general use, it had lost a great part of its higher vocabulary, for which it had to use French words, such as *sir*, *duke*; *captain*, *army*, *battle*; *sermon*, *preach*. Even when the English word was kept, the same idea was often expressed by a French word, whence numerous synonyms such as *work* and *labour*, *weak* and *feeble*.

Latin Influence.

31. In Old French itself we must distinguish between **popular** and **learned** words. The popular words in Old French, such as *sire* 'lord,' from Latin *senior* 'older,' are simply Latin words which have undergone those changes which take place in every language whose development is natural and unimpeded. But as Latin was kept up as an independent language throughout the Middle Ages, Latin words were imported into Old French as well as the other Romance languages, being used first in books, then in ordinary speech. These learned words were kept as much as possible unchanged, being pronounced as they were written. It often happened that a Latin word which had assumed a popular form in French, was re-imported direct from Latin, so that chronological doublets were formed, such as *caitif* 'wretched' and *captif*, both from Latin *captīvus*, whence the English *caitiff* and *captive*.

32. These learned French words were introduced into ME in great numbers. Hence when Latin words came to be imported directly into English, they were put into a French shape on the analogy of those Latin words which had really been brought in through French. Thus when a word in *-tio*, such as *nōminātiō*, was taken direct from Latin, it was made into *-tion* (MnE *nomination*) on the analogy of the older importations, such as *nation* (ME *nācioun*).

Modern English.

33. In the Middle period literary English was still distinctly an inflectional language. In the Modern period it became mainly uninflectional, with only scanty remains of the older inflections.

34. The Modern period is that of the complete ascendency of the London dialect, which henceforth is the only one used in writing throughout England. Henceforth the other dialects of England continued to exist only as illiterate forms of speech confined within narrow areas.

35. The spread of Modern London English—or 'Standard English,' as we may now call it—was greatly aided by the introduction of printing in 1476. The publication of Tindal's translation of the New Testament in 1525 paved the way for the Authorized Version of 1611, which made Early Modern London English what it has ever since been—the sacred or liturgical language of the whole English-speaking race.

Influence of other Languages.

36. In the Early Modern period, the Renascence—the revival of the study of the classical authors of Greece and Rome—led to the adoption of an immense number of Greek as well as Latin words, the Greek words being generally Latinized, just as the Latin words imported into Middle English were Frenchified.

37. As the first prose writings were mostly either translations from Latin, or else the work of scholars to whom Latin was in some respects a more natural means of expression than English, it was inevitable that Early MnE prose was greatly influenced by Latin, not only in vocabulary, but also in grammatical structure and idioms. In a few generations many Latin—and some Greek—words and expressions which were at first purely learned and technical passed into the language of everyday life; while, on the other hand, many others became obsolete.

38. As the relations of England with other countries became more extended, many words were imported into English from almost every European language, especially Dutch, French, Italian, Spanish, and Portuguese, and from many other languages besides, such as Arabic, Persian, and Turkish, and the native languages of America.

39. Standard English has always been influenced by the different English dialects. The literary revival of Broad

Scotch—which is really Modern Northumbrian—at the end of the last century by Scott and Burns has introduced many Scotch words into literary English.

Periods.

40. The main general difference between Early and Late MnE is that the former is the period of experiment and comparative licence both in the importation and in the formation of new words, idioms, and grammatical constructions. The Late MnE period is, on the other hand, one of selection and organization. The most marked differences in detail are the great sound-changes undergone by the spoken language—changes which have been completely disguised by the fixity of the orthography.

PHONOLOGY.

PHONETICS.

41. Phonetics is the science of speech-sounds.

42. As the ordinary spelling does not always show the real pronunciation, it is necessary to use a **phonetic** spelling, which, to prevent confusion, we enclose in ( ).

Analysis.

43. The foundation of speech-sounds is breath expelled from the lungs, and variously modified by the vocal organs—throat, nose, mouth, lips.

Throat-sounds: Breath and Voice.

44. The first modification the breath undergoes is in the throat. If the vocal chords, which are stretched across the inside of the throat, are kept apart so that the air can pass through with but little hindrance, we have **breath**, as in ordinary breathing or sighing, and in the consonant (h), as in *high*. If the chords are brought together so as to vibrate, we have **voice**, as in murmuring or in the word *err*.

Nasal Sounds.

45. If the passage into the nose is left open, we have a **nasal** sound, such as (m) in *am*. In the formation of all sounds that are not nasal, such as the (b) in *amber*, the nose-passage is closed.

Consonants.

46. If the mouth-passage is narrowed so as to cause audible friction—that is, a hissing or buzzing sound—or if it is completely stopped, a **consonant** is produced.

Vowels.

47. If the mouth-passage is left so open as not to cause audible friction, and voiced breath is sent through it, we have a **vowel.** Every alteration in the shape of the mouth produces a different vowel.

Vowel-like Consonants.

48. Some consonants have hardly any friction when voiced, and are called **vowel-like** consonants. Such consonants are (l), as in *little* (litl), and (m).

Synthesis.

49. We have now to consider the **synthesis** of sounds, that is, the different ways in which they are joined together in speech.

Quantity.

50. By quantity, sounds are distinguished as **long, half-long** or medium, and **short,** 'long' being often used to include half-long as well. In phonetic notation long and half-long vowels are doubled, short vowels being written single, as in (məəmə) *murmur*. The length of consonants is only occasionally marked by doubling.

Stress.

51. There are three main degrees of stress or loudness: **strong, half-strong** or medium, and **weak.** Thus in *contradict* the last syllable is strong, the first half-strong, the next weak. We mark strong stress by (·), half-strong by (:), these marks being put before the sound on which the stressed syllable begins, weak or unstressed syllables being left unmarked: (:kontrə·dikt). Weak stress is marked when necessary by prefixing (-), as in (-it reinz) 'it rains.'

52. Sounds which occur only in unstressed syllables, such as the short (ə) in (məəmə) *murmur*, are called **weak.**

Intonation.

53. Intonation or tone is either **level, rising,** or **falling,** marked respectively (¯, ´, ˋ). The level tone is not much used in speech. The rising tone is heard in questions, such as *what´*, the falling in answers such as *noˋ*.

Glides.

54. Glides are sounds produced during the transition from one sound to another. Thus in (kii) *key* we have the glide from the (k)-position to the (ii)-position, which does not, however, require to be written, as it is implied by the position of (k) and (ii).

55. Consonants are often joined together without any glide, not only in such combinations as (nd) in *hand*, where the (d) is formed by continuing the (n), the nose-passage being closed at the same time, but also in such words as the English *act* (ækt).

Syllables.

56. A syllable is a vowel, either alone or in combination with consonants, uttered with a single impulse of stress.

Every fresh impulse of stress makes a new syllable, the beginning of the syllable corresponding with the beginning of the stress. Thus (ə·tæk) *attack* has two syllables, the first syllable consisting of the vowel (ə) uttered with weak stress, the second of (tæk) uttered with a new impulse of stress beginning on the (t). Vowel-like consonants often form syllables in the same way as vowels, as in *battle*=(bæt-l).

Diphthongs.

57. If two vowels are uttered with one impulse of stress, so as to form a single syllable, the combination is called a **diphthong**, such as (oi) in *oil*. Most diphthongs have the stress on the first element. A simple long vowel, such as (əə), is called a **monophthong**.

We now have to consider sounds more in detail.

Vowels.

58. As every alteration in the shape of the mouth produces a different vowel, the number of vowels is infinite. Hence what we call the vowels, (a), (i) etc., are really **groups** of an indefinite number of vowels differing very slightly from one another.

Rounding.

59. The shape of the mouth-passage by which vowels are formed depends partly on the position of the tongue, partly on that of the lips. If the lip-opening is narrowed while the tongue is in a certain position, the resulting vowel is said to be **rounded**. Thus (y) in French *lune* is the round vowel corresponding to the unrounded (ii), which is nearly the sound in English *he*, both vowels having the same tongue-position.

Tongue-Retraction.

60. The tongue-positions depend partly on the degree of **retraction** of the tongue, partly on its **height** or distance from the palate.

61. If the root of the tongue is drawn back, we have a **back** vowel, such as the (aa) in *father*. If the fore part of the tongue is advanced, we have a **front** vowel, such as (ii). If the tongue is left in its neutral position, intermediate between back and front, we have a **mixed** vowel, such as (əə).

Tongue-Height.

62. If the tongue is raised as close to the palate as is possible without making the vowel into a consonant, a **high** vowel is formed. Thus (i) is a high-front vowel, (u), as in *full*, a high-back-round vowel. There are two other degrees of height, **mid** and **low**. For convenience we may include mid and low vowels under the common name 'un-high' vowels, distinguishing them as **close** and **open**, according to the degree of openness of the mouth-passage. We denote open vowels, when necessary, by italics. French *é* in *été* is the mid-front-close vowel, or, more briefly, the front-close vowel, for when a vowel is not expressly called high, we assume it to be un-high. English (*e*) in *men* is the corresponding mid-front-open vowel. Very open vowels are called **broad**. (æ) in *man* is a broad front vowel. The distinction of close and open applies also to the high vowels. Thus French (i) in *fini* is the close high front vowel, English (*i*) in *finny* is the open high front vowel.

The Vowels in Detail.

The following are the most important vowels.

(A) Unrounded vowels.

63. (a) 'clear back': (a·haa) *aha!*

64. (ɐ) 'dull back': (sɐn) *son, sun.*

65. (ə) 'mixed' or 'neutral' vowel: (məəmə) *murmur.*

66. (i) 'high front.' Close (i) in French *fini*, the short E. *i*, as in *finny*, being always open. Long close (ii) is the older E. sound in such words as *see, sea, receive, machine*, and this sound is still preserved in Scotland and the North of England. In the South of England it is diphthongized into (*i*) followed by very close (i), which is nearly the sound of the consonant (j) in *you*, so we write (sij), etc.

67. (e) 'front.' French *é* is close front. The E. vowel in *men* is open front (*e*). Before (ə)—with which it forms a diphthong—it is still opener, as in (feə) *fare, fair.* The long close front (ee) is still preserved in Scotch in such words as *name, day*, where Standard E. has the diphthong (*e*i).

68. (æ) 'broad front': (mæn) *man.*

(B) Round vowels.

69. (u) 'high back round.' Close in French *sou*, the E short (*u*) in *full, good* being always open. The older close (uu) in such words as *moon, move, you* (juu) is still kept in Scotland and the North of England, but in the South of England it becomes (*u*w) with a distinct (w). Weak open (u), as in *value*, is the high mixed round vowel, which, when necessary, we write (ü)—(væljü).

70. (o) 'back round.' Close in French *beau* (bo). Close (oo) in Scotch *no, know*, where Standard E. has the diphthong (*o*u). The (o) in the diphthong (*o*i), as in *boy*, is the same open sound. Weak (o), as in *October*, is the open mixed vowel, which, when necessary, we write (ö)—(öktoubə).

71. (ɔ) 'broad back round.' This is the sound of the E. short vowels in *not, what.* The long broad vowel is heard in such words as *naught, fall.* For convenience we write the short vowel (o), the long (ɔ) in Standard E.—not (nɔt).

72. (y) 'high front round' = rounded (i). French *une.* German *über.*

73. (œ) 'front-round.' Close in French *peu*, whose vowel is a rounded French *é.* Open in French *peur.*

Nasal Vowels.

74. If a vowel is formed with the nose-passage open, it is said to be **nasal**, which we mark by (*n*). Thus we have nasal (a, æ) in French *sang, sans* (sa*n*), *vin* (væ*n*).

Diphthongs.

75. We call (ei, ou; ij, uw) **half diphthongs**, because they are not very distinct, their two elements differing only in height.

76. **Full diphthongs**, on the other hand, such as (ai, au, oi) are made up of vowels as distinct as possible from one another.

77. There is another class of **murmur diphthongs** ending in (ə), as in *hear, here* (h*i*ə), *fare, fair* (*e*ə), *poor* (p*u*ə), *pure* (pj*u*ə), *more* (mɔə). There are also murmur triphthongs, as in *fire* (faiə), *loyal* (loiəl).

78. The following table will show the relations of the

chief vowels more clearly. Those marked * do not occur in English:—

high back	*high mixed*	*high front*
*ʌ	*ɪ	i
back	*mixed*	*front*
a ; ɐ	ə	e ; æ
high back round	*high mixed round*	*high front round*
u	ü	*y
back round	*mixed round*	*front round*
o, ɔ	ö	*œ

79. The relations of the English vowels may be shown thus:

Short: . . .	ɐ	ə	i	e, æ	u	o
Long: . . .	aa	əə				ɔ
Half diphthongs:			ij	ei	uw	ou
Full diphthongs: .	ai, au					oi
Murmur diphthongs:			iə	eə	uə	ɔə

Consonants.

80. Consonants admit of a two-fold division (*a*) by **form**, (*b*) by **place**.

Form.

By form there are five classes:—

81. (*a*) **Open,** in which the passage is narrowed without stoppage, such as (s).

82, (*b*) **Side,** formed by stopping the middle of the passage and leaving it open at the sides, as in (l).

83. (*c*) **Stopped,** formed by complete closure. The

voiceless stops (k, t, p) are in English followed by a breath glide or slight puff of breath, thus *cat* almost=(khæth).

84. (*d*) **Nasal** consonants are formed with complete closure of the mouth-passage, the nose-passage being left open, as in (m).

85. (*e*) **Trills** are the result of vibration of the flexible parts of the mouth. Thus in the trilled Scotch (r) the point of the tongue vibrates against the gums, the E. (r) in *red* being an open consonant without any trill.

Place.

By place there are also five classes :—

86. (*a*) **Back,** formed by the root of the tongue, such as (k, ŋ) in *king* (kiŋ). The back open consonant (x) is the sound of *ch* in the Scotch and German *loch.* The corresponding voice consonant (ʒ) is heard in German *sage.*

87. (*b*) **Front,** formed by the middle of the tongue, such as the front open voice consonant (j) in *you,* which is really a consonantal (i). The corresponding breath consonant (ç) is heard in German *ich* and Scotch *hue, Hugh* (çuu), which in Southern E. is pronounced (hjuw).

88. (*c*) **Point,** formed by the tip of the tongue. In the **point-gum** consonants, such as E. (t, d, n, l) the point of the tongue is brought against the gums just behind the teeth; in the **point-teeth** consonants, such as the point-teeth-open (þ) in *thin,* it is brought against the teeth. The voice consonant corresponding to (þ) is (ð) in *then.*

89. (*d*) **Blade,** formed by the blade of the tongue—that part of it which is immediately behind the point. (s, z) are blade consonants. In the **blade-point** consonants, such as the blade-point open (ʃ) in *she,* the blade position is modified by raising the point of the tongue. The corresponding voice consonant (ʒ) is heard in *measure* (meʒə).

90. The point and blade consonants are included under the name of **forward** consonants.

91. (*e*) **Lip,** formed by the lips, such as (p, m). The lip-open consonant (ɸ) is the sound produced in blowing out a candle; the corresponding voice consonant occurs in German in such words as *quelle* (kβelə); (f, v) are **lip-teeth** consonants. (w*h*), as in *why*, and (w) are **lip-back** consonants, formed by narrowing the lip-opening and raising the back of the tongue at the same time, (w) being a consonantal (u). In Southern E. (w*h*) is often pronounced (w).

Compound Consonants: Rounding, Fronting.

92. (w*h*, w) are really **compound** consonants, formed in two places at once. If instead of back-modifying the lip-open consonant, as in (w*h*), we lip-modify or **round** the back-open consonant (x), we get the back-round consonant (x*w*) in German *auch*. Other consonants may be rounded in the same way, which we express by adding (*w*); thus (r*w*ed) is *red* pronounced with a rounded (r).

93. When a consonant is modified by raising the front of the tongue, it is said to be **front-modified** or fronted, which we express by adding (*j*). Thus the lip-open front-modified consonant is the sound in French *huit* (β*j*it); it is almost a consonantal (y).

The Aspirate.

94. The aspirate (h) is partly an open throat consonant, partly a breath vowel-glide. Thus (h) in *hook* is mainly formed by unvoicing the beginning of the (u), almost as if we were to write the word (w*h*uk).

95. The following is a table of the chief consonants. Those marked * do not occur in E.

	Throat.	Back.	Front.	Point.	Blade.	Blade-Point.	Lip.	Lip-Back.	Lip-Teeth.
	BREATH.								
Open	h	*x	*ç	*r_h_, þ	s	ʃ	*ɸ	w_h_	f
Side	—			*l_h_					
Stop		k	*c	t			p		
Nasal	—	*ŋ_h_	*ñ_h_	*n_h_			*m_h_		
	VOICE.								
Open	—	*ʒ	j	r, ð	z	ʒ	*β	w	v
Side	—			l					
Stop	—	g	*q	d			b		
Nasal	—	ŋ	*ñ	n			m		

96. We generally write (rh), etc., instead of (r_h_) for the sake of convenience.

R IN ENGLISH.

97. (r) in E. occurs only before a vowel following it without any pause, as in *here he is* (hiər ij iz); before a consonant or a pause it is dropped, leaving only the preceding (ə), as in *here she is, he is here* (hiə ʃij iz, hij z hiə). This (ə) is absorbed by a preceding (əə, aa), as in *err, erring, far, far away* (əə, əəriŋ, faa, faar əwei). After (ɔ) the (ə) is kept finally, but dropped before the (r), as in *pour, pouring* (pɔə, pɔriŋ), being also dropped before a consonant in the same word, as in *poured* (pɔd).

LAWS OF SOUND-CHANGE.

98. Sound-changes fall under two main classes—internal and external.

99. **Internal** changes are either organic or acoustic. **Organic** changes are due to the natural tendencies of the organs of speech, as in the change of OE *stān* into MnE *stone* through the natural tendency to pronounce a back vowel without opening the mouth fully, and so to round it.

100. **Acoustic** changes are the result of the impressions which sounds make on the ear, as when one sound is substituted for another because of their likeness to the ear: thus children often make *through* (þruw) into (fruw), and point (r) is changed into back (ʒ) in French and other languages. These are **imitative** changes.

101. **External** changes are those which are independent of organic and acoustic tendencies. Thus the change of *spake* into *spoke* in MnE is not the result of any tendency to change *ā* into *ō* in MnE, but of the influence of the preterite participle *spoken* (**566**).

102. Internal changes are further distinguished as isolative and combinative. **Isolative** changes, such as that of OE *ā* into MnE *ō*, affect a sound without regard to its surroundings, while in **combinative** changes one sound is modified by another one close to it, as in the change of ME (au) in *saw* into MnE (sɔɔ) through (sɔu) or (s*o*u). Here we have two distinct combinative changes: first the rounding of the (a) by the influence of the following (u), and then the lowering of the high (u) till it is merged into the (ɔ). We see that the influence of one sound on another is either **backwards**, as in the change of (au) into (ɔu), or **forwards**, as in the change of (ɔu) into (ɔɔ).

103. All combinative changes are, besides, either convergent or divergent. **Convergent** changes, as of (au) into (ɔu) are organic, being due to the tendency to save trouble by making the passage from one sound to another as short and easy as possible.

104. Complete convergence or **assimilation** in diphthongs makes them into monophthongs, as when (ɔu) becomes (ɔɔ), and in this case is called **smoothing**.

105. Divergent changes are often partly acoustic, being due to the striving for distinctness, as when the half diphthong (ou) in *no* is made into full (au) in Cockney E. But **cleaving**, by which a long vowel is made into a diphthong, is an isolative organic change; it consists generally in forming the first half of the vowel with greater openness—either of the mouth- or the lip-passage—than the second. We see the beginning of cleaving in the E. change of (ii, uu) into (ij, uw), which by divergence could easily become (ei, ou) or (əi, öu) and then (ai, au).

OLD-ENGLISH SOUNDS.

Orthography.

106. The Anglo-Saxons brought with them to England their national Runic alphabet, which was founded on one of the Old Greek alphabets or possibly the Latin. On their conversion to Christianity they adopted the Latin alphabet in its British form, to which they afterwards added the two Runic letters þ=*th* and ƿ=*w*. In the British-Latin alphabet

—and consequently in the OE alphabet as well—several of the letters had peculiar forms, *g* for instance being written ʒ.

107. Each letter of the Latin alphabet was used to denote the OE sound nearest to that which the letter had in the pronunciation of British Latin, which was more archaic than that of the Continental Latin.

108. Spelling in OE was purely phonetic: the OE scribes wrote as they spoke, as far as the defects of their alphabet would allow them to do so.

109. In this book we supplement the defective distinctions of the OE orthography by adding diacritics, which gives the following new letters—*ę*, *ǫ*, *ċ*, *ġ*, *ā*, etc., (¯) denoting vowel-length.

Pronunciation.

110. The vowels had the same sounds as in our phonetic notation, the unmodified vowels being all close except *a*. *a*=(a), as in *faran* 'go,' 'travel'; long in *stān* 'stone.' *e*= close (e), as in *etan* 'eat'; long in *mē* 'me.' There was also an open *e*, which we write *ę*, as in *męte* 'food.' *i*=close (i), as in *witan* 'know'; long in *wīn* 'wine.' *o*=close (o), as in *God* 'God'; long in *gōd* 'good.' There was also an open broad *o*, which we write *ǫ*, as in *lǫng* 'long.' *u*= close (u), as in *sunu* 'son'; long in *hus* 'house.' *y*=close (y) as in *synn* 'sin'; long in *fȳr* 'fire.' *æ*=(æ), as in *fæder* 'father'; long in *hǣlan* 'heal.' *œ* had the sound of close (œ), as in *blœtsian* 'bless'; long in *fœ̄t* 'feet.' The diphthongs *ea*, *ēa*, *eo*, *ēo*=(·æa, ·ææa, ·eo, ·eeo): *heard* 'hard,' *dēad* 'dead'; *eorþe* 'earth,' *dēop* 'deep.' In *ie* the two elements were originally pronounced separately, but in ordinary West-Saxon the diphthong was smoothed into open (*i*), as in *ieldra* 'older,' 'elder'; long in *hīeran* 'hear.'

111. The following consonants require notice. *c*=(k), as in *cēne* 'bold.' *ċ*=(c), resembling in sound our *ch*=(tʃ), as in *ċiriċe* 'church.' *g* when not initial was pronounced (ʒ), as in *dagas* 'days,' *burg* 'city,' *hālga* 'saint,' except in the combination *ng*, which was pronounced (ŋg), as in *lang* 'long,' *singan* 'sing.' *ġ* in the combination *nġ* was a front stop, this combination having the sound (ñq), as in *sęnġan* 'singe,' where the OE *g* has a sound very similar to that of the MnE *g* in *singe*. *ċġ* had the sound (qq), as in *bryċġ* 'bridge,' where, again, the OE sound closely resembles the (dʒ) of *bridge*; the *c* in this digraph is intended to indicate the front sound, the less frequent (gg) being generally written *gg*, as in *frogga* 'frog.' Initial *ġ* also had the sound (q), but seems also to have been pronounced (j): *ġeard* 'yard,' 'court,' *ġenumen* 'taken.' Non-initial *ġ* had the sound (j), except in the combinations *nġ*, *ċġ*; *dæġ* (day), *sęġeþ* 'says,' *hęrġian* 'ravage.'

112. *x*=(ks), but in many words it was originally pronounced (xs), as in *weaxan* 'grow.'

113. *f*, *s*, *þ* had the voice sounds (v, z, ð) between vowels and between *r*, *l* and vowels, as in *drīfan* 'drive,' *frēosan* 'freeze,' *eorþe* 'earth.'

114. Initial *h* had the same sound as in E. *hw*, as in *hwīt* 'white,'=(w*h*). So also *hl*, *hr*, *hn* represented the voiceless sounds of (l, r, n) respectively, as in *hlūd* 'loud,' *hring* 'ring,' *hnutu* 'nut.' In *hw* etc. the *h* and the *w* were originally pronounced separately. Non-initial *h*—'strong *h*'—had the sound of (x) in Scotch *loch*, as in *þurh* 'through'; in some words it had the sound of (ç) in German *ich*, especially after a front vowel, as in *ġe·sihþ* 'sight.'

115. *r* was always trilled, as in Scotch. *c*, *g*, *w* were pronounced clearly before consonants in such words as *cnāwan* 'know,' *gnagan* 'gnaw,' *wrītan* 'write,' *wlæc* 'lukewarm.'

116. Double consonants were pronounced double, or long, as in *mann* 'man'—distinct from *ge·man* 'I remember,' where the *n* was quite short—*sunne* 'sun' (the *nn* as in *pen-knife*) distinct from *sunu* 'son.'

Stress.

117. In OE the general principle of word-stress is to put the strong stress on the first syllable of a word, as in *·fiscas* 'fishes,' *·fisċere* 'fisher,' *·misdǣd* 'misdeed.'

118. In compounds the modifying word came first, and took the chief stress, as in *horshwæl* 'walrus,' literally 'horse-whale,' *ryhtwīs* 'rightly wise,' 'righteous,' *cwicseolfor* 'quicksilver,' literally 'living silver.'

But there are some exceptions to this rule of putting the stress on the first element of compounds :—

119. Group-compounds of preposition + noun, such as the adverbs *of·dūne* 'down,' literally 'off-the-hill,' as in *hē ēode ofdūne* 'he went down,' *on·bæc* 'back,' literally 'on-the-back,' *tō·dæġ* 'today,' were of course originally independent word-groups.

120. Adverbs of full and distinct meaning took strong stress when followed by another word with which they form a group, as in *·wīde ge:sīene* 'widely seen,' 'seen far and wide' [compare the compound *wīdcūþ* 'widely known']. So also when a verb follows, as in *·inn :gān* 'go in,' *·bī :standan* 'stand by,' 'help.' But if the verb precedes, it takes the principal stress: *hē ·ēode :inn.* 'he went in,' *hē ·stōd him· bī* 'he helped him.' When these particles precede their verbs, they are felt to form compounds with them through the group having the same stress as compounds in general, so that we may write these groups as single words—*inngān*, *bīstandan*. But as these particles are, as we see, liable to be separated from their verbs in other constructions, we call them **separable** particles.

121. But if these particles are compounded with nouns or adjectives instead of verbs, they cannot be shifted, as in ·*inngang* 'going in,' 'entrance,' *bīspell* 'by-tale,' 'parable,' whose elements can no more be separated than those of *ryhtwīs*, etc.

122. In OE there is also a class of **inseparable** particles, such as *for-* in *forġiefan* 'forgive,' which has no connection with the preposition *for* 'for,' never occurring as an independent word. These inseparable particles ought strictly speaking to be regarded as derivative elements, like the *un-* in ·*uncūþ* 'unknown,' but as many of them lost their independence only at a comparatively recent period in OE, it is allowable to regard *forġiefan*, etc., as compounds. The inseparable prefix *be-* in *be·sęttan* 'beset' is, indeed, the same word as the preposition *be* 'by,' although they have diverged in meaning.

123. While abstract nouns compounded with inseparable particles throw the stress on to the particle in the usual way, as in ·*forwyrd* 'destruction,' parallel to *inngang*, the corresponding verbs take the stress on the verb itself, as in *for*·*weorþan* 'perish,' *forġiefan*. This shifting of stress is often accompanied by phonetic weakening of the particle; thus to the strong form of the prefix in ·*bīgang* 'going round,' 'cultivation,' 'worship,' corresponds the weak *be-* in *be·gān* 'go round,' 'cultivate,' etc., *besęttan*.

Quantity.

124. Long vowels in weak syllables were shortened in OE, as in *begān* (**123**).

125. On the other hand, short final strong vowels were lengthened, as in *hwā* 'who,' *þū* 'thou'=Germanic *hwa*, *þu*. Hence the short vowel of the unstressed article *se* in *se mann* 'the man' is lengthened when the word is used in the sense of 'he,' as in *sē þe* 'he who.'

126. In Anglian, short vowels were lengthened before vowel-like consonants followed by another consonant—'group-lengthening'—as in *āld* 'old,' *lǭng* 'long,' *blīnd* 'blind,' *dūmb* 'dumb'=Early West-Saxon *eald*, *lǫng*, *lang*, *blind*, *dumb*. These lengthenings appear also in Late West-Saxon.

Vowels.

127. a (**ǫ**), **æ**, **ea.** These vowels all correspond to Germanic *a*, still preserved in Modern German; thus OE *mann*, *fæder*, *heard*=German *mann*, *vater*, *hart*. Germanic *a* in the Oldest E. was kept only before nasals, as in *mann*, *hand*, *lang*. Everywhere else it was fronted to *æ*, as in *wæs* 'was,' *æcer* 'field,' *fæder*. Before 'group *r* and *l*,' that is, before *r* and *l* followed by a consonant, and before strong *h* the voice-glide (ə) was developed, as in E. (hiəriŋ), which afterwards by phonetic divergence developed into full (a), as in *heard*, *earm* 'arm'; *eall*, *eald* 'old'; *ġeseah* 'saw,' *eahta* 'eight,' *weaxan* (**112**). Before a back vowel in the next syllable *æ* became the back vowel *a*, as in *dagas* 'days,' *dagum* 'to days' dat., compared with *dæġ* 'day,' gen. *dæġes*. These are the West-Saxon forms. In Anglian *a* before nasals became *ǫ*—as also often in Early West-Saxon—and *æ* before group *l* became *a*, so that the Anglian forms are *mǫnn*, *hǭnd* (126), *lǭng*; *heard*, etc.; *all*, *āld* (126).

128. i, e, eo. In Germanic, *e* before group-nasals became *i*, whence OE *bindan* 'bind,' *singan* 'sing' compared with *helpan* 'help.' In OE itself *e* also became *i* before single nasals, as in *niman* 'take' compared with *stelan* 'steal.' The vowel in such words as *witan* 'know' is Germanic and Arian *i*. In OE *e* before group *r* became *eo* much in the same way as *æ* became *ea* (127), as in *steorra* 'star,' *eorþe*. *e*, *i* became *eo*, *io* before a back—especially a back round—vowel in the next syllable, as in *heofon* 'heaven,' *cliopian* 'call,' the forms *hefon*, *clipian* also occurring.

129. u, o. In Germanic, *o* became *u* before group-nasals; and in OE itself *o* became *u* before single nasals, whence OE *ġebunden* 'bound' compared with *ġeholpen* 'helped,' *ġenumen* 'taken' compared with *ġestolen* 'stolen.' In such a word as *sunu* 'son,' the *u* s are Germanic and Arian.

130. The Germanic vowel *ǣ* is preserved in West-Saxon, as in *fǣr* 'danger,' *ǣfen* 'evening,' being narrowed to *ē* in Anglian and Kentish—*fēr*, *ēfen*.

Mutation.

131. Mutation is the influence exercised by a vowel on the vowel of a preceding syllable, by which the first vowel is modified in the direction of the second one. Thus in OE *ġecoren* 'chosen' = Old High German *gikoran*, compared with OE *curun* later *curon* 'they chose,' *u* has been lowered to *o* by the influence of the *a*. This is therefore an *a*-mutation of *u*.

132. But the most important mutations in OE are the front mutations, caused by Germanic *i* and *j*, which after they had caused the mutation were generally lost or modified in OE.

133. The following are the mutations in their Early West-Saxon forms:—

e . . . i. *beran* 'carry,' *bireþ* (Oldest E. *biriþ*) 'carries'; *cweþan* 'say,' *cwide* (Oldest E. *cwidi*) 'saying,' 'speech.'

a (æ) . . . ę. *faran* 'go,' 'travel,' *fęrian* 'convey'; *mann* 'man,' *męnn* (Germanic *manni*) 'men.'

ā . . . ǣ. *hāl* 'whole,' 'sound,' *hǣlan* 'heal'; *ān* 'one,' *ǣniġ* 'any.' This 'mutation *ǣ*' remains in the non-West-Saxon dialects, which change Germanic *ǣ* into *ē*. For convenience we will in future distinguish the West-Saxon Germanic *ǣ* by writing it *ǽ*, as in *ǽfen* contrasted with *hǣlan*. Mutated Germanic *ǣ* remains unchanged in West-Saxon, as in *lǽċe* 'physician' (Oldest E. *lǽċi*), *dǽd* 'deed' (Germanic *dǣdi*), and becomes *ē* in the other dialects: *lēċe*, *dēd*.

ea, eo . . . ie. *eald* 'old,' *ieldra* 'older,' *nieht* (Germanic *nahti*) 'night'; *heord* 'herd,' *hierde* 'shepherd.' In Late West-Saxon this *ie* becomes *y* or *i*: *yldra*, *niht*, *hyrde*. In Anglian the one *ie* appears as *ę*, the other as *i*: *ęldra*, *ēldra*, *nęht*; *hirde* (Oldest Anglian *hirdi*).

ēa, ēo . . . īe. *ġelēafa* 'belief,' *ġelīefan* 'believe,' *ēaca* 'increase' (noun), *ēac* 'also,' *īeċan* 'to increase'; *ġesēon* 'see,' *ġesīene* 'visible.' *īe* in Late West-Saxon becomes *ȳ*, *ī*: *ġelȳfan*, *īċan*, *ġesȳne*. In the other dialects it becomes *ē*: *ġelēfan*, *ēċan*, *ġesēne*.

u . . . y. *full* 'full,' *ġefyllan* 'to fill,' *cyning* 'king.' *y* in Late Kentish becomes *e* by lowering and unrounding, as in *ġefellan*.

ū . . . ȳ. *cūþ* 'known,' *cȳþan* 'proclaim,' *mūs* 'mouse,' *mȳs* 'mice.' *ȳ* becomes *ē* in Late Kentish, as in *mēs*.

o . . . œ. *dohtor* 'daughter,' dat. *dœhter*. *œ* was unrounded into *e* in Late OE, the change beginning already in Early West-Saxon: *dehter*. As Germanic *o* became *u* before *i* in the same way as *e* became *i* (133), *y* is the most usual OE mutation of *o*, as in *gold* 'gold,' *gylden* (older *guldīn*) 'golden,' *fox* 'fox,' *fyxen* 'vixen.'

ō . . . œ̄. *fōda* 'food,' *fœ̄dan* 'feed,' *fōt* 'foot,' *fœ̄t* 'feet.' *œ̄* afterwards became *ē*, the change beginning in Early West-Saxon: *fēdan*, *fēt*.

Consonant Influence.

134. In West-Saxon the front glide between *ċ*, *ġ* and a following vowel often developed into a full *e* forming a diphthong with the vowel.

135. ċæ-, ġæ- passed into *ċea-*, *ġea-*, as in *sċeal* 'shall,' *ġeaf* 'gave' [compare *cwæþ* 'said']=non-West-Saxon *sċæl*, *ġæf*. This *ea* was mutated into *ie* in West-Saxon in such words as the noun *ċiele* 'chill' compared with *calan* 'be cold,' *ġiest* 'stranger' [compare German *gast*]=non-West-Saxon *ċęle*, *ġęst*.

136. ċǣ-, ġǣ- became *ċēa-*, *ġēa-*, as in *sċēap* 'sheep,' *ġēafon* 'they gave' [compare *cwǣdon* 'they said']=non-West-Saxon *sċēp*, *ġēfon*.

137. ċe-, ġe- became *ċie-*, *ġie-*, as in *sċield* 'shield,' *ġiefan* 'give' [compare *cweþan*]=non-West-Saxon *sċeld*, *sċēld*, *ġefan*.

138. Through similar changes *ġ* followed by a diphthong in West-Saxon often corresponds to Germanic *j*, which in OE seems to have been made into the stop consonant (q), as in *ġēar* 'year' Anglian *ġēr*, *ġeoc* 'yoke,' *ġeong* 'young,' compared with German *jahr* (=Germanic *jǣr*), *joch*, *jung*.

139. In Anglian, the back consonants *c*, *h*, *g* smooth a preceding diphthong. *ea* became *æ*, as in *ġesæh*, *wæxan*= non-Anglian (West-Saxon and Kentish) *ġeseah*, *weaxan*. *eo* became *e*, as in *fehtan* 'fight,' *werc* 'work' (noun)=West-Saxon *feohtan*, *weorc*. *ēa*, *ēo* became *ē*, as in *ēc*, *ēge* 'eye,' *hēh* 'high,' *flēgan* 'to fly'=West-Saxon *ēac*, *ēage*, *hēah*, *flēogan*.

140. *w* often changes a following *eo* into *o* or *u*, especially in Late OE, as in *sweostor* 'sister,' later *swustor*, *sweord*, *sword*, *swurd* 'sword.'

Consonants.

141. In OE *h* between vowels or between vowel-like consonants and vowels was dropped, often with lengthening of the preceding vowel, as in *furh* 'furrow,' dat. plur. *fūrum*, *Wealh* 'foreigner,' 'Welshman,' plur. *Wealas*, *Wēalas*, *Wielisċ* 'Welsh.' When two vowels came together in this way, they were often made into a diphthong, as in *ġesēon* 'see' from **ġeseohan* [compare *ġeseah* 'saw'].

142. Open *g*, *ġ* became *h* before a breath consonant, as in *byht* 'bending' [*būgan* 'bend'].

143. Final open *g* was also unvoiced in Late West-Saxon, as in *troh* 'trough,' *ġenōh* 'enough,' *burh*=earlier *trog*, *ġenōg*, *burg*.

144. *r* is often transposed, as in *iernan* 'run'—the original form being preserved in *ġerinnan* 'run together,' 'coagulate'—especially in Late Northumbrian, as in *þirda* 'third'= West-Saxon *þridda* [compare *þrēo* 'three'].

145. *s* is often transposed in the same way, as in Late West-Saxon *āxian* 'ask,' *cirps* 'curly'=earlier *āscian*, *crisp*.

146. *r* in some words does not correspond to Germanic *r* but to a Germanic modification of *s*, as in *wǣron* 'were' compared with *wæs* 'was,' *ġecoren* 'chosen,' *cyre* 'choice' compared with *ċēosan* 'choose.' So also *g* and *d* often represent Germanic modifications of *h* and *þ* respectively, as in *cwǣdon*, *cwide* compared with *cweþan*, *slæġen* 'struck,' *slaga* 'slayer' compared with *slēan* [from **sleahan*] 'strike,' 'kill.' These changes are the result of weak stress of the syllable containing *s*, *þ*, *h* in Early Germanic. Hence we call the resulting *r* 'weak *r*' to distinguish it from *r*=Germanic *r*, and so with the other consonants.

147. *þ* in the combinations, *tþ*, *dþ*, *sþ* becomes *t*, to which a preceding *d* is assimilated, giving the combinations *tt*, *st*, as in Early West-Saxon *bītt*=*bīteþ* 'bites' and *bīdeþ* 'waits,' *ċiest* 'chooses' from *ċēosan*.

148. Double consonants in OE often represent a Germanic single consonant+*j*, as in *sęllan* 'give,' *sċęþþan* 'injure,' *sęttan* 'set'=Gothic *saljan*, *skaþjan*, *satjan*, the single consonant appearing in such forms as *sęleþ*, *sċęþeþ*, *sęteþ* 'he gives,' etc., which point to older **saliþ*, etc. Germanic *kj*, *gj*, *fj* appear in OE respectively as *ċċ*, *ċġ* and *bb*, as in *wręċċa* 'one exiled,' *lęċġan* 'lay,' *hębban* 'raise' compared with *wracu* 'state of exile,' *læġ* 'he lay,' *hafen* 'raised.' Germanic *rj*, on the other hand, appears as *ri* in OE, as in *dęrian* 'injure' [cp. *daru* 'injury'].

149. In OE itself, *c*, *t*, *p* are often doubled before *r* and *l*, as in *biter*, *bitter* 'bitter' [cp. *bītan* 'bite'], *æppel* 'apple' [cp. *apulder* 'apple-tree'], *nǣdre*, *nǣddre* 'serpent,' *fōd(d)or* 'food'; and in the later forms *miċċle* plur. of *miċel* 'great,' *dēoppra* adj., *dēoppor* adv. 'deeper.'

Gradation.

150. By gradation we understand certain traditional connections between the vowels—most clearly shown in the conjugation of the 'strong' verbs—which enable us to classify them under the following **gradation-series**:—

a . . . ō. *faran* 'proceed,' *fōr* 'proceeded'; *fōr* 'journey,' *ġefǣra, ġefēra* 'companion.'

e (i, eo) . . . a (æ, ea) . . . u (o). *windan* 'wind,' *wand* 'he wound,' *wundon* 'they wound'; *wendan* 'turn.' *beran* 'carry,' *bær, geboren* 'carried,' *byr-þen* 'burden.' *beorgan* 'protect,' *bearg, burgon, geborgen*; *beorg* 'mountain,' *burg* 'fortress,' 'city,' *borg* 'pledge,' 'security,' *borgian* 'borrow.'

ȧ (æ, ea) . . . ǣ. *bær* 'he carried,' *bǣron* 'they carried'; *bǣr* 'bier.' *spræc* 'he spoke,' *sprǣcon* 'they spoke'; *sprǣċ* 'speech.'

ī . . . ā . . . i. *wrītan* 'write,' *wrāt* 'he wrote,' *writon* 'they wrote'; *gewrit* 'writing' (noun). *belīfan* 'remain'; *lāf* 'residue,' 'remains,' whence by mutation *lǣfan* 'leave.'

ēo (ū) . . . ēa . . . u (o). *ċēosan* 'choose,' *ċēas* 'he chose,' *curon* 'they chose,' *gecoren* 'chosen'; *cyre* 'choice.' *for-lēosan* 'lose'; *lēas* 'devoid of,' *ā-līesan* 'release'; *losian* 'be lost,' 'perish.' *būgan* 'bend,' 'bow,' *bēag, bugon, ġebogen*; *bēag* 'ring'; *boga* 'bow' (noun), *byht* 'bending.'

MIDDLE ENGLISH.

Orthography.

151. In the ME period the OE was superseded by the Old French orthography—Norman at first, but afterwards Parisian.

152. Old French orthography was founded on the traditional pronunciation of Latin; but by the time French was first written down—probably in the 9th century—the tradition of the Old Latin pronunciation had been partially lost.

153. In the 9th-century pronunciation of Latin, *y* had lost its old value, having been unrounded into (i), and so had come to be a mere orthographic variant of *i*. So when Latin *ū* was fronted to (yy) in French, as in *lune* (lyynə) from Latin *lūna*, the *u* was kept as the symbol of the new sound (y). And when the French orthography was introduced into England, the sound of OE *y* was represented by *u*, which we write *ü* to distinguish it from ME *u*=OE *u*. Hence in early Southern ME *sunne* 'sun' and *sünne* 'sin'=OE *synn* were written alike. In Old French there was a diphthong *ui*=(yi), which in Anglo-French was smoothed into (yy), and so was used—together with simple *u*—to express (yy) not only in French words, such as *fruit*, *frūt* 'fruit,' but also in E. words, such as *fuir*, *fūr* 'fire,' *builden* 'build'=OE *fȳr*, *byldan*, *bȳldan*.

154. *y*, being thus superfluous, was almost completely disused for a time in Early ME, but in Late ME—as in Late Old French—it was written in many cases instead of *i*; because *i* was written without any dot, and so was liable to be mistaken for a part of another letter, especially *n*, *m*, *u*. Hence it became usual to write *y* in such words as *bynden*, *wyues*=OE *bindan*, *wīfes*. It also became usual to write *y* at the end of words, as in *many*, *day*=Early ME *mani*, *dai*.

155. In Early Norman French *o* in many words had a sound between close (o) and (u), and as *u* represented the sound (y) as well as (u) in ME as in French, it was found convenient to use *o* for the sound (u)—in which case we write it *ŏ*—especially in combination with such letters as *n*, *m*, *u* (=*v*) where *u* would cause graphic confusion, as in *cŏmen* 'come,' *lŏue* 'love'=OE *cuman*, *lufu*; also before single consonants followed by a vowel, as in *bŏte* 'but,' *cŏrāge* 'courage,' because the earlier ME spellings *bute*, *curage* seemed to suggest (yy).

156. In Late Parisian the older diphthong (ou) was smoothed into (uu), as in *douz* (duuts) 'sweet,' and so *ou* was introduced into Late ME as the symbol of (uu), as in *hous*=earlier *hus*=OE *hūs* 'house,' the actual sound remaining unchanged.

157. In Late Latin *e* was written instead of *ae*, *oe*, which fell into disuse, the classical *caelum*, *poena*, for instance, being written *celum*, *pena*; and so in Old French *e* was used to express open as well as close (e), and this usage passed into ME. We write the long ME open sound *ę̄* to distinguish *dę̄d* 'dead' from *dēd* 'deed,' the latter having the close sound. So also we express the long open *o* by *ǭ*, as in *stǭn* 'stone' distinguished from *mōne* 'moon,' the two sounds not being generally distinguished—any more than the two *e* s—in ME orthography. The Old French diphthong *ie* was smoothed into close (ee) in Anglo-French, and so came to express the latter sound in such words as *meschief* 'mischief,' *lief* 'dear.'

158. In Parisian French, Latin *c*=(k) before front vowels, as in *ciel*, passed through (ts) into (s). In some cases it developed into (tʃ), which combination was expressed by *ch*, as in *chien*. Latin *g*=(g) became 'soft' (dʒ) before front vowels, as in *geste* 'exploit' from Latin *gesta*. Latin *j*=(j) also developed into (dʒ), as in *ja*=Latin *jam*. Latin *qv*, *gv* =(kw, gw) soon dropped their (w) in Old French, so that *qu*, *gu* came to be regarded as symbols of 'hard' (k, g) respectively, especially before front vowels, as in *qui*, *langue* from Latin *qvī*, *lingva*, the former being also expressed by *k*=*ki*.

159. Hence in ME the old *c* was written *k* before front vowels, as in *king*, as also when doubled, as in *þikke* 'thick,' *cw* being expressed by the Early Old French *qu*, as in *quene* 'queen' = OE *cwēn*. *c* was kept before back vowels and generally before consonants, as in *cumen*, *cŏmen*, *clēne* 'clean.' The ME development of OE *ċ* having nearly the sound of French *ch*, this digraph was used to express it, as in *chirche* = OE *ċiriċe*. *c* = (s) was used only in French words, such as *fāce*.

160. In ME the difference in form between the OE ʒ (**106**) and the French *g* was utilized phonetically. The letter *g* was assigned to (g), as in *gōd* 'good,' and the soft French *g*, as in *geste* 'exploit,' and also to the ME development of OE stopped *ġ*, which had nearly the sound of (dʒ), as in *senġen* 'singe,' *briġġe* 'bridge' = OE *sęnġan*, *brycg*. Hard *g* was also expressed by the French *gu*, as it still is in *tongue* = OE *tunge*. *j* = (dʒ) was written only in French words, such as *juġġen* 'judge.' ʒ, on the other hand, was restricted to the open sounds, both back and front, as in *daʒes*, *ʒung* = OE *dagas*, *ġeong*, the latter sound being afterwards expressed by *y*, as in MnE: *yǒng*, *young*.

161. After much fluctuation OE strong *h* was written *gh*, as in *right*, *doghter*.

162. Latin *z* still kept its sound (dz) in Early Old French —where it was also used to express (ts), as in *douz* 'sweet'— and did not become simple (z) till a later period. Hence it is not till the end of the ME period that they began to write *z* instead of *s* = (z) in E. words, as in *wezele* 'weazel,' generally written *wesele*.

163. The Latin sound (w), which was expressed indifferently by the angular v or the round u, became (v) in Old French, the old symbol being kept, so *u*, *v* became the symbol of voiced OE *f* in ME, as in *luve* = OE *lufu*. The sound (w) was introduced again into Old French from Old German in such words as *warde*, from Old Low German *warda* (=OE *weard* 'custody'), developing into (gw), later (g) in Parisian—*guarde*. In those Old French dialects which kept German (w) it was expressed by two angular *u*s joined together, whence we still call the ligature 'double *u*.' In ME *w* soon superseded the OE ƿ (106). As *w* in OE *snāw* 'snow' was practically an (u), in ME *w* came into general use in diphthongs, as in *snow, how*=OE *hū*, the *ow*=(uu) in the latter being only a written diphthong.

164. The other Runic letter *þ* was used throughout the ME period, but the digraph *th* soon came into use to express the voice as well as the breath sound of *þ*, as in *brēþen, brethen* (breeðən) 'breathe,' *brēþ, breth* (breeþ) 'breath.' In Old French *th* was written only in learned words, proper names, etc., and had the sound (t), which it often kept in ME as well; we still pronounce such words as *Thomas* with a (t), as in ME. Old French *ph*=(f) was also used only in learned words and names, *f* being often substituted for it; it was used in ME in such learned words as *phisik* 'physic,' also written *fisik*.

Stress.

165. In ME the noun- and adjective-prefixes *al-, mis-, un-* throw the stress forward, as in *al·mihti, mis·dēd, un·cūþ* 'unknown'=OE *·ælmihtiġ, ·misdǣd, ·uncūþ*.

166. In Old French the stress generally fell on the same syllable as in Latin, as in *na·ture*=Latin *nā·tūram*. Through the dropping of final Latin syllables many French words thus came to have the stress on the last syllable, as in *o·nour* =*ho·nōrem, pi·te*=*pie·tātem*. When first introduced into ME French words kept their original stress: *nā·tūre, o·nūr, pi·tē*;

but such words afterwards threw the stress back on to the first syllable by the analogy of the native E. words, such as *·fader*, *·bodi*, becoming *·nātūre*, etc.

167. In longer French words, where it would have been inconvenient to throw the stress back to the first syllable, it was drawn back from the end to the middle of the word, as in *sǒve·reynetē*, *con·dicioun* (kon·disiuun) and the other words in *-ioun*=Latin *-iōnem*.

168. Many words of French origin compounded with particles, such as *a·vow* (a·vuu), *de·fense*, *dis·ęse* (dis·eezə), keep their original stress by the analogy of native words such as *a·rīsen*, *be·cumen*.

Quantity.

169. The first quantity-change that took place in ME was the lengthening of OE short consonants after a short strong vowel, so that OE *in* 'in' and *inn* 'dwelling' were levelled under the latter form; and as it was no longer necessary to mark the distinction, the OE double consonants were written single, as in *al*, *man*=OE *eall*, *mann*. But double consonants before vowels were kept in ME in pronunciation as well as spelling, so that, for instance, *sunne* 'sun'=OE *sunne* was kept distinct from *sune* 'son'=OE *sunu*, these two words never rhyming on one another in verse.

170. The OE group-lengthenings were kept up in ME, as in *ǭld*, *lǭng*, *blīnd*, *dūmb*, *doumb*=Old Anglian *āld*, *lǭng*, *blīnd*, *dūmb*. Otherwise OE long vowels were generally shortened before two consonants, as in *askien*, *wisdōm* [compare ME *wīs* 'wise'], *kepte* 'kept' pret.=OE *āscian*, *wīsdōm*, *cēpte*. But length was often preserved before *st*, as in *lęst* 'least,' *prēst* 'priest'=OE *lǣst*, *prēost*.

In the transition from ME to MnE the long vowels before *ng* and *mb* were shortened, whence MnE *long*, *young* (jɐŋ), *dumb* compared with *old* (ould), *blind* (blaind). Hence also OE *-anc*, *-ǫnc* appears as *-ank* in MnE, while OE *-ang*, *-ǫng* appears as *-ong*, as in *lank* = OE *hlanc* compared with *long* = OE *lang*.

171. In Late ME short vowels before a single consonant followed by another vowel were lengthened, as in *nāme*, *mę̄te* 'meat,' *brǭken* 'broken' = Early ME *name*, *mete*, *ibroken* = OE *nama*, *mete*, *ġebrocen*. We call these lengthened vowels 'new-longs' as opposed to the 'old-longs' in such words as *wīn* 'wine' = OE *wīn*. But the high vowels *i*, *ü*, *u* were never lengthened, as in *writen* 'written,' *düde* 'did,' *sune* = OE *ġewriten*, *dyde*, *sunu*.

172. Vowels were not lengthened in final strong syllables, as in *smal*, *swan*, *yaf* 'gave,' *God* = OE *smæl*, *swan*, *ġeaf*, *God*, because the final consonants had already been lengthened (169).

173. Short vowels are often preserved in Late as well as Early ME before a single consonant followed by the full vowel *i*, as in *mani*, *peni*, *bodi*, or weak *e* + a vowel-like consonant (r, l, n, m), as in *hamer*, *feter*, *coper*; *sadel*, *hovel*; *seven*, *troden*, all of which still have short vowels in Present English. This is called **back-shortening**. Originally long vowels are sometimes back-shortened in ME, as in *laþer* from OE *lēaþor*. But there are several exceptions to the general principle of back-shortening, as in Late ME *āker*, *crādel*, *stǭlen* = OE *æcer*, *cradol*, *ġestolen*.

Vowels.

174. In ME the OE weak vowels are generally levelled under *e*, especially when final: ME *name*, *beren*, *sune* = OE *nama*, *beran*, *sunu*. There was a tendency to drop weak *e* altogether after another weak syllable, as in *lādi*, 'lady' from OE *hlǣfdige*.

175. Many words which in OE end in a consonant, take final *e* in ME, which they get from the OE inflected forms; thus ME *quēne* 'queen' comes not from the OE nom. sing. *cwēn*, but from the acc. sing. *cwēne*, plur. nom. *cwēna*, etc. Other examples are *sinne* 'sin,' *dale* 'valley,' *bede* 'prayer' =OE *synn*, *dæl*, *ġebed*, plurals *synna*, *dalu*, *ġebedu*. Such forms as *narwe* 'narrow,' *yelwe* 'yellow'=OE *nearu*, *ġeolu*, plurals *nearwe*, *ġeolwe* arose in the same way.

176. a. In the strong vowels the most marked and earliest change is the smoothing of the OE diphthongs, shown in Late ME *hard*, *sterre* 'star,' *brę̄d* 'bread,' *dēþ* 'deep'=OE *heard*, *steorra*, *brēad*, *dēop*.

177. In Early ME *ea* became (æ), which was generally written *e*, which we write *ę*, as in *hęrd*, *węs*=OE *heard*, *wæs*. This broad (æ) was then still further broadened to (a), giving Late ME *hard*, *was*. OE *a* was kept throughout in such words as *man*, *faren*=OE *mann*, *faran*. ME *a* in such words as *al*, *half*, comes from Anglian *all*, *half*, not from West-Saxon *eall*, *healf*.

178. i, ü. In North-Thames E. *i* corresponds not only to OE *i*, as in *smiþ*=OE *smiþ*, but also to OE *y*, as in *sinne*, *dide*. But (y) was still preserved in the Southern dialect, as in *sünne*, *düde*, being represented by *e* in Middle, as well as Old Kentish, as in *senne*. The London dialect generally has *i*=OE *y*, but some words have the Southern, and the few the Kentish forms: *sinne*, *büsi*, *kernel*=OE *synn*, *bysiġ* 'occupied,' *cyrnel*, 'kernel.' In some words (y) was broadened to (u), especially after lip-consonants, as in *wŏrien* 'worry,' *mŏche* 'much'=OE *wyrġan*, *myċel*, *miċel*.

179. e. OE close (e) became open (*e*) in Early ME, so

that OE *e* and *ę* were levelled under the latter sound, which we write simply *e* in ME, as in *helpen, eten, rest, mete*=OE *helpan, etan; ręst, męte.* OE *eo* also became open *e* in Late ME, as in *erþe, hevene.* All these *e*s are liable to be lengthened in Late ME (171), as in *ę̄ten, mę̄te.*

180. u. OE *u* was kept unchanged in ME, as in *sune.*

181. o. OE close *o* became open in Early ME, as in *folk, nose, bodien* 'proclaim'=OE *folc, nosu, bodian,* being liable to lengthening in Late ME, as in *nǭse, bǭdien.*

182. The OE long vowels *ī, ē, ǣ, ū, ō* were generally preserved unchanged in ME, *ē, ǣ* being also the representatives of OE *ēo, ēa* respectively (176): *wīn, kēne* 'bold,' *dēp, sę̄* 'sea,' *hę̄ved* 'head,' *hūs, hous, gōd* 'good'=OE *wīn, cēne, dēop, sǣ, hēafod, hūs, gōd.* So also ME *fīnden, fēld* 'field,' *hūnd* 'dog,' *wōrd* 'word'=Anglian *fīndan, fēld, hūnd, wōrd* (126). *ī* is sometimes the result of raising Anglian *ē* before open *ġ* and front *h*, as in *ie* 'eye,' *hīh* 'high'=Old Anglian *ēġe, hēh,* West-Saxon *ēage, hēah,* the open *ġ*=(j) being absorbed. So also open *g* was absorbed in ME by a preceding *u* or *ū*, as in *fūel* 'bird,' *būen* later *bowen* 'bend'=OE *fugol, būgan.* It is to be observed that ME *ē* represents not only the common OE *ē* in *cēne,* but also the Anglian *ē*=West-Saxon *æ̂* and *īe,* as in *ēven* 'evening,' *dēde* 'deed,' *hēren* 'hear,' *isēne* 'seen'=West-Saxon *æ̂fen, dæ̂d, hīeran, ġesīene.* But *ę̄*=*æ̂* is frequent before and after *r*, as in *drę̄den* 'dread,' *þę̄r* 'there,' *wę̄ren* 'were'=West-Saxon *on·dræ̂dan, þæ̂r, wæ̂ron.*

183. In South-Thames E. *ǣ* and *æ̂* when shortened pass through *æ* into *a*, while in Northern not only Anglian *ē*=*æ̂* but also *ǣ* shorten to *e*, Midland generally showing the same tendency. Hence such words as OE *hlǣfdige* 'lady,' *lǣdde* 'led,' *næ̂ddre* 'serpent,' *ondræ̂dde* 'feared' appear in Southern as *lavedi*, *lādi*, *ladde*, *naddre*, *dradde*, in Northern as *lefdi*, *ledi*, *ledde*, *neddre*, *dredde*. But Southern has *e* in some words, such as *flesh*=OE *flǣsċ*.

184. OE *ā* remained unchanged in the Northern dialect, as in *gā* 'go,' *stān*=OE *gān*, *stān*. In South-Thames E., and to a great extent in Midland, it was rounded into broad *ǭ*: *gǭ*, *stǭn*. So also in *lǭng*=OE *lāng*. This change took place before the introduction of such French words as *dāme*, *cŏrāġe*, which therefore kept their *ā* in South-Thames E. as well as Northern.

185. OE *ȳ* became *ī* in North-Thames E., as also in the London dialect, but was preserved in the Southern dialect, as in *fǖr* 'fire,' *kǖþen* 'make known'=OE *fȳr*, *cȳþan*, which also preserved Late West-Saxon *y*=older *ie*, as in *hǖren* 'hear,' *brǖsen* 'bruise'=Early West-Saxon *hīeran*, *brīesan*. Kentish kept its *ē*, as in *mēs* 'mice.' *ǖ* was brought into London E. in French words containing *u*, *ui*, as in *dǖc*, *cǖre*, *fruit*, *frǖt*; when final or before a vowel it became *ēu*, as is shown by such spellings as *vertew*, *crewel*=*vertu*, *cruel*.

186. Most of the ME diphthongs are the result of the weakening of OE *w* and open *g* and *ġ* after vowels, *w* and open *g* becoming *u*, as in *dēu*, *dew*, *drauen*=OE *dēaw*, *dragan*, open *ġ* becoming *i*, as in *wei* 'way'=OE *weġ*. The glide between a back vowel and a following *h* developed into diphthongic *u*, which was sometimes written, sometimes not, as in *broghte*, *broughte* 'brought'=OE *brohte*. The following are the ME diphthongs:—

ai=OE *æġ*, as in *dai*, *saide* 'said'=OE *dæġ*, *sæġde*.

ei=OE *eġ*, *ęġ*, as in *wei*, *leide* 'laid'=OE *weġ*, *lęġde*.

ēi=OE *ēġ*, as in *hēi* 'hay'=OE *hēġ*. *grēi*=Anglian *grēġ*, West-Saxon *grǣġ*. But OE *ēġ* generally becomes *ī* in ME (**182**).

ęi=OE *ǣġ*, as in *kęie* 'key'=*cǣġ*.

oi occurs only in French words, such as *joie*, *vois*.

au=OE *ag*, as in *drauen*. In such words as *laughter* from Scandinavian *hlahtr* it is the result of glide-development. In words of French origin *au* corresponds sometimes to Old French *au*, as in *cause*, sometimes to Old French nasal *a* before a nasal consonant, as in *chaumbre*, *servaunt*=Old French *chambre* (tʃaa*n*mbrə), etc., the spellings *chambre*, etc. without *u* occurring also in ME, where the pronunciation varied between pure (aa*n*) and (au), which was an E. imitation of the former.

ēu=OE *ēw*, *ēow*, as in *nēwe* 'new'=Old Anglian *nēowe*, West-Saxon *nīwe*. French *ū* had this sound in certain cases (185).

ęu=OE *ǣw*, *ēaw*, as in *dęu*.

ou=OE *ow*, *og*, as in *tow*, *bowe*=OE *tow*, *boga*.

ōu=OE *ōw*, as in *stōu* 'place,' *blōwen* 'bloom'=OE *stōw*, *blōwan*. In Early ME this diphthong also results from the development of a glide before *h*, as in *inōuh*—also written *inōh*—'enough,' from OE *genōh*, earlier *ġenōg* (143); this *ōu* becomes *uu* in late ME: *ynough* (i·nuux).

ǫu=OE *āw*, *āg*, as in *blǫwen* 'blow' (wind), *ǫwen* 'own' =OE *blāwan*, *āgen*.

Consonants.

187. In Old French *h* was silent in most words of Latin origin—being often dropped in writing as well as pronunciation—but was always pronounced in certain words—mostly of German origin—which, of course, kept their *h* when imported into ME both in spelling and pronunciation, the silent French *h* being sometimes written, sometimes not, but never pronounced. ME had silent French *h* in such words as *onūr, honour, hour, horrible.*

188. OE *hr-, hl-, hn-* became voiced in ME, as in *ring, lūd, nǒte*; *hw-* was kept, being written *wh*, as in *what.*

189. The hisses were voiced initially in all native words in South-Thames E., as shown by such spellings as *volk, zingen*, but not in French words, such as *fēste* 'feast,' *saùf* 'safe,' because this change had been carried out before the introduction of French words. Southern *v* was introduced into the London dialect in a few words, such as *vixen*=OE *fyxen*, feminine of *fox, vat*=OE *fæt* 'vessel.'

190. OE *ċ* and stopped *ġ* developed into the compound consonants (cç, qj)—that is, nearly into their MnE sounds (tʃ, dʒ)—as in *chīld, senġen*, OE *ċċ, cg* being written *cch, gg*=(ccç, qqj), as in *wrecche, seġġen* 'say'=OE *wrēċċa, sęcgan.*

191. Open OE *g* was rounded into (ʒ*w*), which passed into (w) and then (u) (**186**). *w*=OE *g* was kept after a consonant, as in *folwen* 'follow'=OE *folgian.*

192. Strong *h* was rounded into (x*w*) in the same way, as shown by its influence on preceding vowels (**186**). As final *h* in ME often corresponded to medial *w* in such pairs as *inōh* sing., *inōwe* plur.=Late OE *ġenōh, ġenōge*, OE final *h* was changed by this analogy into *w* when an *e* was added —as was frequently the case (**175**): thus ME *furwe* 'furrow,' *holwe* 'hollow'=OE *fúrh, holh.* When final *e* was dropped at the end of the ME period, a resulting final *w* was changed to *u*: *folu, holu.*

193. Open *ġ* was generally weakened to *i* after consonants as well as in diphthongs: *bürien* 'bury,' *beli* 'belly'=OE *byrġan, bęlġ.*

194. Final OE front *h* was voiced in ME when a vowel

was added; thus *hīh* 'high' has pl. *hīȝe*, *hīe* (182), from which a new uninflected form *hī* was formed.

195. In OE the Anglian dialects seem to have changed medial *ċ*, *ġ* to *c*, *g* before a back vowel, as in Anglian *sēcan*= West-Saxon *sēċan*. Hence in ME we often find North-Thames *k*, as in *sēke*, corresponding to South-Thames *ch*, as in *sēche*, MnE having the Northern form in *seek*, the Southern in *beseech*. So also MnE *cold*, *gall* point to Anglian *cāld*, *galle*, *chalk* to Southern *ċealc*.

196. Scandinavian words keep their (k) and (g), as in *ketel* 'kettle,' *gerþ* 'girth.' The Northern forms *mikel* 'great,' *give*, etc.,=Southern *müchel*; *yiven*, may also be due to Scandinavian influence.

197. In some cases the fluctuation between the two classes of consonants is due to change of vowel in inflection. Thus the Standard ME *gate* 'gate' points to the OE pl. *gatu*, the Northern *yate* to the sing. (Anglian) *ġæt*. So also *beginnen*=OE *beġinnan* owes its *g* to the pret. and past partic. *begann*, *begunnen*.

198. *ng* kept its (g) not only in such words as *finger*, *English*, but also in *sing*, *singer*, etc.

199. *sċ* passed through (sj) into (ʃ), written *sch*, *ssh*, *sh*, as in *short*, *shrūd*, *fish*=OE *sċort*, *sċrūd*, *fisċ*. Scandinavian *sk* was kept before all vowels, as in *skin*, *skī*=Icelandic *skȳ* 'cloud.'

200. The combinations *lr*, *nr* are made into *ldr*, *ndr* in ME by making the second half of the *l* and *n* into a stopped consonant, so as to facilitate the transition to the *r*, as in *alder* (the tree), *þunder* from OE *aler* genitive *alre*, *þunor* genitive *þunres*. So also *ml* became *mbl* in *þimbel* 'thimble' from OE *þȳm*(*e*)*le* 'thumbstall,' literally 'little thumb,' from *þūma* 'thumb.'

201. Several of the consonants were liable to be dropped in weak syllables. Thus to the strong *ich* 'I'=OE *iċ* there corresponded a weak *ī*, which in Late ME almost supplanted the strong *ich*. Weak final *n* was frequently dropped, as in *gāme*, *bīnde* infin., *ibūnde* past partic.=OE *gamen*, *bindan*, *ġebunden*. So also the dropping of *l* in *muche*=OE *miċel*, *ęch*=OE *ǣlċ* 'each,' of the *w* and *l* in *such*=OE *swelċ*, seems to have begun in weak (unstressed) forms of these words.

English Vowels.

OE	ME	MnE
mann	man	mæn
sæt	sat	sæt
heard	hard	haad
nama	nāme	neim
witan	witen	wit
helpan	helpen	help
heofon	hevene	hevn
stelan	stę̄len	stijl
sęttan	setten	set
męte	mę̄te	mijt
sunu	sune	sɐn
synn	sinne	sin
oxa	oxe	oks
open	ǭpen	oupn
stān	stǭn	stoun
dǣl	dę̄l	dijl
drēam	drę̄m	drijm
wīn	wīn	wain
grēne	grēne	grijn
dēop	dēp	dijp
hūs	hūs	haus
mōd	mōd	muwd
fȳr	fīr	faiər

Modern English Vowels.

ME	fMn		sMn	thMn	PE
a	*man*	æ, a	æ	æ	æ
	path	æ, a	ææ	ææ	aa
i	*wit*	*i*	*i*	*i*	*i*
e	*end*	*e*	*e*	*e*	*e*
u	*son*	*u*	ʌ̣	ɐ	ɐ
o	*ox*	*o*	ɔ	ɔ	ɔ
ā	*name*	ææ, aa	*ee*	ee	*e*i
ī	*wine*	əi	əi	əi	ai
ē	*green*	ii	ii	ii	*i*j
ę̄	*deal*	*ee*	ee	ee, ii	
ū	*house*	öu	əu	əu	au
ō	*moon*	uu	uu	uu	*u*w
ǭ	*stone*	*oo*	oo	oo	*o*u
ai	*day*	ai, *ee*	æi, *ee*	ɛe	*e*i
ei	*they*	*e*i, *ee*	*ee*		
ǫi	*boil*	oi, ui	oi, ʌi	oi, əi	*o*i
ąų	*saw*	au, ɔɔ	ɔɔ	ɔɔ	ɔɔ
ēu (ǖ)	*new*	yy(u), iu	yy, iu	juu	j*u*w
ę̄u	*few*	*e*u	*e*u, iu		
ōu	*grow*	ou	ou, oo	oo	*o*u
ǭu	*know*				

MODERN ENGLISH SOUND-CHANGES.

202. The sound-changes in MnE are so great that their history requires a threefold division of the period into

First MnE	1500–1600
Second MnE	1600–1700
Third MnE	1700–

These divisions are necessarily somewhat arbitrary. In reality, First MnE extended some way into the following century.

Orthography.

203. In First MnE weak *e* was generally dropped—always when final—as in (naam, fal, stoonz)=ME *nāme, falle(n), stǭnes*. At the same time double consonants between vowels were shortened, as in (ʃiliŋ, fulər, sitiŋ)=ME *shilling, fuller, sittinge*. But as the doubling served to show that the preceding vowel was short, the ME spellings were retained, and the doubling was extended to words which in ME had a single consonant, as in *penny, herring, copper* = ME *peni, hering, coper*. Final *e* being now silent was often omitted in writing, so that such words as ME *belle* were written *bell* with a final double consonant, which led to a frequent doubling of final ME consonants to show shortness of the preceding vowel, as in *all, small, glass* = ME *al, smal, glas*. But this doubling was not carried out uniformly. So as the dropping of final *e* in such words as *hate* (haat), *hope* (hoop)= ME *hātien, hǭpien* would have led to confusion with such words as *hat, hop*, final *e* was kept in them, and came at last to be regarded as a mark of the length of the preceding vowel; and accordingly was added to many words which had no final *e* in ME, as in *wine, stone, foe* = ME *wīn, stǭn, fǭ*. *e* was always kept after *v* whether the preceding vowel was long or short, because *v* was generally written *u*, and such a word as *loue*=ME *lŏve* would have been mistaken for *low* if the *e* had been dropped.

204. The writing of *y* for *ı* was carried to great lengths in Early MnE. *y* or *ie* was always written finally as in *many, manie, citie*, but otherwise the two letters were written almost at random.

205. The close and open ME vowel-pairs *ē, ę̄* and *ō, ǭ* diverged more and more in sound in Early MnE, so that it became necessary to distinguish them in writing. In ME *ee, oo* were used to express the close and open sounds indiscriminately, but in Early MnE they were gradually restricted to the close sounds, as in *see, moon*=ME *sē, mōne*, OE *sēo*(*n*), *mōna*, the open sounds being expressed by the addition of the open vowel *a*, as in *sea, boat* = ME *sę̄, bǭt*, OE *sǣ, bāt*. The latter sound was, however, more frequently expressed by single *o* with length-*e* after the following consonant, as in *stone*. Single *e*+length-*e*, on the other hand, expressed the close sound, especially in less familiar words, such as *complete, extreme, ee* being rarely written in such words.

206. In Early MnE *i* and *j*, *u* and *v* were still written almost indifferently both as vowels and consonants, so that, for instance, *us, vine, join*, could be written *vs, uine, ioyne*; but an arbitrary distinction began to be made, by which descending *i* and angular *u* were used only as consonants, as at present. This reform came from Italy through France.

207. In First MnE the orthography was still quite unsettled, but after a time it was found more convenient to keep one spelling for each word, even when there were differences of pronunciation; and as the number of books and readers increased, the fixed orthography adopted by printers became more and more general, till in the Third MnE period it settled down into its present shape, except in a few isolated words such as *cloathes*, *tyger*, which in the beginning of the present century were made into *clothes*, *tiger*.

208. But as the sounds of the language went on changing with even greater rapidity than before, the difficulty of mastering the traditional spelling has increased year by year; so that although a knowledge of the standard orthography is the main test of education and refinement, few even of the upper classes have a perfect mastery of it.

209. We express this divergence between spelling and pronunciation by calling the present English spelling **unphonetic**. The orthography of Old English was, on the contrary, a **phonetic** one—in intention, at least, and as far as the defects of the Roman alphabet on which it was based would allow. Even in the Early MnE period the spelling was still in intention mainly phonetic: people tried to make their spelling represent their actual pronunciation, whereas now we learn the spelling of each word mechanically, by eye, without paying much regard to its pronunciation.

210. The first beginnings of intentionally unphonetic spellings appear at the end of the Old French period, when **etymological spellings** were introduced, by which, for instance, French *dete*, *dette* was made into *debte* by the influence of its Latin original *debitum*, and *parfet*, *parfit* (Modern French *parfait*) was made into *parfaict* by the influence of Latin *perfectum*. So also Old French *autour* (Modern French *auteur*) came to be written *auctour* by the influence of its Latin original *auctōrem*. This Latinizing often led to etymologically incorrect spellings. Thus the Latin *rhētŏr* 'orator' (from Greek *rhētōr*) was written *rethor*, because *th* was a more familiar combination of letters than *rh*. By the influence of *rethor*, *autour* was made into *authour*, so as to give the word a more learned appearance. All these innovations made their way into English, where some of them were further developed. Thus the two spellings of *autour* were blended into the form *aucthour* by the side of *auctour*, *authour*, and ME *parfit* was latinized into *perfit*, *perfect*. None of these spellings had, at first, any influence on the pronunciation either of French or English. Modern French has, indeed, discarded these 'silent' letters in most of the above words. This writing of silent consonants in French was probably first suggested by *s* having been dropped in pronunciation before another consonant in Old French itself in such words as *isle* 'island' from Latin *īnsula*, which in late old French was pronounced (iilə) = Early Old French (izlə), the vowel being lengthened, so that by degrees *s* was often inserted without regard to etymology as a sign of length, as in *pasle* 'pale' = earlier *pale* from Latin *pallidum*. When the French *isle* was introduced into English, the silent *s* was introduced in the native word *iland*, which was written *island*, the two words having really nothing in common except their meaning. Other native English words were misspelt in this way. Thus *antem* from OE *antefn* (from Greek *antíphōna* through some Low Latin form) was written *anthem*, to give it a more learned appearance.

211. In course of time these false spellings began to influence the pronunciation. Thus although in Early MnE *perfect* was still pronounced (perfet), by degrees the pedantic pronunciation (perfekt) came into general use. So also with many other latinized words.

212. In Latin *th* occurs only in words of Greek origin, and in the popular language it was made into (t), so that both in OE and. MnE *th* in Latin, and consequently in foreign, words generally was pronounced (t), being often written so. Even in Early MnE this pronunciation was still very frequent, not only in such words as *author*, but also where the *th* was etymological, especially in proper names, such as *Thomas*. Even in Second MnE we still find such pronunciations as *apothecary* (potikəri), *Catherine* (kætərn). We still keep (t) in *Thomas*, and even write it in the shortened forms *Tom*, *Kate*; but in most of the other words—including *author*, *anthem*, etc.—the influence of the spelling has introduced the (þ)-sound.

213. We are now able to answer the question, Why is English spelling unphonetic? The main reason is that it has not followed the changes of pronunciation. The present English spelling represents not the sounds of Present English but those of Early MnE or rather Late MnE. Such a spelling as *knight* is not in itself unphonetic; on the contrary, it is a phonetic representation—though an imperfect one—of the sound-group (kniçt), which in ME was the pronunciation of one of the words which we now pronounce (nait), the other one having been pronounced (niçt) in ME, and written accordingly *night*. Such a spelling as *island* is, on the other hand, unphonetic from every point of view, because it inserts a letter which is not pronounced now, and never was pronounced. Such a spelling as *author* was also originally unphonetic, though it has now become phonetic—but only by corrupting the pronunciation and obscuring the etymology of the word.

Vowels.

214. The most convenient way of dealing with the MnE vowels is to take each Late ME vowel separately, and trace its history down to the present time.

215. a was gradually advanced to the broad (æ), so that such words as *man, sat* had exactly their present pronunciation in Second MnE. But in First MnE the old (a)-sound was still kept by many speakers. Before *l* not followed by a vowel *a* kept its back sound and the glide between it and the *l* developed into an (u), so that such words as *fall, calm* became (faul, kaulm), being sometimes written *faull* etc. (a) was also kept after (w, wh), as in *was, what,* where it was rounded in Second MnE, whence the present (woz, whot), although there was no rounding when a back consonant followed, as in *wax, wag.* In Second MnE (æ) was lengthened before (s, þ) and in some other cases, as in *glass, path* (glææs, pææþ). At the end of the Third MnE period this (ææ) was broadened into (aa), which is the present sound—(glaas, paaþ).

216. i, e have generally remained unchanged. But in First MnE *er* final or before a consonant became (ar) as in *star, hart, heart*=ME *sterre, hert, herte.* Not in the weak *her.*

217. u was preserved in First MnE, as in *full, come* (kum). In Second MnE it was unrounded to (ʌ), which was afterwards lowered to its present sound (ɐ)—(fɐl, kɐm). But before this lowering took place the (ʌ) was generally rounded back again to (u) between a lip-consonant and (l), as in *full, wool*=ME *wŏlle,* and in other words after lip-consonants, as in *wood*=ME *wŏde, put.*

218. ü generally appears as *i* in MnE, into which it had already been unrounded in the London dialect of ME. Thus

MnE has *fill*, *sin*=OE *ġefyllan*, *synn*. But (y) was preserved in First MnE in some words still written with the French *u*, such as *busy*, *bury*=OE *bysiġ*, *byrgan*.

219. o kept its ME sound (*o*) in First MnE, as in *top*, *ox*, and was broadened to its present sound in Second MnE, being lengthened before the same consonants which lengthen (æ), as in *froth*, *cross*, *off*. In Early MnE a glide-(u) developed between (o) and *l* not followed by a vowel, as in *bowl* (boul) =OE *bolla*—where it was expressed in writing—*folk* (foulk) where it was not written any more than in the parallel *fall* (215).

220. ā underwent the same changes as *a*, being gradually narrowed till it passed from (ææ) into (*ee*), as in *name*, *take*, this last change being completed before the Second MnE lengthening of (æ) in *path*, etc. In Third MnE (*ee*) was further narrowed into close (ee), which in the present century was cleft into (ei, *e*i).

221. ī was diphthongized in First MnE by lowering and retracting the tongue in the first half of the vowel (**105**) till it became (əi), as in *wine*, *vice*, with a very high close (ə), which was broadened in the next two periods, till the diphthong became almost (ai), as at present.

222. ē, ę̄. Late ME *ē* probably had a very close sound between (ee) and (ii), and when in First MnE the old *ī* had become (əi), the old *ē* developed into full (ii), as in *see*, *field*= ME *sē(n)*, *fēld*, ME *ę̄* keeping its open sound (*ee*), as in *sea*, *there*, this (*ee*) being narrowed to (ee) in Second MnE, which by the middle of the Third MnE period was further narrowed to (ii), ME *ē* and *ę̄* being thus levelled, as in (sii)=*see*, *sea*. But the change into (ii) was arrested by a preceding *r* in *break*, *great* (breik, greit), which were, however, also pronounced (briik, griit) in the last century. In First MnE *ę̄* was often shortened to (e), especially before stops, as in *bread, heavy.*

223. ū was diphthongized in the same way as ī, becoming (öu) with very close (ö), as in *house, crown*, the first element being gradually unrounded and broadened into its present sound—between (ə) and (æ).

224. ō, ǭ. When *ū* had become (öu), ME *ō*—which was probably a very close sound between (oo) and (uu)—was moved up into the place of the old *ū*, as in *too, moon* (tuu, muun). *ǭ* kept its open sound (*oo*) at first, as in *go, stone*, and was narrowed to close (oo) in Second MnE, which in the present century was cleft into (ou, *o*u). The older sound has been preserved in *broad* (brɔd) through the influence of the (r). (uu)=ME *ō* was shortened in some words in First MnE, as in *flood* (flud), *mother, gum*=OE *flōd, mōder, gōma*, whence the present forms (flɐd) etc. There was another shortening of (uu) in Second MnE, especially before stops, as in *good* (gud), *book, bosom.* These words did not change their (u) into (ɐ), because this change was already completed.

225. ai, ei. In MnE the ME diphthongs *ēi, ę̄i* shortened their first elements, and so were levelled under *ei.* As *ai* became (æi) in First MnE by the regular change of (a) into (æ)—which in this case was hastened by the fronting influence of the (i)—*ai* and *ei* became very similar in sound, so that there was a tendency to level *ei* under *ai*, as in *way, hay, clay*=ME *wei, hēi, clę̄i*=OE *clǣġ*. The weak *they, their* kept *ei*, as also several other words, especially before *gh*, as in *neighbour, eight.* In Second MnE these diphthongs were smoothed into (*ee*), so that *tail* and *tale*, etc. had the same sound, and went through the same changes.

226. oi was sometimes kept in First MnE, but in some

pronunciations the (i) raised the preceding (o) to (u), such words as *boil* having the two pronunciations (boil) and (buil). In Second MnE this (u) underwent its regular change into (ʌ, ɐ); and the resulting (ɐi) was so similar in sound to the (əi) of *wine*, etc., that it was levelled under it, and *boil* etc. was pronounced (bəil) and (boil), the former being the more usual pronunciation. In the next period (boil) etc. again got the upper hand by the help of the spelling, and the noun *bile*=OE *bȳle* 'ulcer' was mistakenly made into *boil*.

227. au was kept in First MnE, but soon passed into open (ɔɔ)—the long of our vowel in *not*—as in *saw*, *fall* (**215**), which in the Third period was narrowed to its present sound. In some words *au* lost its (u), as in *laugh*, which in Second MnE passed through (læf) into (lææf), whence the present (laaf), *half*—also written *haulf*—*halve*. *au*=French *a* before nasals (186) generally went through the same changes, as in *aunt*, *comma(u)nd*, *la(u)mp*.

228. ēu, ū̄; ęu. At the end of the ME period the cleaving of final *ū̄* into *ēu* (**185**) had been extended to non-final *ū̄* as well, so that this sound was completely levelled under *ēu*, which in First MnE became (iiu, iu) by the regular change of *ē* into (ii), as in *duke*, *fruit*, *new*, *true*—also written *trewe*=ME *dūc*, *frūt*, *nēwe*, *trēwe*. ME *ęu* remained in First MnE, but with the usual shortening of the first element, as in *few* (feu)=ME *fęwe*, and became (iu) in Second MnE, all the three ME sounds *ū̄*, *ēu*, *ęu* being thus levelled under (iu). In the Third period (iu) shifted the stress on to the second element, becoming (i·uu, juu). The (j) was afterwards dropped after (r, ʃ, ʒ) and often after (l), as in *true*, *chuse*—now written *choose*—*juice*, *lute*. In Cockney and New-England American it is dropped after all the other consonants as well, as in *new*, *duty*, being kept only initially, as in *union*.

229. ōu, ǭu both became (*oo*u) or (*o*u) in First MnE, as in *grow, know, soul* = ME *grōwen, knǭwen, sǭule*, which in the Second period was smoothed into (*oo*) and then narrowed into (oo), as in *go* (**224**), so that *know* and *no* etc. had the same vowel.

Weak Vowels.

230. In First MnE long weak vowels were generally shortened, as in *honour* (onur), *image* (imadʒ, imædʒ), *nation* (naasjun, nææsjun) = ME *onūr, imāge, nāciūn*. Weak diphthongs were kept, as in *nature* (naatiur)=ME *nātūre, certain*. Short vowels were generally kept, as in *moral, person, sorrow* (soru), but *e* before *r* was obscured to (ə), as in *better*, and occasionally other vowels as well in such words as *scholar, honour, nature*. But there was also an artificial pronunciation which tried to follow the spelling, pronouncing not only (skolar) etc. but also (naasjon, kondisjon) etc., although the *o* in *nation* was only another way of spelling (u) as in *son* = OE *sunu*. *ou, ow*=ME (u, uu) was also often pronounced (o) or even (ou) in *honour, emperour, sorrow*, etc.

231. In Second MnE the natural pronunciation got the upper hand again. Weak (u) passed by regular change into (ɐ), as in (neeʃɐn) *nation*, and such pronunciations as (piktər)=*picture*, which are now vulgarisms, were in general use. As (ɐ) was very similar in sound to (ə), there was a tendency to make (ə) the general weak vowel, although the older clear weak vowels were still kept in many cases, as in (næʃɐnæl, næʃonæl) *national*, now pronounced (næʃənəl). In Second MnE weak initial vowels wére often dropped, especially in long words, as in *apprentice* (prentis), *estate* (steet), *opinion* (pinjən). We still keep the short form of the first word in the expression *'prentice hand*, but the vowel has generally been restored by the influence of the spelling.

Consonants.

232. During the transition from ME to MnE the hisses *þ*, *s*, *f*, became voiced in weak syllables, especially in inflectional *-es*, as in the gen. sing. *mannes* and the plur. *stǭnes*, whence MnE (mænz, stounz), the breath sounds being preserved in strong monosyllables such as *gēs*, *pens*=MnE (gijs, pens) contrasting with *penies*=MnE (peniz). The same change was carried out in weak monosyllables, so that numerous doublets were formed. Thus the emphatic adverb *of*=MnE *off* preserved its (f), while the preposition *of* was weakened to (ov). There were similar doublets of *wiþ*, *is*, *his*, etc. Initial *þ* was voiced in the weak forms of some very frequent—mostly pronominal words—such as *þe*, *þē*, *þīn*, *þat*, *þouh*=MnE (ðī, ðij, ðain, ðæt, ðou), the strong forms being now lost.

233. The voicing of weak (tʃ) into (dʒ) in *knowledge*=ME *knǭwlęche* is quite parallel to the voicing of weak (s) in *stones*. We have the same weakening in the Present English pronunciation of such words as *ostrich* (ostridʒ) and the ending *-wich* in *Greenwich*, *Norwich*.

234. Towards the end of the First MnE period (s) preceded by a weak vowel and followed by a strong vowel became (z), whence the Present English distinction between *exert* (ig·zəət) and *exercise* (·eksəsaiz), the (s) being preserved unchanged in the latter word because it is followed by a weak vowel. Other examples are *exhibit* compared with *exhibition*, *example*, *anxiety* (æŋ·zaiiti) compared with *anxious* (æŋʃəs), where the change of (s) into (ʃ) is a later one (**241**), *dessert, disease, dissolve, transact.*

Exceptions to this rule are the result of analogy. Thus *to absent* (əb·sent) owes its (s) to influence of the adjective *absent* (·æbsənt), *research* to the influence of *search.*

235. Initial (h), which was preserved through First and Second MnE, began to be dropped at the end of the last century, but has now been restored in Standard E. by the combined influence of the spelling and of the speakers of Scotch and Irish E., where it has always been preserved. It is also preserved in American E., while it has been almost completely lost in the dialects of England, including Cockney E.—as also in vulgar Australian.

236. But (h) is always dropped in weak syllables when not at the beginning of the sentence, as in (-hij sed -ij wəz redi) *he said he was ready*, whence the distinction between the emphatic (·him) and the unemphatic (·im).

The dropping of *h* in weak syllables is very old. Even in OE we find such spellings as *eora, Eadelm*=*heora* 'their,' *Eadhelm* (a man's name).

237. As we have seen, strong *h* appears in ME in the form of (ç) and (x*w*). In First MnE the former was weakened to a mere breath-glide, and then dropped, the preceding vowel being lengthened, so that ME *night* (niçt) passed through (niht) into (niit), whence by the regular change (nəit). But the older (niht) was still kept up by some speakers, and the co-existence of (nəit) and (niht) gave rise to the blending (nəiht) or (nəiçt), which, although artificial, seems to have been not uncommon in speech. The *gh* in *high, nigh, weigh,* etc. = ME *hīgh, hī* was generally silent. The back-*gh* was kept in such words as *laugh, thought, enough* (laux*w*, þoux*w*t, þox*w*t, inux*w*), and in many words the lip element was exaggerated in Second MnE till it became (f)—(læf, lææf, þoft, þoot, inɐf)—which in *draft* by the side of *draught*—both from ME *draght*—has been adopted in the spelling.

238. **r** was kept unchanged in First MnE, being afterwards gradually weakened till it lost its trill everywhere. Towards the end of the Third period it began to be dropped everywhere except before a vowel, as in the present Standard E.

239. Already in First MnE (r) had developed a glide before it in such words as *fire*, *flower* (fəiər, flöuər)=ME *fīr*, *flūr*, and had broadened a preceding *e* into (a), as in *star* (**216**). In Second MnE it began to modify preceding vowels in the direction of (ə), so that *er*, *ir*, *ur* came to be levelled under (ər) or (ɐr), as in *her* (hɐr) *fir*, *bird*, *fur*, *turn*. In Third MnE it modified preceding (ee)=*ā*, *ai*, *ei* to (*ee*), as in *care* (keer), *fair*, *their* contrasting with *name* (neem), *fail*, *veil*; and towards the end of this period it broadened a preceding (æ) into (a), as in *star*, *hard*. ME *ęr*, *ǭr* appear in Third MnE sometimes as (iir, uur), as in *fear*, *moor*, being sometimes broadened into (*ee*r, ɔr), as in *there*, *bear*, *floor*. In the present century (r) has been dropped everywhere except before a vowel, *r* final or before a consonant being represented only by a preceding glide-(ə), as in (faiə)= Early MnE (fəiər)=ME *fīr*. This (ə)=*r* has broadened preceding (ij, uw) into (i, u), as in *here* (hiə), *poor*, *cure* (kjuə) contrasting with *he* (hij), *pool* (puwl). The glide-(ə) before (r) was finally absorbed by a preceding mixed or broad vowel, (ɐr) in *her* etc. passing through (ɐə) into (əə), (aə, oə) into (aa, ɔ), as in *star*, *floor*.

240. 1. Already in First MnE (l) began to be dropped between (u) and a following consonant, as in *half* (haul̥f, hauf), *folk* (foulk, fouk); also in *should* (ʃuuld, ʃuld, ʃud), *would*, *could*, where the (l) was at first dropped only when these words were weak.

241. s, z. In Second and Third MnE the combinations (sj, zj) became (ʃ, ʒ), as in *nation* (*nee*ʃɐn)=Early MnE (nææsjun)=ME *nācioun* (naasi-uun), *sure* (siur, sjuur, ʃuur), *usual* (iuziuæl, juuʒuæl), such words as *nature*, *verdure* passing through (næætjur, *nee*tjər, verdjur, verdjər) into the present (neitʃə, vəədʒə).

242. w· in First MnE was kept before (r), which it rounded, and was then dropped itself, as in *write* (r*w*əit), the (r) being afterwards unrounded.

243. In Second MnE *w* was dropped in weak syllables, especially in *-ward*, *-wards*, as in *Edward* (edərd), *backwards* (bækərdz). We still drop the *w* in *towards* (tɔdz), but it has been restored in the other words through the influence of the spelling, except in vulgar speech. The weak ending *-wich* drops the *w* in all familiar place-names, such as *Greenwich* (grinidʒ).

244. k was kept initially before (n) in First MnE., as in *know* [compare *acknowledge*], the (n) being unvoiced, and the (k) afterwards dropped, so that in Second MnE (kn*o*u, kn*h**o*u) became (n*h*oo), this (n*h*) being afterwards levelled under the more frequent (n) in *no*, etc.

245. g was dropped before (n) in Second MnE as in *gnaw*.

246. In First MnE medial (ŋg) was shortened to (ŋ) in such words as *singer* (siŋər), *singing*=ME (siŋger), etc. by the analogy of final (ŋ) in *sing*; but (ŋg) was kept in the comparison of adjectives, as in *longer*, *longest*.

247. t, d. In Second MnE (t) preceded by the hisses (s, f) and followed by the vowel-like consonants (l, n, m) was regularly dropped, as in *thistle* (þisl), *fasten* (fææsn), *chestnut*, *Christmas*, *often*.

248. In First MnE (d) preceded by a vowel and followed by (r) was opened into (ð) in many words, such as *father*, *together*, *hither*=OE *fæder*, Late ME *fader*, *fāder* (173), OE *tōgædre*, *hider*. Conversely (ð) often became (d) in First MnE in combination with (r) and (l), as in *murther*, *murder*, *rudder*, *fiddle*=OE *morþor*, *rōþor*, *fiþele*.

249. b. In First MnE final (b) was dropped after (m), as in *lamb*. Hence *b* was added in writing to words which in ME had only *m*, as in *limb*, *numb*=ME *lim*, *inumen* 'taken,' 'seized'=OE *genumen*.

PRESENT ENGLISH.

Stress.

Word-Stress.

250. The characteristic features of Present English stress are some of them of OE origin, while others developed themselves in ME and in the different periods of MnE, some being apparently of very recent origin.

251. In Present English, as in OE, the most general principle of stress is that subordinate words—especially form-words—have weak stress. Thus in *he is a man of the world*, the subordinate words *he*, *is*, *a*, *of*, *the* all have weak stress. Hence the weakened stress in *a :piece of bread*, and the distinction between *-some bread* and *·some ·people*.

252. The OE principle of putting the stress on the first syllable of a word generally resulted in the principal stress being on the root-syllable of inflected or derived words.

This principle is still maintained in MnE in native words, as in *fearful*, *fearfully*, *fearless*, *fearlessness*, *fisher*, *fishery*, *fisherman* (fiʃəmən).

253. We have seen that already in ME many long words of French origin with the stress on the last syllable threw it back on to the first syllable by the analogy of the native stress (**167**). In MnE this tendency has become stronger and stronger, so that the first-syllable stress in such words as *honour*, *pity*, *emperor*, *justify*, which in Late ME was only occasional, has now become fixed. Even in the present century many of these words have thrown back their stress to the first syllable, such as *balcony*, *crystalline*, *recondite*, which in the last century were stressed on their second syllables.

254. Native words which had weak stress on the first syllable in OE and ME, such as *arise*, *become*, *forgive*, *to-day*, still keep this stress in MnE, as also those French words which preserved a similar stress in ME through their resemblance to the above native words, such as *avow*, *defend*.

255. Many other foreign words have also preserved their advanced stress. There are many foreign derivative endings —chiefly Greek and Latin, often modified in their passage through French—which regularly take the stress, such as *-esque*, *-tion*, *-sion* etc., *-bility*, *-graphy*, as in *picturesque*, *grotesque*, *imagination*, *position*, *possibility*, *photography*, in all of which the stress is taken away from the root-syllable, on which it falls in the shorter forms *imagine*, *possible*, *photograph* etc. Many words which were imported from French and other foreign languages in the MnE period keep their advanced stress even when the analogy of other words points to throwing it back on the first syllable, such as *machine*, *caprice*—which show their French origin by the pronunciation of *i* as (ij)—*champagne, canoe, gazelle.* Words which were imported straight from Latin generally keep the Latin stress, as in *pa·pyrus*, even when the final syllable is dropped, as in *cre·ate, se·vere.* Words of Greek origin follow the Latin accentuation as well as the Latin spelling, so that the original Greek stress is preserved in English only when it happens to be preserved in Latin also, as in *genesis, museum* =Greek *génesis, mouseíon.*

256. But foreign words even of recent introduction are always liable to have their stress thrown back on to the first syllable, or, at any rate, towards the beginning of the word, as soon as they become pópular, which in Latin words is generally shown by their shortening or dropping their endings, as in *·auditor*=Latin *au·dītor*, *·discipline*=Latin *discip·līna*, *phi·losophy*=Latin *philo·sophia* from Greek *philosophíā.*

257. When a foreign word is used in different senses, it often happens that in its more familiar meaning it throws the stress back, keeping the original stress in the less familiar meaning. Thus we keep the original Latin stress in the adjective *au·gust* and the name *Au·gustus*=Latin *au·gustus*, but throw it back in the month-name *·August.* So also the adjective *mi·nute* keeps its Latin stress, which is thrown back in the more familiar noun *·minute.*

258. In many cases where the same foreign word is used both as a noun and a verb in English, it keeps its end-stress when used as a verb by the analogy of the native verbs which have the same stress, while the corresponding noun- or adjective-form takes the stress on the first syllable, so that the distinction between such words as the noun *·accent* and the verb *to ac·cent* is really ultimately due to the analogy of the OE pairs *·forwyrd, for·weorþan* etc., which analogy was greatly aided by the fact that many verbs of French and

Latin origin also threw forward their stress; thus the contrast between the foreign verbs *in·duce, in·vade* etc. and the native nouns *·income, ·insight* etc. led to the distinction between the noun *·insult* and the verb *in·sult* from Latin *īnsul·tāre.* The following are additional examples of such pairs:—

·absent	*to ab·sent*	*·compound*	*to com·pound*
·abstract	*to ab·stract*	*·extract*	*to ex·tract*
·affix	*to a·ffix*	*·frequent*	*to fre·quent*
·object	*to ob·ject*	*·produce*	*to pro·duce*
·present	*to pre·sent*	*·rebel*	*to re·bel*

In some cases, however, the noun- and adjective-forms keep the verb-stress, as in *ad·vice* (*to ad·vise*), *ce·ment.*

259. The normal stress of a word is always liable to be changed by considerations of emphasis, even a weak word or syllable being capable of taking strong stress if emphasized, as in *that is ·the thing to do,* especially in cases of contrast, as in *to give and ·forgive, not ·subjective but ·objective,* against the normal stress *for·give, sub·jective, ob·jective.*

Quantity.

260. In MnE there is a general tendency to shorten long vowels. As we have seen (**222**, **224**), long vowels are often shortened before certain consonants in native words, as in *blood* (blɐd) = OE and ME *blōd.*

261. There is also a tendency to shorten long vowels—or keep strong short vowels from being lengthened—when followed by a single consonant and a weak vowel, in words of French origin, whether popular or learned, as in *cavern, cavity* compared with *cave*; *gratify, gratitude* compared with *grateful*; *perish, method, benefit, relative, astonish, philosophy,* *astronomy*, *pleasure* (pleʒə) compared with *please*, *courage* (kɐridʒ), *flourish*.

262. But when the consonant is followed by two weak vowels, the preceding strong vowel is often lengthened, as in *atheist*, *radiant*, *patient*, *tedious*, especially in the derivative endings *-tion*, *-sion*, etc., preceded by a strong vowel, as in *nation*, *admiration*, *adhesion*, *notion*, *corrosion*, although *i* is not lengthened under these circumstances, as in *hideous*, *petition*. Short vowels are also preserved when the two short vowels are preceded by certain consonants, such as *n* and *sh*, as in *companion*, *fashion*.

263. There is also a variety of other exceptions, especially before certain endings, such as *-al*, *-ive*, *-y*, *-n* and *-r* preceded by weak vowels, as in *fatal*, *decisive*, *navy* compared with *navigate*, *bacon*, *paper*, *labour*, those in *-n* and *-r* being probably the result of the influence of native words, such as the preterite participles *taken*, *shaken*, etc., and the numerous derivatives in *-er*, such as *maker*.

264. But some of these words with long vowels shorten them when another syllable is added, as in *national* compared with *nation*, *tyrannous* compared with *tyrant*.

265. In words which have been imported direct from Latin and Greek, the vowels are generally long under the circumstances described above, as in *basis*, *ether*, *regent*, *crisis*, *focus*, *strophe*. But there are several exceptions, such as *simile* (simili), *chemist*, the quantity varying in some words, such as *pathos* (peiþos, pæþos).

ACCIDENCE.

NOUNS.

Old English.

Gender.

266. There are three genders of nouns in OE—**masculine, feminine,** and **neuter.** The genders of nouns are most clearly shown by the accompanying definite article 'the'—masculine *se*, feminine *sēo*, and neuter *þæt*. The gender is partly natural, partly grammatical. It is to be noted that by natural gender names of children and young animals are neuter: *þæt ċild* 'child,' *þæt ċealf* 'calf.' In the same way diminutives are neuter: *þæt mæġd-en* 'maiden,' 'girl.' Names of things and abstractions are often neuter, but as often masculine or feminine: *þæt hēafod* 'head'; *se hęre* 'army'; *sēo wynn* 'joy.' Names of living beings sometimes have a grammatical gender which contradicts the natural gender; thus *þæt wīf* 'woman,' 'wife' is neuter.

267. Compound nouns follow the gender of the last element. Hence *se wīfmann* 'woman' is masculine, because *se mann* 'human being' is masculine.

Strong and Weak.

268. All nouns belong to one of two classes—strong and weak. **Weak** nouns are those which inflect mainly with *-n*, such as *se steorra* 'star,' plural nominative *steorran*. All others are **strong**, such as *se stān* 'stone,' plural nominative *stānas*.

Cases.

269. OE nouns have four cases, **nominative, accusative, dative, genitive**, which are not always clearly distinguished.

Declensions.

The following are the regular noun-declensions:—

Strong Masculine.

		Sing.	Plur.	Sing.	Plur.
270.	Nom.[1]	*stān*	*stānas*	*ęnde* 'end'	*ęndas*
	Dat.	*stāne*	*stānum*	*ęnde*	*ęndum*
	Gen.	*stānes*	*stāna*	*ęndes*	*ęnda*

Strong Neuter.

		Sing.	Plur.	Sing.	Plur.
271.	Nom.	*hūs*	*hūs*	*sċip* 'ship'	*sċipu*
	Dat.	*hūse*	*hūsum*	*sċipe*	*sċipum*
	Gen.	*hūses*	*hūsa*	*sċipes*	*sċipa*

272. Some neuters have a plural ending *-ru*, such as *ċild*, plural *ċildru, ċildrum, ċildra*. The neuter plural ending *-u* is dropped after a long syllable, that is, one containing a long vowel, as in *hūs* 'houses,' or containing a vowel followed by more than one consonant, as in *folc* 'nations.'

Strong Feminine.

273.		Sing.	Plur.	Sing.	Plur.
	Nom.	*caru* 'care'	*cara*	*synn* 'sin'	*synna*
	Acc.	*care*	*cara*	*synne*	*synna*
	Dat.	*care*	*carum*	*synne*	*synnum*
	Gen.	*care*	*carena*	*synne*	*synna*

[1] Wherever the accusative is not given separately, it is the same as the nominative.

274. The *-u* of the nom. sing. is, like the *-u* of the neuter plur. nom., kept only after a short syllable.

Weak Masculine.

275.

	Sing.	Plur.
Nom.	*nama* 'name'	*naman*
Acc.	*naman*	*naman*
Dat.	*naman*	*namum*
Gen.	*naman*	*namena*

	Weak Neuter.		Weak Feminine.	
	Sing.	Plur.	Sing.	Plur.
Nom.	*ēage* 'eye'	*ēagan*	*ċiriċe* 'church'	*ċiriċan*
Acc.	*ēage*	*ēagan*	*ċiriċan*	*ċiriċan*
Dat.	*ēagan*	*ēagum*	*ċiriċan*	*ċiriċum*
Gen.	*ēagan*	*ēagena*	*ċiriċan*	*ċiriċena*

276. There are besides a number of **irregular** strong nouns. The most important of these are the **mutation-nouns**, such as the masculine *mann* 'man,' *fōt* 'foot,' *tōþ* 'tooth,' plur. *mȩnn*, *fēt* (*fœ̄t*), *tēþ*, the feminine *gōs* 'goose,' *mūs* 'mouse,' plur. *gēs*, *mȳs*.

Masculine Mutation-nouns.

277.

	Sing.	Plur.	Sing.	Plur.
Nom.	*mann*	*mȩnn*	*fōt*	*fēt*
Dat.	*mȩnn*	*mannum*	*fēt*	*fōtum*
Gen.	*mannes*	*manna*	*fōtes*	*fōta*

Feminine Mutation-Nouns.

278.

	Sing.	Plur.
Nom.	*mūs*	*mȳs*
Dat.	*mȳs*	*mūsum*
Gen.	*mūse*	*mūsa*

279. The relationship-words in *-er*, *-or*, such as *fæder* 'father,' *mōdor* 'mother,' *brōþor* 'brother' are partly regular, partly indeclinable, the dat. sing. generally having mutation :—

	Sing.	Plur.	Sing.	Plur.
Nom.	*fæder*	*fæderas*	*brōþor*	*brōþor, brōþru*
Dat.	*fæder*	*fæderum*	*brēþer*	*brōþrum*
Gen.	*fæder, fæderes*	*fædera*	*brōþor*	*brōþra*

280. Some nouns are indeclinable, such as the abstract fem. nouns in *-u*, such as *ieldu* 'old age,' *strengu* 'strength.' The fem. *nieht* 'night' is indeclinable in the sing. and in the nom. plur., the masc. *mōnaþ* 'month' being also indeclinable in the nom. plur.; we still preserve these unchanged plurals in the compounds *fortnight*=OE *fēowertīene nieht* 'fourteen nights' and *twelvemonth.*

The inflection of nouns is attended by various modifications which fall under the general head of OE sound-changes:—

281. Nouns ending in weak *-el, -ol, -en, -er*, etc. often drop their vowel before an inflection beginning with a vowel, thus *se fugol* 'bird,' *þæt wǣpen* 'weapon' have plurals *englas, fuglas, wǣpnu.*

282. For the change of *æ* into *a* in such nouns as *se dæġ* 'day,' gen. sing. *dæġes*, plur. nom. *dagas*, *þæt dæl* 'dale,' 'valley,' gen. sing. *dæles*, plur. nom. *dalu*, see § **127**.

283. For the dropping of *h* in such nouns as *se Wealh* 'Welshman,' plur. *Wēalas*, see § **141**.

284. In Late OE final *h* and medial *g* alternate in such words as *se troh* (earlier OE *trog*), plur. *trogas*, *sēo burh*, gen. sing. *burge* (**143**).

285. Final *-u* in the nom. sing. of some nouns, such as *þæt meolu* 'meal,' *sēo sċeadu* 'shadow,' 'shade,' *sēo sinu* 'sinew' is a weakening of original *w*, which reappears before an inflection beginning with a vowel, as in the gen. sing. *meolwes, sċeadwe, sinwe.* This *-u* is dropped after a long syllable, as in *sēo mǣd* 'meadow,' plur. *mǣdwa.*

286. The dropping of *h* before vowels (**141**) leads to contraction, as in *þæt feoh* 'money,' gen. sing. *fēos.*

Early Middle English.

287. In Early Southern the old gender-distinctions in nouns were still partially kept up. By degrees, however, the inflections of the adjectives and the definite article were dropped; and when the Earliest Southern *þe, þēo, þęt* were levelled—as they soon were—under the uninflected *þe*, so that *þēo sünne*=OE *sēo synn* and *þęt hūs* became *þe sünne, þe hūs*, the old genders were gradually forgotten, simply because there was nothing to mark them.

288. The first great change in the old system of inflections was the levelling of weak vowels under *-e* (**174**). By this change the distinctions of gender in the OE weak forms *mōna, sunne, ēage* were levelled in the Early Southern forms *mōne, sunne, ēie* as far as the endings were concerned. The distinctions of case were almost entirely effaced by this change in such words as OE *caru*, acc., dat., and gen. sg. *care*, nom. plur. *cara*. So also the inflections in OE *stāne* (dat. sing.), *stāna* (gen. plur.), *scipu* (nom. plur.) were levelled under the same final *-e*.

289. The only endings which could withstand this levelling were the gen. sing. *-es*, the nom. plur. *-as*, which both became *-es* in ME, as in *stǭnes*=OE *stānes, stānas*, the weak *-an*, which became *-en*, the gen. plur. *-ena*, which became *-ene*. The dat. plur. *-um* became *-em*; but as this was the only case ending in *m*, the consonant was levelled under the more frequent *n*, so that ME *-en* represented OE *-um* as well as *-an*, as in *ivēren*=OE *gefēran, gefērum*.

290. The general result of these changes was not only to obscure the distinctions of the cases, but also in some classes of nouns to obscure the distinction between singular and plural. The confusion was most marked in the feminine nouns, where the changes we have been considering gave the following as the endings corresponding to those of the OE nouns *caru*, *synn*, *sunne* respectively:—

Sing.	Nom.	*-e*	-*	*-e*.
	Acc.	*-e*	*-e*	*-en**
	Dat.	*-e*	*-e*	*-en**
	Gen.	*-e*	*-e*	*-en**
Plur.	Nom.	*-e**	*-e**	*-en*
	Dat.	*-en*	*-en*	*-en*
	Gen.	*-ene*	*-e*	*-ene*

291. It is evident that the forms marked * in the above table are in the minority, while at the same time most of them obscure the distinction between singular and plural. They were accordingly got rid of by the analogical extension of those forms which were in the majority and more distinctive. The *-e* of *care* and *sunne* was extended to the OE nom. *synn*, which became ME *sünne*. The plural *-en* of *sunnen*=OE *sunnan* was extended to all feminine nouns—ME *caren*, *sünnen*=OE *cara*, *synna*. As *-en* was now the distinctive mark of the plural, it was given up in the singular of *sunne*, whose oblique cases took the same form as the nominative, as in the other two classes. The final result was that all feminine nouns were uniformly declined as follows:—

	Sing.	Plur.
Nom.	*-e*	*-en*
Acc.	*-e*	*-en*
Dat.	*-e*	*-en*
Gen.	*-e*	*-ene*

292. As might be expected, the gen. plur. *-ene* was often levelled under the other plural cases, becoming *-en*.

293. Weak masculines and neuters were declined in the same way—sing. *name*, *ēie*, plur. *namen*, *ēien*. The only distinction between masculine and neuter weak nouns—namely in the acc. sing. (OE *naman*, *ēage*) was thus lost.

294. -*e*=the OE neuter plur. ending -*u* was made into -*en* for the sake of distinctness, as in *dēoflen*, *children*=OE *dēoflu*, *ċildru*, sing. *dēovel*, *chīld*. In many of these words -*e*=OE -*u* was extended to the singular, as in *dale* 'valley,' *bede* 'prayer,'=OE *dæl*, *ġebed*, plur. *dalu*, *ġebedu*. These OE plurals became *dalen*, *beden* in ME.

295. The remaining masculine and neuter nouns kept their original strong forms. The dat. sing in -*e* was kept at first, but often dropped, because such forms as *weie*, *wŏrde*=OE *weġe*, *worde* suggested a weak singular, and so the dat. sing. was levelled under the nom. in such words—*wei*, *wōrd*—in accordance with the general ME tendency. The dat. plur. -*en*=OE -*um* was disused for a similar reason—because it suggested a weak plural. The gen. plur. -*e*=OE -*a* was sometimes kept, but the more distinct weak ending -*ene* was often used instead—*kingene*, as in *alre kingene king* 'king of all kings,' *wŏrdene* instead of *kinge*, *wŏrde*—both of these forms being gradually supplanted by the nominative. In the neuter plur. the OE undeclined forms were still kept—*hūs*, *wōrd*—but the strong masc. ending was often extended to the neuters, so as to distinguish the two numbers—*hūses*, *wŏrdes*.

The following are then the regular Early Southern ME noun-inflections, those which are liable to be dropped being in ( ):—

Strong Masculine and Neuter.

296.

	Sing.		Plur.	
Nom.	*stǭn*	*wōrd*	*stǭnes*	*wōrd*, *wōrdes*
Dat.	*stǭn*(*e*)	*wōrd*(*e*)	*stǭnes*	*wōrd*, *wōrdes*
Gen.	*stǭnes*	*wōrdes*	*stǭne*(*ne*), *stǭnes*	*wōrde*(*ne*), *wōrdes*

297. The neuter *chīld* has plur. *children*, corresponding to OE *ċildru*.

Strong and Weak Feminine.

298.	Sing.	Plur.
Nom.	*sünne, chirche*	*sünnen, chirchen*
Dat.	*sünne, chirche*	*sünnen, chirchen*
Gen.	*sünne, chirche*	*sünnen(e), chirchen(e)*

Weak Masculine and Neuter.

299.	Sing.		Plur.	
Nom.	*ivēre*	*ēie*	*ivēren*	*ēien*
Dat.	*ivēre*	*ēie*	*ivēren*	*ēien*
Gen.	*ivēre*	*ēie*	*ivēren(e)*	*ēien(e)*

300. The relationship-words *vader, mōder, süster* generally remained unchanged in the sing., having the regular plurals *vaderes, mōdren, süstren.* *brōþer* of course lost the OE mutation in the dat. sing., which became *brōþer*. But this mutation was transferred to the plur. on the analogy of *fēt, men*, etc., so that *brōþre*=OE *brōþru* became *brēþre*, and then, by the usual change of plural *-e* into *-en*, *brēþren*.

301. Final *e* was dropped after a weak vowel, as in *lęfdi* 'lady'—OE *hlǣfdiġe*. The plural ending *-s* without a vowel occurs only in long French words, as in *parlūrs* 'parlours,' *vestimenz* 'vestments,' where *z*=(ts).

In Old French such a word as *vestiment* is inflected thus—

Sing. Nom.	*vestimenz*	Plur. Nom.	*vestiment*
Acc	*vestiment*	Acc.	*vestimenz*

As the distinction between nom. and acc. had been lost in ME., the French *-s* was naturally identified with the English plur. inflection *-es*.

302. In Early Midland and Northern the distinctions of grammatical gender were entirely lost during the transition from OE, the distinction between strong and weak forms being also done away with, except in a few isolated forms. The natural consequence was that the *-es* of the genitive was extended to weak nouns and to all feminine nouns, the plur. *-es* being then extended in the same way, first to strong neuters, then to weak nouns and feminine nouns generally. The final result was that the only regular inflections left were gen. sing. *-es*, plur. nom. and gen. *-es*, the distinction between nom. and gen. plur. being kept up only in irregular plurals such as *men*, gen. *mennes*.

Late Middle-English.

303. Standard ME follows the Early Midland dialect in its noun-inflections: it has only one case, the genitive; the original nominative, accusative, and dative being now merged in one 'common case':—

Sing.	Common	*wōrd*,	*sinne*	*man*
	Gen.	*wōrdes*,	*sinnes*	*mannes*
Plur.	Common	*wōrdes*,	*sinnes*	*men*
	Gen.	*wōrdes*,	*sinnes*	*mennes*

304. The *e* of *-es*—the gen. as well as the plur. ending—is often dropped in English as well as French words after a weak syllable, as in *fāders* (also *fādres*), *lādys* (also *lādyes*), and after a strong vowel, in order to avoid hiatus, as in *fǭs* 'foes.' Also in *pens* = earlier *penies*, of which *pens* was originally the weak form, the word having lost its stress in such combinations as *twǭ penies*.

305. The whole ending *-es* is often dropped in French words and proper names ending in a hiss-consonant, as in the gen. sing. *Troilus*, *Vęnus*, and the plurals *cās* 'cases,' *vers* (also *verses*).

This is the result of French influence, for in Old French such a word as *vers*, whose *s* is part of the body of the word, was necessarily indeclinable:—

Sing. Nom. *vers*	Plur. Nom. *vers*
Acc. *vers*	Acc. *vers*

306. Originally feminine nouns sometimes keep their earlier *s*-less gen. sing., as in *þe chirche dǭre, his lādy grāce.* We still preserve this form in *Lady-day* compared with *Lord's day.*

307. Many originally neuter nouns with unchanged plurals still keep these, such as *folk, dēr, hors, shēp, swīn, pound.* It must be observed that most of these plurals have a collective meaning; thus the plur. *folk* is oftener used in the sense of 'people in general' than in that of 'nations,' and in MnE *swine* is used exclusively in the collective plural sense, not being used in the singular at all. *fōt* when used as a measure was made invariable in the plural on the analogy of the old neuter *pound*, and the invariable *night* in *fourte-night* (280), etc.

308. In its general meaning *fōt* keeps its mutation-plural *fēt.* So also *man, wŏm(m)an* (OE *wīfmann*), *tōþ*, etc. have plurals *men, wŏm(m)en* (OE *wīfmęnn*), *tēþ*, etc.

309. The weak plural-ending *-en* is preserved not only in *oxe* plur. *oxen*, but also in other words which have now lost it in the spoken language, such as *asche, aschen, hǭse, īe* 'eye,' *ien, fǭ* 'foe,' *fǭn, tǭ* 'toe,' *tǭn, schō* 'shoe,' *schōn.* In other words this ending is a ME extension, as in *brēþren, children, dohtren, sustren. cow* has plur. *kȳn*=OE *cū*, plur. *cȳ*, the northern dialect keeping the older form *kī.*

Modern English.

310. By the beginning of the MnE period the *s* of inflectional *-es* had been voiced (232), (s) being kept only in monosyllables such as *geese*, *pence*. In Early MnE the *e* was kept after a hiss-consonant for the sake of distinctness, as in *horses* (horsez), and was dropped everywhere else, the (z) being necessarily unvoiced after voiceless consonant, as in *beasts* (beests) from *beastes* (beestez), while it was of course preserved after vowels and voiced consonants, as in *days*, *heads* (heedz).

311. The ME dropping of *-es* after hiss-consonants is still kept up in a few phrases such as *for old acquaintance sake*, *for Jesus' sake*; but in the spoken language the *-es* is generally kept, as in *St. James's Square*, where it is also written. Such genitives as *Æneas'*, *Socrates' wife* occur only in the literary language; in the spoken language the full *-es* is added, or else the construction *of Æneas* etc. is used.

One result of the contraction of inflectional *-es* in MnE is that radical *s* has been sometimes mistaken for the plural inflection, so that an original singular has been made into a plural, as in the case of *alms*, *eaves*, *riches*, *summons*: these 'apparent plurals' correspond to the OE singulars *ælmesse*, *efese* (plur. *efesan*) and the Old French singulars *richesse*, *semonse*.

Most of these apparent plurals are not used in the singular; but *summons* is used in the sing. without any change—*a summons*. There are some plurals which form a curtailed singular by throwing off the radical final *s*. Thus the collective plural *pease*=the OE weak plural *piosan* has developed a singular *pea*, whence a new orthographic plural *peas* has been formed.

Inflectional plurals often come to be used as singulars by change of meaning, such as *news*, *sixpence*. They may then form new plurals, such as *sixpences*.

312. The ME (and OE) alternation of breath and voice consonants in the inflection of such native words as *wif*, gen. sing. *wives*, plur. *wives*, has been kept up only partially in MnE. It has been entirely abandoned in the gen. sing., which is now formed afresh from the common case—*wife's*. We still keep the voice consonant in such plurals as *wives*, *paths* (paaðz), but such a plural as the earlier MnE *turves* has been made into *turfs*.

We still keep the gen. sing. *calves* in the compounds *calves-head*, *calves-foot* expressing articles of food; otherwise *calf* has the regular gen. sing. *calf's*.

The following are the main types of noun-inflection in Present English:—

313. *Sing. Common*	hɔs	dog	kæt	waif	guws	mæn
Gen.	hɔsiz	dogz	kæts	waifs	guwsiz	mænz
Plur. Common	hɔsiz	dogz	kæts	waivz	gijs	men
Gen.	hɔsiz	dogz	kæts	waivz	gijsiz	menz

Like *horse* are inflected words ending in the hisses (s, z; ʃ, ʒ), such as *piece*, *box*, *size*, *adze*, *fish*, *church* (tʃəətʃ), *age* (eidʒ).

Like *dog* are inflected nouns ending in a vowel or any voiced consonant except (z, ʒ), such as *day*, *lady*, *neighbour* (neibə), *mile*, *dove*, *son*, *lord*.

Dice (for gaming) and *pence*, the plurals of *die* and *penny* have (s) because they were shortened to monosyllables already in ME, *dies* (for coining) and *pennies* being new-formations from the singulars on the analogy of the regular plurals *days*, *ladies*, etc.

Like *cat* are inflected nouns ending in any breath consonant except (s, ʃ), such as *earth*, *cliff*, *clerk*, *bishop*.

314. All the nouns inflected like *wife*—'voice-breath nouns'—show a long syllable before the inflection in Late ME, as in *slaves*=Late ME *slāves* (Early ME *staves*), *wolves*

=ME *wulves.* Hence nouns with original short *i* never make this change—*piths* (piþs), *cliffs.* The only voice-breath noun ending in (s) is *house*, plural *houses* (hauziz). The chief voice-breath nouns in (þ) are *bath* (baaþ), *baths* (baaðz)=Late ME *baþ*, *bāþes* (baþ, baaðes), *path*, *oath*, *mouth.* *clothes* was originally the plural of *cloth*, which now forms a regular plural of its own—*cloths.* The great majority of nouns in (þ) keep the breath-sound in the plural; such nouns are *moth*, *death*, *hearth*, *health*, *birth.* Some, such as *lath*, *truth*, *youth*, have both pronunciations, that with voice consonants in the plural being, of course, the older one. Nouns in *-f* show the change more frequently: after long Late ME vowels, as in *life*, *knife*, *wife*, *thief*, *leaf*, *loaf*; after *l*, as in *half*, *calf*, *elf*, *self*, *shelf*, *wolf.* Nouns in *-rf*, such as *dwarf*, *scarf*, *turf*, *wharf*, made this change in Early MnE—*dwarves*, etc.—but they now generally keep the *f* in the plural—*dwarfs*, etc. Nouns in *-oof* also keep the *f*, as in *hoofs*, *roofs.* So also *belief.* But the French noun *beef* still keeps its plural *beeves*, which, however, is now isolated from its singular, through the latter having lost its original meaning 'ox.' *staves* was originally the plural of *staff* (Late ME *staf*, *stāves*), but having diverged from it in meaning, it has now developed a new singular *stave*, while *staff* itself has developed a new plural *staffs*, as in *army staffs.*

Irregular Plurals.

315. The following **mutation-plurals** are still in common use: *man*, *men*; *woman*, *women* (wumən, wimin), this plur. being Southern in spelling, though Midland in pronunciation; *foot*, *feet*; *goose*, *geese*; *tooth*, *teeth*; *louse*, *lice*; *mouse*, *mice.*

316. The only **n-plurals** in common use are *ox, oxen*; *child, children*. *brother* now has the regular plural *brothers*, the old plural *brethren* being used only in a metaphorical sense. *cow* also has a regular plural *cows*, the older *kine* occurring only in the higher literary language.

317. *sheep* and *deer* keep their **unchanged plurals**.

318. These are the only absolutely invariable words. In all other invariable words the unchanged plural implies either measure or collectiveness. As in Late ME, so also in MnE many nouns of measure have an unchanged plural only when preceded by a numeral, as in *two dozen knives* compared with *dozens of knives*; and many of them keep it only in groups or compounds such as *ten-pound note* compared with *ten pounds*, the earlier MnE *ten pound* being now obsolete or vulgar. It is only when a noun of measure is used also as an ordinary descriptive noun that it occasionally keeps its unchanged plural under all circumstances, as in *how many stone does he weigh?*

319. While the use of the unchanged plural of measure has been gradually restricted in MnE, the unchanged collective plural has been extended. *swine* has now lost its singular, the sing. and separative plur. being expressed by *pig, pigs*. But in most cases the collective and separative plurals are used side by side, as in *to catch fish* compared with *the story of the three fishes*.

Foreign Plurals.

320. Many foreign words—especially Latin and Greek—keep their original plurals, but some of them have also regular English plurals; some have the two plurals in different meanings. Some are used only in the plural. Some are unchanged in the plural.

321. The most important **Latin** endings are:—

-a . . . **-æ**: *formula, formulæ.*

-us . . . **-i**: *fungus, fungi.*

-um . . . **-a**: *desideratum, desiderata.*

-is . . . **-es**: *analysis, analyses.*

-es . . . . **-es**: *species.*

-ix, -yx, -ex . . . **-ices**: *appendix, appendices; calyx, calyces; vortex, vortices.*

There are other isolated Latin plurals: *genus, genera; stamen, stamina.*

322. **-on** . . . **-a** is a Greek plur.: *phenomenon, phenomena.*

323. We have Italian plurals in *bandit, banditti; dilettante, dilettanti; virtuoso, virtuosi.*

324. The Hebrew plurals *cherubim, seraphim* are collective, and are occasionally used as singulars in Early MnE—*a cherubim.*

325. The French plural ending *x* in *beaux, flambeaux,* has the same sound as the regular *-s.*

326. The plural of *Mr.* is expressed by the different word *Messrs.*, in full *Messieurs. Mr.* is a weak form of ME *meister* from old French *meistre,* the corresponding strong form being *master. Messieurs* is the French *mes Sieurs* 'my Lords,' the sing. of which is *Monsieur.* The plural of the feminine *Madam*=French *ma Dame* 'my Lady' is *Mesdames*=French *mes Dames* 'my Ladies,' which, however, is not much used in English.

327. The tendency of the language now is to get rid of foreign plurals as much as possible, except where the foreign plur. marks a difference of meaning. Many words which have foreign plurals, form their plurals also regularly, sometimes with a distinction of meaning, as in *appendixes* and *appendices.*

ADJECTIVES.

Inflections.

Old English.

328. In OE the adjectives have the three genders of nouns, and the same inflections, though with partially different forms, together with the distinction of strong and weak. Adjectives (as also pronouns) also show traces of an **instrumental** case, which is, however, generally expressed by the dative.

329. Adjectives agree with their nouns in gender, number, and case: *hīe cōmon mid langum sċipum, nā maniġum* 'they came with long ships, not many.'

330. The weak form is used after the definite article and other defining words, as in *se gōda cyning* 'the good king,' *se hālga* 'the holy (man),' whence the weak masc. noun *hālga* 'saint,' *þās hālgan cyningas* 'these holy kings,' compared with *sum gōd cyning* 'a certain good king,' *hālġe męnn* 'holy men.'

331. The following are the strong inflections of *gōd*, the forms which differ from those of the nouns being marked * :—

		Masc.	Neut.	Fem.
Sing.	Nom.	*gōd*	*gōd*	*gōd*
	Acc.	*gōdne**	*gōd*	*gōde*
	Dat.	*gōdum**	*gōdum**	*gōdre**
	Instr.	*gōde*	*gōde*	*gōde*
	Gen.	*gōdes*	*gōdes*	*gōdre**
Plur.	Nom.	*gōde**	*gōd*	*gōde**
	Dat.		*gōdum*	
	Gen.		*gōdra**	

332. The weak forms are identical with those of the weak nouns, except in the gen. plur., which, however, sometimes appears as *-ena* with the same ending as in the nouns, instead of taking the ending of the strong adjectives :—

	Masc.	Neut.	Fem.
Sing. Nom.	*gōda*	*gōde*	*gōde*
Acc.	*gōdan*	*gōde*	*gōdan*
Dat.	*gōdan*	*gōdan*	*gōdan*
Gen.	*gōdan*	*gōdan*	*gōdan*
Plur. Nom.		*gōdan*	
Dat.		*gōdum*	
Gen.		*gōdra**	

333. The *-u* of the strong fem. nom. sing. and the strong neut. nom. plur. is kept under the same circumstances as in the noun-inflections; thus *sum* 'some' has *sumu* in the above cases, as opposed to the long-syllable *gōd.* Adjectives in *-el, -en,* etc. drop the *e* as in noun-inflection; thus *hālig, micel, āgen* 'own,' have plurals *hālge, micle, āgne.* Where final *-u* is a weakening of *-w*, the *w* is restored before an inflection beginning with a vowel, as in *nearu* 'narrow,' *salu* 'sallow,' *ġeolu* 'yellow,' plurals *nearwe, salwe, ġeolwe.* In late OE final *-h* alternates with medial *g* in such forms as *genōh* 'enough' [earlier *ġenōg*], plur. *ġenōge.* The dropping of weak *h* between vowels leads to contraction; thus *hēah* 'high,' Mercian *hēh*, has plural *hēa* (from *hēahe*).

Middle English.

334. The levelling of noun-inflections in ME and the loss of gender distinctions naturally led to the disregard of concord. Hence the case-endings in the singular of strong adjectives began to fall off at the beginning of the ME period. The distinction between singular and plural and between strong and weak inflection was preserved in the adjectives as well as in the nouns. *gōd* represented the strong singular, *gōde* the strong plural and the weak singular. As the weak form of the adjective was generally followed by a noun, it was superfluous to mark the distinction of number in the adjective, and consequently the weak singular ending *-e* was used also in the plural. The result was that in Late ME the adjective had only two inflections:—

Strong Sing.	*gōd*	Weak Sing.	*gōde*
Plur.	*gōde*	Plur.	*gōde*

335. The weak form is used much as in OE: *þe yŏnge sŏnne* 'the young sun,' *þis ilke mŏnk* 'this same monk.'

336. In the Northern dialect all adjectives became indeclinable already in the Early period through loss of final weak *-e*.

337. The old cases were partially preserved in the Earliest ME. The gen. plur. ending *-re*=OE *-ra*, as in *alre kingene king*=OE *eallra cyninga cyning*, lingered longest, because of its distinctiveness. In Late ME *alder*, from earlier *alre* through *aldre*, became a sort of prefix to superlatives, as in *alderbest* 'best of all'; in Early MnE Shakespere still has *alderliefest* 'dearest of all.'

Modern English.

338. In MnE the loss of final *-e* made the adjectives indeclinable as far as case and number are concerned. Adjectives thus became formally indistinguishable from adverbs, except by their syntactical relations, the only change of form that was left to them—namely comparison—being shared by adverbs. But Early MnE still preserved a trace of the ME inflections in the distinction between *enough* sing., *enow* plur. =ME *inōh, inōwe.*

Comparison.

Old-English.

339. In OE the comparative is formed by adding *-ra*, and is declined like a weak adjective, as in *lēof-ra* 'dearer' masc., *lēofre* fem. and neut., the corresponding adverbs ending in *-or*: *lēofor, heardor.* The superlative is formed by adding *-ost*, and may be either strong or weak: *lēofost* 'dearest,' *se lēofosta mann.* The uninflected form of the superlative is used also as an adverb: *lēofost, heardost.* Some adjectives form their comparison with mutation, the superlative ending in *-est*, as in *lang* 'long,' *lęngre, lęngest, nēah* 'near,' superlative *nīehst, nīext* (Anglian *nēh, nēst, nēxt*). In some comparisons the comparative and superlative are formed from a word distinct from that which constitutes the positive: *gōd* [adverb *wel*], *bętera* [adverb *bęt*], *bętst.* The positive of some comparatives and superlatives is represented only by an adverb; thus to *ǣrra* 'former' (in time) *ǣrest* 'first' corresponds the adverb *ǣr* 'formerly.' Many of these form the superlative with *-m*, which is an older form than *-st.* The original form of this superlative is seen in *for-ma* 'first,' the positive of which is represented by the adverb *fore* 'before.' But in most cases the meaning of this old superlative ending was forgotten, and the ending *-st* was added—generally with mutation—giving the double superlative *-mest.* Thus from *forma* the new superlative *fyrmest* 'most foremost,' 'first' was formed. Other examples are *innemest, norþmest* from *inne* 'inside,' *norþ* 'north.'

Middle-English.

340. In Early ME the endings are *-re*, *-ere* [adverbial *-er*], *-est*: *lēof*, *lēofre* [adverbial *lēover*], *lēovest*. In Late ME the final *-e* of *-ere* was dropped, so that the distinction between adjective and adverb was levelled.

Modern English.

341. In MnE the endings are the same as in Late ME—*-er*, *-est*. We have also a **periphrastic comparison**, which consists in prefixing the adverbs *more*, *most*, as in *beautiful*, *more beautiful*, *most beautiful* by the side of *hard*, *harder*, *hardest*. Periphrastic comparison appears already in Early ME. At first the two methods of comparison were used indiscriminately; but by degrees the periphrastic comparison has come in MnE to be applied chiefly to longer and more unfamiliar adjectives, the inflectional comparison being restricted more and more to the shorter adjectives.

342. In Early ME such comparisons as *more sad*, *most sad*, *beautifuller*, *beautifullest* were frequent; and they are still used in poetry and the higher prose.

343. **Double comparison** was frequent in Early MnE, as in *more braver*, *most unkindest*. This now survives only as a vulgarism.

Irregular Comparison.

344. In ME and MnE the old mutation in such comparisons as OE *lang* (*lǫng*, *lǭng*), *lęngre*, *lęngest* was gradually got rid of by the introduction of the vowel of the positive, whence the MnE *longer*, *longest*. Mutation is preserved only in a few irregular and isolated forms. Other irregularities are the result of ME sound-changes—*late*, *latter*—of various confusions and mixtures of originally distinct words and forms—*far*, *further*—and of the retention of different-word comparatives and superlatives—*good*, *better*.

345. The double superlative ending *-mest* was naturally associated with *mǣst* 'most,' and already in Late OE we find such forms as *ȳtmǣst* by the side of *ȳtemest* from *ūte* 'outside'; in ME we find the endings *-mest* and *-mǭst* side by side, the latter ultimately getting the upper hand. In the few cases of mutation the vowel of the positive was gradually extended to the other two degrees; already in OE we find *ūtemest* instead of *ȳtemest*. So also OE *fyrmest* was made into *formest* in ME by the influence of *forma* and *fore*, whence the MnE *foremost*. In OE the positives of *æftemest* 'last' and *niþemest* 'lowest' were represented by the adverbs *æfter* 'after' and *niþer*, *neoþor* 'downwards,' 'down,' these being themselves old comparatives. In ME the full forms of the positives *after*, *neþer* were introduced into the superlatives, whence the MnE *aftermost*, *nethermost*, a new superlative *undermost* being formed on the analogy of *nethermost*. A superlative ending *-ermost* having thus established itself, other superlatives of place were formed directly from comparatives by adding *-most*, as in *lowermost*, *uppermost* in imitation of *nethermost* and *undermost*, *uttermost* by the side of *utmost*, *innermost*. So also from *further* was formed a superlative *furthermost*, from which again was formed a double comparative *furthermore*, perhaps partly by the influence of *evermore*. The OE *midmest* was made into *middlemost*, and on the analogy of this form superlatives such as *highmost* were formed direct from adjectives, *highmost* being perhaps regarded as a transposition of *most high*. To the OE superlatives *norþmest*, *sūþmest* correspond as positives the adverbs *norþ*, *sūþ*, which were also used as nouns. Hence in MnE we have superlatives in *-most* formed directly from nouns, such as *topmost, endmost.*

The following are the irregular comparisons of MnE:—

346. *old* { *elder* *eldest* / *older* *oldest* }

OE *eald* (*āld*), *ieldra* (*ẹldra*), *ieldest* (*ẹldest*). The comparisons *elder, eldest* are used to express differences of age from a more abstract point of view than *older, oldest,* as in *elder brother* compared with *he is older than he looks.*

347. *late* { *latter* *last* / *later* *latest* }

OE *læt* 'slow' [adv. *late* 'slowly,' 'late'], *lætra* [adv. *lator*], *latost.* *latter*=ME *later* with back-shortening. *last* is a shortening of ME *latest,* not by phonetic change, but apparently by the analogy of *best, least,* etc. When *latter* and *last* developed special meanings, the new comparisons *later, latest* were formed directly from *late.*

348. *out* { *utter* *utmost, uttermost* / *outer* *outmost, outermost* }.

OE *ūte* adv. 'outside,' *ȳterra* [adv. *ūtor*], *ȳtmest, ȳtemest.* Even in OE the vowel of the positive is extended to the other degrees: *ūterra, ūtemest,* whence by back-shortening the MnE *utter,* etc., *outer,* etc., being new-formations from *out.*

349. *far* { *farther* *farthest* / *further* *furthest* }

OE *feorr* adv. and occasionally adj. 'far,' *fierra* [adv. *fierr*], *fierrest.* *feorr* became by regular change ME *fer,* MnE *far.* To the OE adverb *fore* 'before,' 'in front' corresponds the comparative *furþra* [adv. *furþor*], superl. *fyrest, fyrst, forma, fyrmest.* The comparative adverb *fierr* was soon confused with the positive *feorr* in ME through the tendency to give up mutation in comparison, and the more distinct *furþor* took its place, *fierr* and *furþor* having nearly the same meaning. When ME *first*=OE *fyrst* became the ordinal numeral corresponding to *ǭn* 'one'—taking the place of OE *forma* 'first'—a new superlative *furþest* was formed from *furþer*=OE *furþor*. Lastly, the vowel of the positive was extended to the other degrees, giving *farther*, *farthest*. The old superlative *forma* being no longer recognizable as such, was regarded as a positive, whence a new comparative *former* was made in imitation of *latter*.

350.	*nigh*	*near*	*next*
		nearer	*nearest*

OE *nēah* (*nēh*) adverb (rarely adjective), *nēarra* [adv. *nēar*], *nīehst*, *nīext* (*nēxt*). The MnE positive adjective and adverb *near* is the old comparative adverb, made into a positive on the analogy of *here*, *there* as well as *far*. It is compared regularly *nearer*, *nearest*, the old superlative *next* being isolated from it. The old positive is represented by the adjective and adverb *nigh*.

351. *good* (*well*) *better* *best*

OE *gōd* [adv. *wel*], *bętera* [adv. *bęt*], *bętst*. The dropping of the *t* in *best* is not phonetic, but is the result of the influence of *mǣst*, etc.

352. *bad* *worse* *worst*

NE *yfel*, *wiersa* [adv. *wiers*], superl. *wierrest*, *wierst*, Anglian *wyrsa*, etc. In ME *ill* from Scandinavian *illr* came into use concurrently with *üvel*, *ivel*, *evel*, our present *evil* being the Kentish form. In ME a new adjective with the same meaning—*badde*—was developed by change of meaning and shortening from the OE noun *bǣddel* 'effeminate person.' In MnE *bad* has gained the upper hand, though *worse* and *worst* are still comparisons of *evil* and *ill* as well as of *bad*. In the Southern ME *wurse, wurst, u* was developed out of *ü*=Late West-Saxon or Anglian *y* by the influence of the *w*. In Early MnE a new double comparative *worser* was formed. Both *worser* and the double superlative *worsest* occur in Vulgar MnE.

353. *little* {*less* / *lesser*} *least*

OE *lȳtel, lǣssa* [adv. *lǣs*], *lǣst*. The new formation *lesser* is, of course, a double comparative like *worser* (**352**).

354. *much* *more* *most*

OE *miċel, māra* [adv. *mā*], *mǣst*. In Late West-Saxon *miċel* became *myċel* by the influence of the *m*, whence Southern ME *müchel, muche(l)*. In OE *mā*, originally an adverb, is used as a neuter noun governing the genitive in the sense of 'more in number,' as in *mā þāra witena* 'more of the councillors.' In ME *mǭ*=OE *mā* came to be used as an adjective, and in Early ME *moe* was regarded as the comparative of *many*=OE *maniġ*. *moe* has now been levelled under *more*=OE *māra* neut. *māre*, so that *more, most* are the comparisons both of *much* and of *many*. In ME—and already in Late OE—the *ā* of *māra, mā* was extended to the superlative, which became *māst, mǭst*, MnE *most*.

PRONOUNS.

355. In OE the inflections of the personal pronouns of the first and second persons—*iċ* 'I,' *þū* 'thou'—are altogether peculiar and anomalous. The personal pronouns of the third person—*hē* 'he,' *hit* 'it,' *hēo* 'she'—have inflections similar to those of the adjectives: compare acc. sing. masc. *hine*, dat. sing. masc. *him* with *gōdne*, *gōdum*. So also the interrogative pronoun *hwā*, *hwæt* 'who,' 'what,' and the demonstrative pronouns *sē* 'that,' 'the' and *þes* 'this' have inflections similar to those of strong adjectives. The main peculiarities of the pronoun inflections as distinguished from those of the adjectives are (*a*) that they are sometimes made up of different words, thus *ić* acc. *mē*, *sē* acc. *þone*, and (*b*) that the neuter sometimes has a special ending *-t*, as in *hit* 'it' compared with *hē*, *hwæt*, *þæt*, which in OE is the neuter of *sē*. Some of the pronouns have an instrumental case.

356. The remaining OE pronouns have the inflections of ordinary strong adjectives, whether they are used as adjectives or nouns. Thus the adjective-pronoun *sum* in *sum mann* 'a certain man' and the noun-pronoun *sum* 'a certain one' both have plural *sume*, as in *sume męnn cwǣdon*, *sume cwǣdon* 'some (people) said'; and there was a singular neuter noun-pronoun *eall*, as in *sęle eall þæt þū hæfst* 'sell all that thou hast,' as well as a plural *ealle*, as in *ealle wundrodon* 'all wondered.' So also *hwęlć* 'which,' *swęlć* 'such,' *ōþer* 'other,' *ǣniġ* 'any,' *nān* 'none,' 'no,' had the plurals *hwęlće*, *swęlće*, *ōþre*, *ǣniġe*, *nāne*, which were used both as adjectives and nouns. OE pronouns only occasionally take weak inflection, as in *ić selfa* 'I myself' compared with *ić self*, acc. *mē selfne*.

357. In ME the old plurals in *-e* were kept, as in *alle men* 'all men,' *alle þat liveþ* 'all that live.' But in MnE the *-e* was dropped in accordance with the general rule, so that these pronouns became invariable in the plural, as in *some think differently*, *beloved by all*, *of such is the kingdom of heaven*.

358. The regularly inflected pronouns had a gen. sing. masc. and neut. in *-es* in OE. The OE noun-genitive *ōþres* 'another man's' survives in the MnE *other's, another's.* So also *either's*=OE *ǣġþres* from *ǣġþer*=*ǣġhwæþer.* The MnE genitive *one's* is a new-formation. It is probably the old genitive *other's*—together with the desire of distinctness—which led to the formation of a new plural *others* instead of the invariable *other*, which was still preserved at the beginning of the Early MnE period, as in *when other are glad, then is he sad.* The plural *ones* of the prop-word *one*, as in *the young ones*, is, of course, a still later formation.

Personal Pronouns.

Old-English.

359. The following are the inflections of the personal pronouns—including, for convenience, the interrogative *hwā* —later forms being in ( ) :—

Sing.	Nom.	*iċ*	*þū*	*hē*	*hit*	*hēo*
	Acc.	*meċ* (*mē*)	*þeċ* (*þē*)	*hine*	*hit*	*hīe* (*hȳ*)
	Dat.	*mē*	*þē*	*him*	*him*	*hire*
	Gen.	*mīn*	*þīn*	*his*	*his*	*hire*
Plur.	Nom.	*wē*	*ġē*		*hīe* (*hȳ, heo*)	
	Acc.	*ūsiċ* (*ūs*)	*ēowiċ* (*ēow*)		*hīe* (*hȳ, heo*)	
	Dat.	*ūs*	*ēow*		*him* (*heom*)	
	Gen.	*ūre*	*ēower*		*hira, heora*	

Sing.	Nom.	*hwā*	*hwæt*
	Acc.	*hwone*	*hwæt*
	Dat.	*hwǣm* (*hwām*)	
	Gen.	*hwæs*	
	Instr.	*hwȳ*	

360. The change of the plur. *him* into *heom* is the result of the influence of the gen. plur. *heora* together with the desire to distinguish between singular and plural. The late nom. plur. *heo* is the result of levelling under *heom* and *heora.*

361. Many of the above inflections had weak forms, in which long vowels were shortened, such as weak *þu*, *heo*= strong *þū*, *hēo.*

Middle-English.

362. In ME the genitive of the personal pronouns was gradually restricted to the function of a possessive pronoun, though it still retained something of its independence in such phrases as *oure aller hę̄le* 'the salvation of us all'=OE *ūre eallra hǣlu.*

363. In ME the distinction between accusative and dative was done away with, these two cases being levelled under one which we call the 'objective' case, this objective case being really the old dative used also as an accusative. This extension of the dative began already in OE, *mē*, *þē*, *ūs*, *ēow* being the regular accusatives even in Early West-Saxon. The explanation is that as the personal pronouns generally refer to living beings, we naturally think of 'I,' 'you,' etc. not as mere passive objects of striking, calling, sending, etc., but as being to some extent actively interested in these processes; and hence we are inclined to use the interest-case or dative to express the personal complement even of purely transitive verbs. Hence even in OE they began to say *hē slōg mē* 'he struck me' instead of *hē slōg meċ* in the same sense as *hē slōg þone stān* 'he struck the stone,' but from a different point of view. In ME the change was carried out consistently, *him* supplanting *hine* and so on. But with the specifically neuter pronouns the process was reversed: *it* and *what* being mainly thought of as passive complements of verbs, not only kept their old accusatives—which was made still more easy by these accusatives having the same form as the nominatives—but used them to express the much rarer relation of interest, and so the old accusative *it* has come to represent the dative as well as the accusative in MnE, while the old dative *him* serves as accusative as well as dative.

364. In ME—as also in OE—all the third person pronouns had weak forms without *h-*: unemphatic or weak *im* by the side of emphatic or strong *him*, although in writing only the emphatic form was used, just as in MnE we write *I saw him*, whether the *him* is emphatic (him) or weak (im). But even in the earliest Midland we find *it* written everywhere by the side of *he*, etc., showing that this originally weak form had supplanted the strong one. The reason is that it was so rarely necessary to emphasize the impersonal pronoun that the strong *hit* was forgotten and disused. But *hit* was preserved in South-Thames English up to the end of the Late ME period.

365. OE *iċ* split up into the two forms *ich* (North-Thames *ic*) and *ī*. The latter—which was, of course, originally the weak form—gradually supplanted the fuller form, which became extinct in Standard ME, although it still survives in the dialects of the West of England.

366. So also the weak *us* (with short vowel) gradually supplanted the strong *ūs*, *ous*.

367. In ME weak *eo* often became *a* through intermediate *ea*. Already in Early Old-Anglian we find weak *heara* by the side of the older strong *heora*. In Early ME *heara* passed into *hare*, and in the same way Late OE *heom* 'them' became *ham*. The weak OE *heo* 'she,' which in Late OE also expressed 'they,' passed through the same change, becoming *ha*. This weak *ha* was then extended to the masc.

sing. So in Early Southern we find the strong and weak pairs with *a* in the latter: *hē* (*ha*) 'he,' *hēo* (*ha*) 'she,' 'they,' *heom* (*ham*) 'them,' *heore* (*hare*) 'their.' *ha* was liable to drop its *h* by still further weakening, whence the Early MnE *a*=*he* in *quoth'a, quotha, 'a must needs.*

368. Strong *hēo* 'she' passed through *hēō* into (hjoo, j*h*oo), which last is the Early Midland form, written *ȝho* parallel to *wha* 'who'=(w*h*aa). But the feminine demonstrative *sēo* 'that one,' 'she' gradually took the place of *hēo*, at first in the Midland dialect, and then in the Standard ME. *sēo* passed through *seō* (sjoo) into *shō* in some dialects with the change of (sj) into (ʃ). This *shō*, being a weak form, existed side by side with the strong *sēo*, and in some Midland dialects the two were blended together into a new form *shēo*, which became *shē* by the regular change of *ēo* into *ē*. Strong *hēo* was soon discarded, because this vowel-change levelled it under the masculine *hē*.

369. *ēow* in its weak form passed through (joow) into (juuw), written *ȝuw*, which then became *yow*=(juu), the (w) first changing the *ō* into *ū*, and then being itself absorbed by the *ū*. Early Southern has *ōu* with dropping of the *e*, just as in *hore*=*heore*.

370. The Late OE tendency to confuse *hēo* 'she' and *hīe* 'they' under the common form *hēo* led to a more extended use of the demonstrative plural *þā* 'they.' In the ME period this usage was especially developed in North-Thames English. But as *þā* also had the strong demonstrative meaning 'those ones,' 'those,' and as Scandinavian influence was strong in North-Thames English, *þā* in the sense of 'they' was made into *þei* by the influence of Scandinavian *þeir* 'they,' where the *-r* is only the inflection of the nom. masc. plur. The influence of the Scandinavian dat. and gen. plur.

þeim 'to them,' *þeira* 'their' also changed the old *þǣm*, *þāra* into *þeim*, *þeire*, *þeir* in North-Thames E. In Late ME *þei* found its way into the Standard dialect, which, however, still generally kept the Southern dative *hem* and the possessive *here* from the earlier Southern emphatic *heom*, *heore*.

371. The following are, then, the chief forms of the personal pronouns in Early ME, the North-Thames forms being in ( ):—

Sing.	Nom.	*ich*, *ī* (*ic*, *ī*)	*þū*	*whǭ* (*whā*), *whęt* (*what*)
	Obj.	*mē*	*þē*	*wham*
Plur.	Nom.	*wē*	*ȝē*	
	Obj.	*ūs*, *us*	*ōu* (*ȝūw*, *ȝū*)	
Sing.	Nom.	*hē*, *ha*	*hit* (*it*)	*hēo*, *ha* (*ȝhō*, *shō*)
	Obj.	*hine*, *him*	*hit* (*it*)	*hire*
Plur.	Nom.		*heo*, *ha* (*þei*)	
	Obj.		*heom*, *ham* (*þeim*)	

372. The later forms of Standard ME are—

Sing.	Nom.	*ī*, *ich*	*þow* = (þuu)	*whō*	*what*
	Obj.	*mē*	*þē*	*whōm*	*what*
Plur.	Nom.	*wē*	*yē*		
	Obj.	*us*	*yow* = (juu)		
Sing.	Nom.	*hē*	*hit*, *it*	*shē*	
	Obj.	*him*	*hit*, *it*	*hire*, *hir*, *her*	
Plur.	Nom.		*þei*		
	Obj.		*hem*, *þeim*		

373. In Late ME the Early ME *wham* took the vowel of the nom. *whō*, in which Early ME *ǭ* was made into close *ō* by the influence of the *w*.

374. In ME the plural *yē*, *yow* was used in respectful and ceremonious address instead of the singular *þow*, *þē* by imitation of Old French.

Modern English.

375. In Early MnE the use of the ceremonious plural *ye*, *you* was so much extended that it became the usual polite form of address, the singular *thou* being used mainly to express familiarity and contempt, which latter use brought about its complete disuse in the spoken language of the present century, which therefore makes no distinction of number in the personal pronoun of the second person. But we still preserve the old *thou* in the poetical and liturgical language.

376. In Early MnE the objective form *you* came to be used as a nominative, and in Present English *you* has completely supplanted *ye* in the spoken language. The change is partly the result of a general confusion between nominative and objective in MnE, partly of the influence of the singular pronoun *thou*. In Early MnE the ME *þē*, *yē* became (ðii, jii), which were shortened into (ði, ji) when weak. So also ME *þow*, *yow* became Early MnE (ðöu, jöu) by the regular change of (uu) into (öu), the short (u) of the ME weak forms being necessarily preserved unchanged in the Early MnE (ðu, ju). In Early MnE *thou* and *ye* were liable to lose their vowels before another word beginning with a vowel or *h*+vowel, so that *thou art*, *ye are* were shortened into *th'art*, *y'are*, just as *the earth* was shortened into *th'earth*. This gave the following Early MnE forms of the second person pronoun :—

Nom.	(ðöu, ðu, ð)	(jii, ji, j)
Obj.	(ðii, ði)	(jöu, ju)

377. It will be observed that each of these pronouns has two groups of endings which have exactly opposite functions, (-öu), etc. being the nominative ending in the singular *thou*, but the objective ending in the plural *you*, while (-ii) is the objective ending in the singular, the nominative ending in the plural. The natural result of this was that the associations between form and grammatical function became unsettled, and when *ye*, *you* came to be frequently used in a singular meaning, *thou* (ðöu) and *you* (jöu) were associated together, till at last *you* came to be regarded as a nominative. This confusion was increased by the shortened forms *y'are*, etc., in which it was impossible to know whether the *y'* was a contraction of *ye* or of *you*.

378. The phonetic similarity between *thee* and *ye* led to the frequent use of *ye* as an objective, especially in the weak form (ji), which was used indifferently as an objective or a nominative, being often further weakened by dropping the consonant, as in *hark'ee*, *harkee*, *lookee*, *thankee*. Such forms as *I tell ye* (ji) were still frequent a few generations ago, and (i) may still be heard in *how do you do?* (hau d i duw), but such forms as (luki, þæŋki) survive only as vulgarisms.

379. As (ðöu) and (ðu), (jöu) and (ju) diverged considerably in sound, one member of each pair was got rid of in the course of the Early MnE period, namely the weak (ðu) and the strong (jöu), whose place was taken by (juu),—a lengthening of the weak (ju). As this (uu) did not develop till after the change of ME (uu) into (öu) had been completed, it was, of course, preserved from that change.

380. We have seen that the ending *-e(e)* in the second person pronouns is the mark both of the nominative (*ye*) and the objective (*thee*). The same cross-association runs through some of the other pronouns:—

Nom. : *he, she, we, ye*
Obj. : *me, thee*

The fact that in four cases out of six *-ee* is the nom. ending explains how *ye* was able to maintain itself as a nom. in spite of the support given to *you* by the sing. *thou.*

381. Confusions between nominative and objective may occur in any language through misunderstanding grammatical categories. Thus in the Bible we find *whom do men say that I am?*, where what ought to be the nominative is put in the objective through attraction—through being regarded as the object of the verb *say*; and although OE is strict in its distinction between nom. and accusative, yet the OE version shows the same attraction: *hwæne sęcġaþ męnn þat sȳ mannes sunu?* But as long as a language marks the distinctions of case with clearness, such confusions are confined to isolated constructions. In MnE, however, the distinction between nominative and objective was marked only in a few words, and even there was marked in a way which inevitably led to confusion; and even apart from this cross-association there was no uniformity: thus in the pairs *I, me*; *he, him*; *we, us* the objective cases have no formal characteristic in common. Hence in MnE the linguistic sense for the distinction between nominative and objective has been almost as much weakened as that for the distinction between indicative and subjunctive.

382. In Early MnE the usage was more unsettled than it is now, the nominative being as freely substituted for the objective as vice-versa, as in such constructions as *'tween you and I*. *you and I* were so frequently joined together as nominatives—*you and I will go together*, etc.—that the three words formed a sort of group-compound, whose last element became invariable.

383. The tendency of Later MnE is to merge the distinction of nominative and objective in that of **conjoint** and

absolute, that is, to keep the old nominative forms only when in immediate connection with a verb—*I am*; *said he*—so that, as the pronouns in the nominative generally precede the verb, *I*, *he*, etc., are felt almost to be inseparable verb-forming prefixes, as in *I call*, compared with *to call*. When a pronoun follows a verb, it generally stands in the objective relation; hence, on the analogy of *he saw me*, *tell me*, etc., the literary *it is I* is made into *it is me* in the spoken language, so that *me* is felt to be the absolute form of the conjoint *I*, being also used as the answer to the question *who is there?*, etc. In the vulgar language this is carried out consistently, the slightest separation from the verb being enough to elicit the objective form, as in *me and John came home yesterday*=the polite *John and I came home yesterday*, *them that is here*=*they that* . . In Standard spoken English the absolute use of the objective forms is most marked in the case of *me*, which is put on a level with the old nominatives *he*, etc.: *it is me*, *it is he*, *it is she*. But the usage varies, and in more careless speech such constructions as *it is him*, *it is us* are frequent.

384. The tendency to use the nominative forms before the verb has had the contrary effect on the pronoun *who*. Already in Early MnE *whom do you mean?* was made into *who do you mean?* on the analogy of *I mean* . . , *you mean* . . , etc. In Present spoken English *whom* may be said to be extinct, except in the rare construction with a preposition immediately before it, as in *of whom are you speaking?*=the more purely colloquial *who are you speaking of?*

385. The pronouns *thou*, *thee* and *ye* are now confined to the liturgical and the higher literary language. In the singular the distinction between nom. *thou* and obj. *thee* is strictly maintained. In the Bible *ye* is the nom. and *you* is the corresponding obj., but in the present language of poetry there is a tendency to use *ye* in the obj. as well as the nom., in order to avoid the prosaic *you*: *ye see, I see ye.*

386. In Early MnE *them*—which seems to be a weak form of ME *þeim*—finally got the upper hand of ME *hem*, which has survived only as a weak form, being written *'em* from the mistaken idea that it was a shortening of *them.* We still use (əm) as a weak form of *them* by the side of (ðəm), but only in very familiar speech.

387. The MnE *it, her* are also equivalent to ME weak forms.

388. The ME weak *ha* occurs occasionally in Early MnE in the form of *'a, a,* but only in very familiar, careless speech.

389. The following are the present forms of the personal pronouns :—

Sing.	Nom.	*I*	*thou, you*	*who*	*what*
	Obj.	*me*	*thee, you*	*whom*	*what*
Plur.	Nom.	*we*	*ye, you*		
	Obj.	*us*	*ye, you*		
Sing.	Nom.	*he*	*it*	*she*	
	Obj.	*him*	*it*	*her*	
Plur.	Nom.		*they*		
	Obj.		*them ('em)*		

390. The shortening (-s)=*us* occurs only in *let's.* In Early MnE it was more general.

Possessive Pronouns.

Old English.

391. The OE possessive pronouns are the genitives of the corresponding personal pronouns: *mīn* 'my,' *ūre* 'our,' *þīn* 'thy,' *ēower* 'your,' *his* 'his, its,' *hire* 'her,' *hira, heora* 'their.' The possessives of the third person—*his, hire, hira*—together with *hwæs* 'whose,' are indeclinable, those of the first and second person—*mīn, þīn, ūre, ēower*—being declined like strong adjectives: *mid his frēondum* 'with his friends,' *mid mīnum frēondum.*

Middle English.

392. In ME *his* was made declinable on the analogy of *mīn*, etc., that is, it took a plural ending *-e*, as in *alle hise men* compared with OE *ealle his mẹnn.* This being the only inflection of the possessives in ME, those ending in *-e* necessarily remained or became indeclinable. The Early ME *ōwer, ʒūr*=OE *ēower* took final *-e* in Late ME by the analogy of *ūre*, becoming *youre.*

393. *mīn* and *þīn* dropped their final *n* before a consonant in Early ME—*mī fader*—keeping it before a vowel or *h*+vowel: *mīn arm, þīn herte.* In Late ME the *n* was often dropped before a vowel as well. The *n* was, of course, always kept when the possessives were used absolutely, or when they followed their noun: *hit is mīn, brōþer mīn!*

394. In Late ME the possessives ending in *-e* generally take the genitive ending *-s* when used absolutely: *tō mīn hous or tō youres*; *al þis gōld is oures*=OE *tō mīnum hūse* *oþþe tō ēowrum ; eall þis gold is ūre.* This *-s* is an extension of the *-s* of *his* : *his gōld, þat gōld is his.*

395. In the weak forms long vowels were sometimes shortened—*min, mi*—and final *e* was dropped : *hir, our*, etc.

396. In North-Thames English *þei* brought with it the possessive *þeire*=Icelandic *þeira*, which gradually made its way into the London dialect, where it also appears in the weak form *þere* parallel to *þem*=*þeim.*

397. The following are the possessive pronouns in Standard ME, weak forms being in ( ):—

Conjoint : *mīn mī* (*min, mi*) ; *þīn, þī* (*þin, þi*) ; *his* (*hes*) ; *hire, hir* (*her*) ; *oure, our* ; *youre, your* ; *here, her, þeire, þeir* (*þere, þer*).

Absolute : *mīn* ; *þīn* ; *his* ; *hires, hirs, heres, hers* ; *oures, ours* ; *youres, yours* ; *heres, hers.*

All those beginning with *h* were, of course, liable to lose it in their weak forms.

398. The Early ME possessive *whas* became *whōs* in Late ME through the influence of *whō.*

Modern English.

399. In Early MnE *his* was still the possessive of *it* as well as *he* : *it* (the serpent) *shall bruise thy head, and thou shalt bruise his heel* (Bible). But, already in the Midland dialect of ME the want of a special possessive for *it* was supplied by using the uninflected *it* as a possessive instead of *his* ; and this usage appears also in Early MnE : *the hedge-sparrow fed the cuckoo so long that it's had its head bitten off by it young* (Shakespere). Towards the end of the Early MnE period the present genitive *its* came into general use—

a form which does not occur at all in the Bible, and very rarely in Shakespere.

400. The ME distinction between conjoint *mine*, *thine* and *my*, *thy* was still kept up in Early MnE, but the shorter forms were frequently used before vowels: *mine eyes*, *my eyes*. In the higher literary language the distinction is still kept up: *mine eyes*, *mine host*. But many modern poets drop the *n* before sounded (h), as in *my heart*=Early MnE *mine heart*, keeping it only before vowels and silent *h*+vowel, as in *mine honour*.

401. The following are the present forms of the possessive pronouns:—

Conjoint: *my*, *mine*; *thy*, *thine*; *his*; *its*; *her*; *our*; *your*; *their*; *whose*.

Absolute: *mine*; *thine*; *his*; *its*; *hers*; *ours*; *yours*; *theirs*; *whose*.

Self.

Old-English.

402. In OE the emphatic *self* is added to nouns and personal pronouns, being generally inflected like a strong adjective in agreement with its head-word: *God self hit ġeworhte* 'God himself made it,' *swā-swā hīe cwǣdon him selfum* 'as they said to themselves,' *hē forġeat his selfes* 'he forgot himself.' In the nominative the weak-inflected *selfa* is used in the same way: *God selfa, iċ selfa*.

403. In OE the personal pronouns are used also as reflexive pronouns, as they still are in such phrases as *he looked about him* compared with *he must take care of himself*. OE *self* does not make a pronoun reflexive, but simply emphasizes one that is already so, as in *wȳsċton him selfum* the shorter *wȳsċton him* being enough to express the meaning 'wished for themselves.' Hence such a phrase as *hē ofsticode hine* might mean either 'he stabbed him' (some-one else), or 'he stabbed himself.' By degrees *hē ofsticode hine selfne*, which at first meant both 'he stabbed that very man' and 'he stabbed himself,' was restricted to the latter meaning, the simple *hine*, *him*, etc., being restricted more and more to the non-reflexive meaning, so that already in Early ME we find *self* used very much as in MnE.

404. In OE a personal pronoun in the dative is often added reflexively to a pronoun in the nominative, but without materially affecting its meaning, as in *hē ondrēd him þone mann* 'he was afraid of the man,' literally 'feared for himself,' *hīe gewiton him* 'they departed.' This pleonastic dative is often added to *self*, *selfa* in this way: *hē biþ him self ġehwæþer, sunu and fæder* 'he (the phœnix) is himself to-himself both (pronoun), son and father,' *iċ mē self ġewāt* 'I myself departed,' *hē him selfa sċēaf rēaf of līce* 'he to-himself himself pushed the robe from the body'='he took off his robe.'

Middle English.

405. In ME the meaning and function of the datives *mē* and *þē* in the combinations *ich mē self*, *þū þē self*, etc., were soon forgotten, so that these constructions became unmeaning, which led to the change of *mē* and *þē* into the possessives *mī*, *þī*, *self* being regarded as a noun, as shown in such constructions as *mī self haveþ* 'myself has' compared with *þī self havest* 'thyself hast.' On the analogy of *miself*, *þiself* the plurals *ūreself*, *ȝūreself* were formed. The dative was preserved in *himself* 'himself, itself,' plur. *himself* (Late ME also *þemself*). *hireself* 'herself' could of course be regarded either as dative or possessive. The forms *-selve, -selven* also occur: *mīselve, mīselven, himselve, himselven.* *selven* is probably the OE dat. sing. or plur. *selfum, selve* being either a shortening of *selven* or else = OE weak *selfa.*

Modern English.

406. In Early MnE *self* came to be regarded more and more as a noun, which led to such constructions as the Shakesperian *thy fair self, Tarquin's self.* A new plural *selves* was now formed on the analogy of *shelf, shelves,* etc.: *myself, ourselves, to your gross selves* (Shakespere).

407. But the older dative was still preserved in *himself, themselves. itself* must also be regarded as containing the objective (=dative) case of *it* rather than as a contraction of *it's self.* In Present English we have the forms *his self, their selves* in vulgar speech; and even in the Standard dialect these forms are necessary when *own* is added: *his own self.*

408. The following are the forms of the spoken language:—

Sing. *myself*; *yourself*; *himself, itself, herself.*
Plur. *ourselves*; *yourselves*; *themselves.*

To these may be added the indefinite *oneself.*

409. It will be observed that *yourself, yourselves* make a distinction between sing. and plur. which is lost in the simple *you,* the sing. *thyself* being, of course, preserved only in the higher literary language. So also a form *ourself* occurs occasionally in older writers in the sense of 'myself'; but in the present literary language an author speaks of himself as *ourselves,* if he uses the plural.

410. In the literary language *self* is used as an independent noun: *till Glory's self is twilight* (Byron); *then, all forgetful of self, she wandered into the village.*

411. In the spoken language the emphatic and reflexive meanings of *myself,* etc., are distinguished by the stress, these forms having strong stress when emphatic, weak when reflexive, as in *I did it my'self* compared with *he roused himself.*

Demonstrative.

Old English.

412. The OE demonstrative *sē* 'that, this, the, he,' etc., and *þēs* 'this, this one' are inflected as follows:—

		Masc.	Neut.	Fem.	Masc.	Neut.	Fem.
Sing.	Nom.	*sē* (*se*)	*þæt*	*sēo*	*þēs* (*þes*)	*þis*	*þēos*
	Acc.	*þone*	*þæt*	*þā*	*þisne*	*þis*	*þās*
	Dat.	*þǣm, þām*		*þǣre*	*þissum*		*þisse(re)*
	Gen.	*þæs*		*þǣre*	*þisses*		*þisse(re)*
	Instr.	*þȳ*		*þǣre*	*þȳs*		*þisse(re)*
Plur.	Nom.	*þā*			*þās*		
	Dat.	*þǣm, þām*			*þissum*		
	Gen.	*þāra, þǣra*			*þissa, þissera*		

The forms *sē, þēs* are used only as noun-pronouns in the sense of 'this one,' 'he.'

Middle English.

413. In ME the *s* of the OE *sē, se, sēo* was made into *þ* by the influence of the more numerous forms beginning with *þ*, and of *þes, þis, þēos.*

414. The resulting *þe*, *þat*, *þeo* was at first used, as in OE, both as a demonstrative and as a definite article. But by degrees the neuter sing. *þat* and the plur. *þā* were restricted to the demonstrative meaning. In Early Southern *þęt hūs* =OE *þæt hūs* is still used in the sense of 'the house' as well as of 'that house'; but in Late ME *þat* is restricted to the more emphatic meaning, as in MnE. This restriction was still more marked in the plur.; already in the Earliest ME *þǭ men*, *þǭ hūs* were used only in the demonstrative meanings 'those men,' 'those houses.'

415. *þǭ* was now regarded as the plur. of *þat*, and was completely disassociated from the definite article. Hence it became necessary to eliminate the old *þā*-forms—acc. sing. fem. and nom. plur.—from the inflection of the definite article. This was done by extending the nom. sing. fem. first to the acc. sing. fem.—*þeo sünne* = OE *þā synne* as well as *sēo synn*—and then to the plur. nom.: *þeo sünnen*=OE *þā synna*.

416. The old *þās*—the acc. sing. fem. and nom. plur. of *þes*—was now associated with the old *þā*, till at last ME *þǭ* and *þǭs* were completely confused, *þǭs* being regarded as *þǭ* with the plural *-s* added, so that *þǭ men*, *þǭs men* both came to mean 'those men.'

417. The form *þǭs* was now eliminated from the inflection of *þes* in the same way as *þǭ* was eliminated from the inflection of *þe*, the fem. sing. nom. *þeos* being extended first to the acc. fem. sing. and then to the nom. plur.: *þeos sünne*=OE *þēos synn* and *þās synne*, *þeos sünnen*=OE *þās synna*.

418. The following are the full inflections of the Early Southern demonstratives corresponding to OE *se* and *þes*:

	Masc.	Neut.	Fem.	Masc.	Neut.	Fem.
Sing. Nom.	*þe*	*þęt*	*þeo*	*þes*	*þis*	*þeos*
Acc.	*þene*	*þęt*	*þeo*	*þesne*	*þis*	*þeos*
Dat.	*þen*	*þen*	*þer*	*þisse*	*þisse*	*þisse*
Gen.	*þes*	*þes*	*þer*	*þisses*	*þisses*	*þisse*
Plur. Nom.		*þeo*			*þeos*	
Dat.		*þen*			*þissen*	
Gen.		*þer*			*þisse*	

419. But already in Early Southern there was a tendency to make the definite article indeclinable—*þe*. The main causes of this were (*a*) the want of stress of the article, which made its endings indistinct, (*b*) the general loss of the sense of gender- and case-distinctions, and (*c*) the confusion which arose from using *þęt* both as an article and a demonstrative.

420. The new demonstrative *þat* was in like manner extended to the masc. and fem. sing. and then to the oblique cases of the sing., so that *þat hūs, þat man* were sharply distinguished from *þe man, þe hūs*.

421. The neuter *þis* was extended in the same way: *þis man, þis hūs, þis cū*=OE *þes mann, þis hūs, þēos cū*.

422. At first the indeclinable *þat* was not always restricted to its demonstrative meaning, but was used also as an article in all three genders. This usage survived in Late ME in a few combinations: *þat ǭn* 'the one,' *þat ǭþer* 'the other,' *þat ilke* 'the same'=OE *se ilca, þæt ilce*, etc. The final *t* of the *þat* was often regarded as the beginning of the next word, and the *a* was weakened to *e* so as to make the curtailed *þat* into the definite article *þe*, the first two of the above combinations being written *þe tǭn, þe tǭþer*. *The tother* has been preserved to the present day in vulgar English. In Early MnE *the tother* and *the other* were blended into *t'other*, which was still used in the literary language of the last century.

423. In the plural, where there was no distinction of gender, *þǭ*, *þǭs* and *þeos* became indeclinable even sooner than the singulars *þat*, *þis*.

424. The plural *þeos* 'these' was discarded in Late ME, and a new plural was formed direct from *þis* by adding the regular adjective plural ending *e*, giving *þise*, which also appears in the weak form *þese*, like *hese*=*hise*. *þese* may, however, be the result of the influence of the older *þēos*, *þeos*, which in Late ME would become *þēs*, *þes*.

Modern English.

425. Standard MnE finally settled down to the demonstrative forms—

Sing.	*that*	*this*
Plur.	*those*	*these*

426. In Early MnE the article *the* is often shortened to *th'* before vowels and *h*+vowels, as in *th'enemy*, *th'hilt*, and even before other consonants, as in *th'world*, where the *w* was probably dropped.

one, a; none, no.

427. In OE the numeral *ān* 'one,' which was inflected like a strong adjective (but with acc. sing. masc. *ǣnne*), was occasionally used also in an indefinite sense, which sometimes approached very near to that of the indefinite article: *ān mann*='a certain man,' 'a man'; although in most cases the indefinite article was not expressed at all: *on ǣlcre byriġ biþ cyning* 'in each city there is a king.'

428. From *ān* was formed the negative *nān* 'none'=**ne ān* 'not one,' which was used both as a noun—*nǣnne ne* *gehǣlþ* 'he heals no one'—and, more frequently, as an adjective: *nān mann* 'no man,' *nān þing* 'no thing,' 'nothing.'

429. In ME *ān* developed into a regular indefinite article. When used in this way it lost its stress and shortened its vowel, becoming *an*. As this shortening took place before the change of *ā* into *ǭ*, the article *an* was isolated from the numeral *ǭn* 'one.'

430. In ME *ǭn*, *nǭn*, *an* dropped their final *n* in the same way as *mīn* and *þīn* before a consonant, keeping it before a vowel or *h*+vowel: *ǭ man* 'one man,' *ǭn arm*, *shē dōþ nǭn harm tō nǭ man*, *a man*, *an ǭld man*. *ǭn* and *nǭn* kept their *n* of course when used absolutely.

431. In MnE the strong words *ǭn* and *nǭn* levelled these distinctions, but in different ways. In the case of *one* the shortened form was given up, *one* being used before vowels as well as consonants: *one man*, *one arm*. It is to be noted that in Early MnE *one* kept the sound (*oo*n).

432. *none* went the opposite way, the fuller form being preserved only absolutely—*I have none*—the shorter *no* being used as the conjoint form before vowels and consonants alike: *no man*, *no other*.

433. The article *an* has kept the ME variation: *a man*, *an enemy*. In Early MnE the full form was also kept before *h*: *an house*. We now say *a house*, *a history*, etc. But we generally use *an* before *h* in weak syllables, where it is then dropped in pronunciation, as in *an historical event*. As *one* itself is now pronounced (wɐn), it takes *a* before it: *such a one*. So also *u*=(juw, juə) now takes *a* before it, as in *a unit*, like *a youth*. But *an unit*, *an useless waste of life* are still found in the literary language, being traditions of the earlier pronunciation of *u* as (·iu).

In ME the distinction in meaning between *ǭn* and *an* was not always strictly carried out at first, the strong *ǭn* being sometimes used as an indefinite article, and *an* being sometimes used in the sense of 'one.' This latter usage has survived to the present day in a few phrases, such as *a day or two, they are both of an age.*

Interrogative and Relative.

434. The interrogative pronouns in OE are *hwā, hwæt,* whose inflections have been already given (**359**), *hwęlċ, hwilċ,* Late West-Saxon *hwylċ* 'which' (implying 'more than one'), and *hwæþer* 'which of two.' *hwęlċ* is a shortening of **hwaliċ, hwilċ* of **hwiliċ* (with the *a* assimilated to the following *i*), where *hwa-* is the original short form of *hwā* (**125**), and *-lic* is a shortening of *līc*, the original meaning of the compound being 'who-like' or 'what-like.' *hwæþer* was originally formed from **hwa* with the same comparative derivative ending as in *furþor* (**350**). *hwęlċ* is used both as a noun and an adjective, generally in a more definite sense than *hwā, hwæt,* though it must sometimes be translated by *who* or *what,* especially when an adjective, *hwęlċ* being the only adjective form of *hwā* and *hwæt,* as in *hwęlċe mēde hæbbe ġē?* 'what reward have ye?'

435. In ME *hwęlċ* dropped the *l*, probably at first only when unstressed: Early Southern *hwüch* from Late West-Saxon *hwylċ,* Late ME *which* being a Midland form.

436. In OE *hwā* and *hwæt* were used only as nouns, but in ME *what* was used as an indeclinable adjective of all three genders: *what þing, what man.* This early use of *what* as an adjective was helped by its resemblance to *þat.* The OE use of *hwæt* with a noun in the gen. plur., as in *hwæt manna?* 'what kind of men,' 'what men,' also paved the way for the later use of the word as an adjective, just as *mā*+gen. plur. developed into an adjective (**354**). When the language was able to distinguish between *what thing* and *which thing*, the latter pronoun was gradually restricted to its more definite meaning.

437. *hwæþer*, Anglian *hwęþer* from **hwaþir*, was used both as a pronoun='which of two,' and as an adverb and a conjunction='whether.' It now survives only as an adverb, *which* having taken the place of the pronoun. The pronoun *whether* still survived in Early MnE, as in *whether of them twain did the will of his father?* corresponding to the OE *hwæþer þāra twēgra dyde þæs fæder willan?*

438. There were no simple relative pronouns in OE, there being only an indeclinable relative particle *þe*, which was generally joined to the noun-pronoun *sē*: *se mann sē-þe* . . 'the man who . . ,' *þā męnn þǣm-þe* . . 'the men to whom . .' *sę̄* by itself was also used as a relative: *se mann sē* . . , *hē þæt bēacen ġeseah þæt him ġeīewed wearþ* 'he saw the beacon that was shown to him.' In ME *that* became an indeclinable relative as in MnE: *he that will* . .

439. Although the OE interrogative pronouns were not used relatively, they were freely used conjunctively, a usage which naturally grew out of their interrogative meaning, *hwæt wilt þū?* 'what do you wish?' for instance, suggesting such constructions as *hē āscode þone cyning hwæþer hē wolde* 'he asked the king which of the two he wished,' *hē hordaþ and nāt hwām* 'he hoards and knows not for whom.' In ME *whǭ* soon came to be used as a relative, as also in MnE: *the man who* . . , *the woman who* . . , *what* being still restricted to the conjunctive use.

Definite.

440. Besides *sē* and *þēs* there was in OE a third demonstrative pronoun *ġeon*, which however became obsolete already in Early West-Saxon. It was preserved in North-Thames English, being still in common use in the north of England and Scotland in the form of *yon*. In MnE *yon* has been confused with the adverb *yond*, *yonder*—*yond cloud*, *yonder hill*—of which it was supposed to be a shortened form, and was consequently written *yon'*. *yond* is now completely obsolete, and *yonder* is more frequent than *yon* in the literary language, both being obsolete in the spoken language.

441. The OE demonstrative of quality *swęlċ*, *swilċ*, Late West-Saxon *swylċ*=**swalic*, **swilic* 'so-like,' **swa* being the older form of *swā* 'so,' dropped its *l* in ME in the same way as *hwęlċ* did, Southern *swüch* becoming *swuch* by the influence of the *w*, which was then absorbed by the *u*, giving *such*. The tradition of the Midland form *swich* is still preserved in the vulgar *sich*.

Indefinite.

442. The particle *ā* 'always' was in OE prefixed to pronouns and adverbs—especially interrogative ones—to give them an indefinite sense, as in *āhwǣr* 'anywhere,' *āhwæþer* 'either of two.' Interrogative pronouns and adverbs were also used in an indefinite sense without any prefix, as in *ġif hwā þās bōc āwrītan wile* 'if anyone wants to make a copy of this book.' The indefinite meaning grows naturally out of the interrogative, such a question as 'who?' being necessarily indefinite, for if we knew who the person was, we should not ask the question. The indefinite meaning was made more prominent by putting the interrogative word between *swā* . .

swā 'as . . as': *swā-hwā-swā* 'whoever,' *swā-hwæt-swā* 'whatever,' *swā-hwęlċ-swā* 'whichever.' In ME the first *swā* was dropped in these groups: *whǭ-sǭ, what-sǭ*. In Late OE *ǣfre* 'ever,' 'always' is sometimes added like the older *ā*—though more loosely—to express indefiniteness, as in *eall þæt ǣfre bętst wæs* 'whatever was best'; and in ME this usage was much extended, whence the MnE *whosoever, whatsoever*, and, with dropping of the now superfluous *so, whoever, whatever, whichever*, etc.

443. In OE the noun *wiht* 'creature,' 'thing,' came to be regarded almost as a pronoun, and when the indefinite *ā-* was prefixed to it, the origin of the resulting noun-pronoun *āwiht* was forgotten, and it was contracted to *āuht, āht, aht.* The prefix *ā-* also appears in the form of *ō-*, whence the parallel forms *ōwiht, oht*. Hence ME has both *auht, aht*, and *ouht, ọht*. In OE negative forms were obtained by prefixing *n-*: *nāwiht, nāuht, naht, nōwiht, noht*, whence ME *nauht, naht*, and *nouht, noht*. The fluctuation between *au* and *ou* in these words still continued in MnE, even when the two spellings had come to represent the same sound (ɔ). We now write only *au* in *aught*, making an arbitrary distinction between *naught* and *nought*. In OE *nauht*, etc. were used as adverbs='not at all,' 'by no means,' and in ME they became less and less emphatic, especially in the weak forms, which dropped the *h*, becoming *nat, not*, which at last became equivalent to the older *ne* 'not.'

444. some=OE is still used as a plural noun-pronoun, the singular being represented by the compounds *someone, somebody, something*. In ME the two indefinite pronouns *sum* and *what* were combined in *sumwhat* to express the same meaning as *something*; *somewhat* is now used only as an adverb.

445. any=the OE noun and adjective *ǣniġ*, formed from *ān* 'one' by the derivative ending *-iġ*, which causes mutation of the preceding vowel. In late ME *ęni* was back-shortened (**173**) to *eni*, which was often made into *ani* by the influence of *an*. Early MnE has both *eny* and *any*; and MnE keeps the former in speech, the latter in writing. The OE negative *nǣniġ* was supplanted by *nǭn* in ME. *any* is now used only as an adjective, the corresponding noun being represented by the compound *anyone*, *anybody*, *anything*. In Early MnE *any* was still used as a noun: *who is here so vile? . . . if any, speak!* (Shakespere).

446. other = the OE strong noun and adjective *ōþer*: *þæs ōþres nama* 'the other man's name,' *þā ōþre męnn* 'the other men.' For the later inflections of *other* see § **358**.

447. The reciprocal noun-pronouns *one another*, *each other* are now inseparable compounds, but their elements were originally separate words with independent inflections; *they love each other* meant originally 'they love, each-one (nom.) the-other (acc.).' In OE we find such constructions as *ǣġhwæþer ōþerne oftrædlīċe ūtdrǣfde* 'each the-other repeatedly drove out' (said of the five sons of a king); and even in Early MnE we still find reminiscences of the original construction: *with greedy force each other doth assail* (Spenser).

Quantitative.

For *much*, *more*, *most*; *a little*, *less*, *least*, see §§ **353**, **354**. For *enough* see § **338**.

448. both=ME *bǭþe* from OE **bā-þā* 'both those,' 'both the,' *bā* being the fem. and neut. form corresponding to the masc. *bēġen* 'both,' just as the fem. and neut. *twā* 'two' correspond to the masc. *twēġen*.

449. each=OE *ǣlċ* from **āgilīc*, literally 'ever each,' where the *ġe-* has the same collective meaning as in *ġefēra* 'companion,' etc. *ǣlċ* in ME became *ęlch*, and—with the same dropping of the *l* as in *which—ęch*, the Northern form being *ilk*, which was thus confounded with *ilk* 'same'=OE *ilca*. *each* is still a noun as well as an adjective, though there is also a compound noun-form *each one*.

450. every is a ME compound of *ǣfre* (**442**) and *ǣlċ*, the earliest ME form being *ęvręlch*, then *ęvrich*, which in Late ME was shortened to *ęveri*. *every* is now used only as an adjective, the noun being represented by the compounds *everyone*, *everybody*, *everything*.

451. either=OE *ǣġþer*, *ǣġhwæþer* from **āgihwæþer*. OE *ǣġþer* has the meaning of Latin *uterque* 'each of two,' 'both of two,' the meaning 'one of two,' Latin *alteruter*, being expressed by *āhwæþer* without the collective *ġe-*, which often shortened to *āuþer*, *āþer*. The difference of meaning is seen in such sentences as *on ǣġþere healfe ēas* 'on both sides of the river' and *ġif hē āuþer þissa forlǣtt* 'if he gives up either of these two things.' In ME the pronoun *ǭuþer*=OE *āuþer* was gradually disused, and *ęiþer*=OE *ǣġþer* was used to express both meanings. In MnE *either* is now generally restricted to the alternative meaning *alteruter*.

In ME both *ęiþer* and *ǭuþer* continued to be used as conjunctions, weak *ǭuþer* being contracted to *ǭþer*, *ǭr*, *or*. *ǭþer* .. *or* 'either .. or'—in which the first member kept its fuller form because it kept the strong stress—was in Late ME made into *ęiþer* .. *or*, as in MnE.

452. In OE there was a negative form corresponding to *āuþer*: *nāhwæþer*, *nāuþer*, *nāþer*, *nōhwæþer*, *nōþer*. In ME it was preserved as a conjunction, the weak form being shortened to *nor*. The strong form *nǭuþer* was, on the other hand, made into a new-formation *nęiþer* on the analogy of *ȝiþer*, being used both as a pronoun and as the first member of the correlative conjunction-group *nęiþer* . . . *nor*, as in MnE.

453. In MnE *either* and *neither* are used both as adjectives and as nouns.

454. There are a few quantitative pronouns remaining, whose etymology and history deserve notice:—

several has the same form in ME and old French; it comes from the Late Latin *sēparālis*, corresponding to Old Latin *sēparābilis* 'separable.'

few=OE *fēa*, *fēawe* plur.

many=OE *manig*, Late West-Saxon *mǣnig* by the analogy of *ǣnig*. ME *mani*, *meni* with back-shortening. Early MnE (mani, meni).

NUMERALS.

Cardinal.

455. The cardinal numerals 1–12 are expressed by the following isolated words:—

one. OE *ān*.

two. OE masc. *twēgen*, neut. and fem. *twā*. Already in the Earliest ME *twā* was extended to the masc.: *twā men*= OE *twēgen męnn*. But *twēien*, *twēie*=OE *twēgen* was preserved, and, indeed, survives in the present literary English in the form of *twain*, but was used indiscriminately in all three genders. In Late ME *twǫ*=OE *twā* became *twō* by the same influence of the *w* as in *who* (**373**). In Early MnE the (w) of (twuu) was soon absorbed, giving (tuu).

three. OE *þrīe*, neut. and fem. *þrēo*. In ME the latter form was extended to the masc., becoming *þrē* in Late ME.

four. OE *fēower*, which in ME became *fōwer*, *four*, the *e* being absorbed by the two lip-consonants between which it stood.

five. OE *fīf*, absolute *fīfe*. *fīf*, like the other isolated numerals above three, though uninflected when joined to a noun, is generally inflected when used absolutely: *fīf męnn*, *heora wǣron fīfe* 'there were five of them.' In ME both forms were kept, the conjoint *fīf* and the absolute *fīve*, the latter being by degrees extended to the conjoint use, whence the MnE *five*.

six. OE *siex*, *six*, Anglian *sex*.

seven. OE *seofon*.

eight. OE *eahta*, Anglian *æhta*, whence ME *eighte*.

nine. OE *nigon*. ME *nigen*, *nīn*, absolute *nīne*.

ten. OE *tīen*, Anglian *tēn*. ME *ten* with shortening.

eleven. OE *ęndleofan*. ME *enleven*, *elleven*, absolute *elevene*.

twelve. OE *twęlf*, absolute *twęlfe*. ME *twelf*, *twelve*.

456. The teen-numerals 13–19 are compounds of the units with *-tīene*, Anglian *-tēne*:—

thirteen. OE *þrītīene*, *þrittīene*, *þrēotīene*. ME *þrittēne*. The MnE form shows the same consonant-transposition as in *third* (**466**).

fourteen. OE *fēowertīene*.

fifteen. OE *fīftīene*. In ME *fiftēne* the *ī* was shortened before the consonant-group.

sixteen. OE *sixtīene*.

seventeen. OE *seofontīene*.

eighteen. OE *eahtatīene*, Anglian *æhtatēne*. ME *eightetēne*, contracted *eightēne*.

nineteen. OE *nigontīene*. ME *nigentēne*, *nīntēne*.

457. The ty-numerals 20–90 are formed in OE by combining the units with *-tiġ*, which was originally a noun meaning 'a lot of ten,' 'half a score,' so that *twenty* originally meant 'two tens.' The numerals 70–90 also prefix *hund-*:—

twenty. OE *twēntiġ* from **twēgen-tiġ*, *twentiġ*.

thirty. OE *þrītiġ*, *þrittiġ*. ME. *þritti*, Late East-Midland *þirti*, with the same transposition as in *third*.

forty. OE *fēowertiġ*.

fifty. OE *fīftiġ*. ME *fifti*.

sixty. OE *sixtiġ*.

seventy. OE *hundseofontiġ*. ME *seoventig*, *seventi*.

eighty. OE *hundeahtatiġ*, Anglian *hundæhtatiġ*.

ninety. OE *hundnigontiġ*.

458. In OE the ty-numerals are sometimes declined as adjectives, as in *æfter þrītiġra daga fæce* 'after the space of thirty days.' When undeclined they are used in their original function of nouns governing the genitive: *sixtiġ mīla brād* 'sixty miles broad.'

459. The high numerals **hundred** and **thousand** are in OE neuter nouns, *hund*, *hundred* and *þūsend*, governing the genitive: *twā hund wintra* 'two hundred winters (years),' *þūsend manna* 'a thousand men.'

460. In OE there was no numeral higher than thousand. **million**, ME *millioun*, is the French form of Late Latin *millīō*, acc. *milliōnem* formed from Latin *mīlle* 'thousand.' *billion*, *trillion*, etc. are much later formations, in which the Latin prefixes *bi-* and *tri-* (as in *biennial*, *triennial*) were substituted for the initial syllable of *million*, so that *billion* was regarded as a sort of contraction of **bimillion*. *milliard* is a Modern French formation from Latin *mīlle*, or rather from *million*, by substituting the augmentative ending *-ard* for *-on*, so that the word means 'big million,' *million* itself originally meaning 'group of thousands.'

461. Numeral-groups are either **cumulative**, as in *twenty-five* = 20 + 5, or **multiple**, as in *two hundred* = 2 × 100. In such cumulative groups as *twenty-five* the units always came first in OE—*fīf and twentiġ manna*—and we still say *five-and-twenty* as well as *twenty-five*, but only with the lower ty-numerals; thus we hardly ever say *he is five and fifty.*

462. In speaking we generally count by hundreds up to 1900, especially in dates. Thus 1066, 1891 are called *ten hundred and sixty-six, eighteen hundred and ninety-one*, or, more briefly *ten sixty-six, eighteen ninety-one.*

463. The high numerals are not used alone, but require *a* or *one* before them, the latter when emphatic, as in *one hundred, not two hundred. a* in *a hundred, a thousand*, etc. may be the indefinite article, but is more probably the weak *one*, as in *a day or two* (**433.** 1).

464. In MnE all the numerals are treated as adjectives followed by nouns in the plural, *a-hundred*, etc. being a kind of group-adjective: *ten men, twenty men, a hundred men, two thousand men.*

465. But all the numerals can also be used as nouns with plurals in *-s.* They necessarily become nouns when their head-word is suppressed, as in *units, tens, and hundreds, to go on all fours, there were ten of us*; but even when the head-word is expressed, the numeral may be made into a noun whenever it has any independence of meaning, as in *thousands of people.*

Ordinal.

466. Most of the ordinal numerals are derivatives of the cardinal ones, but the first two ordinals are expressed by distinct words:—

first is the OE *fyrest*, which originally meant 'foremost' (349); but this meaning was sometimes so much weakened that *fyrest* became practically equivalent to *forma*, which is the regular OE ordinal corresponding to *ān*.

second was introduced in ME, being the French form of Latin *secundus*. The OE word was *ōþer*, which was discarded because of the ambiguity resulting from it having also the meaning 'other.'

third=OE *þridda*, Late Northumbrian *þirda*, ME *þirde*.

The other OE ordinals below 20 are formed from the cardinals by adding *-þa*, the *þ* becoming *t* after *s* or *f*, and final *n* of the cardinals being dropped:—

fourth=OE *fēowerþa*, *fēorþa*, ME *fōurþe*. [Cp. *fourteen*, *forty*.]

fifth=OE *fīfta*, ME *fifte*, Early MnE *fift*. In later MnE the *th* was restored by the influence of the other ordinals, as also in Early MnE *sixt*.

sixth=OE *sixta*.

seventh=OE *seofoþa* is a Late ME new-formation direct from the cardinal. So also *ninth*, *tenth*, *eleventh*.

eighth=OE *eahtoþa*, Anglian *æhtoþa*, where the *o* is the older form of the *a* in the cardinal *eahta*, *æhta*.

ninth=OE *nigoþa*.

tenth=OE *tēoþa* with the unmutated vowel of the cardinal *tīen*.

eleventh=OE *endleofta*.

twelfth=OE *twelfta*.

467. The OE teen-ordinals end in *-tēoþa*, which in ME was made in *-tēnþe*, a new-formation from the cardinal ending *-tēne*, as in *fiftēnþe*=OE *fīftēoþa*.

468. The OE ty-ordinals end in *-tigoþa*, *-tiogoþa*, which in ME became *-teoþe*, and then *-tiþe* by the influence of the cardinals: OE *twentigoþa*, Late ME *twentiþe*. In Early MnE *e* was introduced by the analogy of the verb-inflection *-eth*, but these ordinals were still pronounced (twentiþ, þirtiþ), etc., although the spelling has now altered the pronunciation into (twenti-iþ), etc.

469. In Early MnE the ordinal ending *-th* was extended to the high numerals, which before had no ordinal forms: *hundredth*, which was pronounced (hundreþ), *thousandth*, *millionth*.

470. The OE ordinals were inflected as weak adjectives.

471. In ordinal groups only the last member of the group takes the ordinal form, the others being left in the shorter cardinal form: *twenty-fifth* or *five-and-twentieth*, *hundred and second*. This usage prevailed already in OE, as in *on þām twā-and-twentigoþan dæġe*, where *twā* is kept in the neuter, although *dæġ* is masculine, because it forms a sort of group compound with the ordinal.

472. The ordinals are used as nouns in MnE in the combination of two ordinals to express fractional numbers, as in *two thirds of an inch*.

VERBS.

Old-English.

INFLECTIONS.

473. There are two main conjugations of verbs in OE, **strong** and **weak**, distinguished mainly by the formation of their preterites and preterite participles. If we compare these parts of the verb with its infinitive, we find that strong verbs, such as *bindan* 'to bind,' form their preterite by vowel-change

—*band* 'he bound'—and add *-en* in the preterite participle with or without vowel-change, *ġe-* being often prefixed, in weak as well as strong verbs—*ġebunden* 'bound'; while weak verbs, such as *hīeran* 'hear,' form their preterite and preterite participle with the help of *d* or *t*: *hīerde, ġehīered.*

474. The following are the chief verb-endings of the active voice, including the preterite participle passive. Where two endings are given, the second is that of the weak verbs. Observe that all three persons have the same ending in the plural, and that the imperative exists only in the second person.

		Indicative.	Subjunctive.
Present Singular	1	*-e*	*-e*
	2	*-st*	*-e*
	3	*-þ*	*-e*
Plural		*-aþ*	*-en*
Preterite Singular	1	*-, -de*	*-e, -de*
	2	*-e, -dest*	*-e, -de*
	3	*-, -de*	*-e, -de*
Plural		*-on, -don*	*-en, -den*
Imperative Singular		*-, -, (-e, -a)*	Infinitive *-an*
Plural		*-aþ*	Gerund *-enne*
Participle Present		*-ende*	
Preterite		*-en, -ed*	

475. Verbs whose root ends in a vowel generally contract; thus *sēon* 'to see,' *gān* 'to go,' conjugate *iċ sēo, iċ gā, wē sēoþ, wē gāþ* compared with *iċ binde, wē bindaþ.*

476. For the plural ending *-aþ*, both indic. and imper., *-e* is substituted when the pronoun comes immediately after the verb: *ġē bindaþ*, but *binde ġē*. So also *gā ġē!* compared with *ġē gāþ.* These forms were originally subjunctives, *binde ġē* being a shortening of *binden ġē.* So also in *gā wē* 'let us go.' This change was often extended by analogy to the ending *-on*, as in *mōte wē* 'may we,' *sohte ġē* 'ye sought' compared with *wē mōton, ġē sohton.*

477. The passive voice, and many forms of the active voice as well, are expressed by the combination of auxiliary verbs with the pret. partic. and, more rarely, the pres. partic. The chief auxiliary verbs are *wesan* 'be,' *weorþan* 'become,' and *habban* 'have,' as in *hē wæs ġefunden, hē wearþ ġefunden* 'he was found,' *hē is ġecumen* 'he has come,' *hē hæfþ ġefunden* 'he has found.'

478. But besides the pret. partic., there is a trace of the old Germanic passive in the form *hātte* from *hātan*, which is both pres. 'is named, called,' and pret. 'was called.'

479. The infinitive was originally an indeclinable abstract noun formed from the corresponding verb, so that *bindan* originally meant 'binding,' 'act of binding.' The gerund is a similarly formed noun in the dative case governed by the preposition *tō*, which always precedes it, as in *hē is tō cumenne* 'he is to come'=Latin *ventūrus est.* It often takes the *a* of the infin.—*tō cumanne.*

480. The pret. partic., as already stated, generally takes *ġe-* before it; but not if the verb already has *ge-* or a similar inseparable prefix, as in *forġiefen* 'forgiven,' *ālīesed* 'redeemed.' In West-Saxon *hīeran* generally takes *ġe-* throughout: *ġehīeran, ġehīered.*

481. Both participles are declined like adjectives: *wē sindon ġecumene, hē hæfþ hine ġefundenne* 'he has found him,' literally 'he possesses him found.' But in the later language the pret. partic. in combination with auxiliary *habban* became indeclinable through the original meaning having been forgotten: *hē hæfþ hine ġefunden.*

482. In the older language the second person sing. ends in *-s*: *þū lufas* 'thou lovest,' *þū lufades.* But already in Early West-Saxon the regular forms are *lufast*, *lufadest*.

483. In Late Northumbrian inflectional *þ* became *s*: *hē bindes*, *wē bindas*.

484. In Late OE the subj. plur. ending *-en* was made into *-on* by the influence of the indic., as in *ġyf hȳ wǣron* 'if they were,' compared with Early West-Saxon *ġif hīe wǣren*.

485. In Late OE the *-st* of the 2nd pers. sing. pret. indic. of weak verbs is extended to the subj.: *ġyf þū lufodest* 'if you loved'=Early West-Saxon *ġif þū lufode*.

Strong Verbs.

486. In the strong verbs the plur. of the pret. indic. often has a vowel different from that of the sing.: *iċ band*, *wē bundon*. The 2nd sing. pret. indic. and the whole pret. subj. always have the vowel of the pret. plur. indic.: *þū bunde*, *ġif iċ bunde*, *ġif wē bunden*. The following are the Early West-Saxon inflections of the strong verb *bindan*:—

		Indic.		Subj.
Pres. Sing.	1	*binde*		*binde*
	2	*bindest*, *bintst*		*binde*
	3	*bindeþ*, *bint*		*binde*
Plur.		*bindaþ*		*binden*
Pret. Sing.	1	*band*		*bunde*
	2	*bunde*		*bunde*
	3	*band*		*bunde*
Plur.		*bundon*		*bunden*
Imper. Sing.		*bind*	Infin.	*bindan*
Plur.		*bindaþ*	Gerund	*tō bindenne*
		Partic. Pres.	*bindende*	
		Pret.	*gebunden*.	

487. Some strong verbs are inflected like weak verbs everywhere except in the preterite forms. Thus *swęrian* 'swear,' pret. *swōr*, is inflected like *fęrian* (504): pres. indic. *swęriġe, swęrest, swęreþ, swęriaþ;* subj. pres. *swęriġe, swęriġen;* imper. *swęre, swęriaþ;* pres. partic. *swęriġende.* Many strong verbs with double consonants, such as *biddan* 'pray,' 'ask' pret. *bæd*, are inflected like *sęttan* (503): pres. indic. *bidde, bitst* (*bidest*), *bitt* (*bideþ*), *biddaþ;* subj. pres. *bidde, bidden;* imper. *bide, biddaþ;* pres. partic. *biddende.*

All of these verbs, both strong and weak, had a *j* before their endings in Germanic (148)—**swarjan, *farjan, *bidjan, *satjan*; and hence all of them mutate their root-vowels. The strong verb *wēpan* 'weep' is also a 'j-verb,' as shown by its mutation, the Anglian form being *wǣpan*, and is declined like the weak verb *hīeran*, which however has the same endings as a strong verb in the infinitive and present tenses, and so there is nothing to distinguish the inflections of *wēpan* from those of the ordinary j-less strong verbs: pres. *wēpe, wēpst* (*wēpest*), *wēpþ* (*wēpeþ*), *wēpaþ*; imper. *wēp*, etc.

488. The Germanic forms of the endings *-st, -þ* were *-is, -iþ*, which are still preserved in the oldest English: *bindis, bindiþ.* In West-Saxon these endings mutated a preceding vowel and then dropped their own vowels, as in *þū lȳcst, hi̇t grēwþ* from *lūcan* 'close,' 'lock,' *grōwan* 'grow.' The resulting consonant-combinations were modified in various ways (147): *tþ, dþ, ddþ* were made into *tt, t*, as in *lǣtt* 'lets,' *bītt* 'waits,' *bitt* 'asks,' *stęnt* 'stands' from *lǣtan* 'let,' *bīdan, biddan, standan*; and *sþ* became *st*, as in *ċiest* 'chooses' from *ċēosan.* Similar changes took place in the 2nd pers. sing.: *þū bitst* 'you ask,' *þū ċiest.* In Anglian the full endings *-es* (*-est*), *-eþ* were restored, the unmutated vowels being at the same time restored: *lēteþ, bīdeþ, bideþ, biddeþ, stǫndeþ; biddes, ċēoses.*

489. The vowel-changes in the strong verbs are generally due to gradation (**150**), which is often accompanied by consonant-change, as in *weorþan, geworden* (**146**). But in some verbs the vowel of the pret. is the result of contraction of Germanic and Arian reduplication; thus *hēold* 'held' (infin. *healdan*) is a contraction of **hehold*, **hehald*. Traces of this reduplication are preserved in a few OE preterites, such as *hē-ht*, later *hēt* (infin. *hātan* 'call,' 'command')= Germanic **hehait* (Gothic *haihait*).

490. The following are the classes under which the strong verbs fall according to their vowel-changes, each class being named after a characteristic verb. A few examples only are given of each class. The special Anglian forms are given in ( ). The forms are given in the order infin., pret. sing., pret. plur., pret. partic.

I. Reduplicative or fall-class.

491. The pret. sing. and plur. has *ēo* or *ē*, the pret. partic. keeping the vowel of the infin.:—

feallan (*fallan*) 'fall'	*fēoll*	*fēollon*	*feallen* (*fallen*)
healdan (*hāldan*) 'hold'	*hēold*	*hēoldon*	*healden* (*hālden*)
cnāwan 'know'	*cnēow*	*cnēowon*	*cnāwen*
grōwan 'grow'	*grēow*	*grēowon*	*grōwen*
bēatan 'beat'	*bēot*	*bēoton*	*bēaten*
hātan 'command'	*hē(h)t*	*hē(h)ton*	*hāten*
lǣtan 'let'	*lēt*	*lēton*	*lǣten*

II. Shake-class.

492. These verbs have in the infin. *a*, *ea*, or, in j-verbs the mutations *ę*, *ie*, in the pret. sing. and plur. *ō*, in the pret. partic. *a*, *æ*:—

faran 'go'	*fōr*	*fōron*	*faren*

sċacan 'shake'	*sċōc*	*sċōcon*	*sċacen*
hębban (148) 'raise'	*hōf*	*hōfon*	*hafen, hæfen*

III. Bind-class.

493. In the infin. *i, ie, e, eo* followed by two consonants one at least of which is nearly always a vowellike consonant—*r, l, n, m*; in the pret. sing. *a, æ, ea*; in the pret. plur. *u*; in the pret. partic. *u, o.*

bindan 'bind'	*band, bǫnd*	*bundon*	*bunden*
ġieldan (*ġeldan*) 'pay'	*ġeald* (*gāld*)	*guldon*	*golden*
helpan 'help'	*healp* (*hālp*)	*hulpon*	*holpen*
berstan (144) 'burst'	*bærst*	*burston*	*borsten*
weorþan 'become'	*wearþ*	*wurdon*	*worden*
feohtan (*fehtan*) 'fight'	*feaht* (*fæht*)	*fuhton*	*fohten*

IV. Bear-class.

494. In the infin. *e, ie, i* followed by a single consonant which is generally vowellike; in *brecan* the vowellike consonant precedes the vowel; in the pret. sing. *a, æ, ea*; in the pret. plur. *ǣ, ēa, ō, ā*; in the pret. partic. *o, u*:—

beran 'carry'	*bær*	*bǣron*	*boren*
brecan 'break'	*bræc*	*brǣcon*	*brocen*
sċieran (*sċeran*) 'cut'	*sċēar* (*sċær*)	*sċēaron* (*sċēron*)	*sċoren*
niman 'take'	*nam, nǫm*	*nōmon, nāmon*	*numen*

V. Give-class.

495. In the infin. *e, ie*, and, in the j-verbs *i*, followed by a single, non-vowellike consonant, this class differing from the last only in the pret. partic., which keeps the vowel of the infin., the mutated *i* of the j-verbs returning to *e*:—

sprecan 'speak'	*spræc*	*sprǣcon*	*sprecen*
ġiefan (*ġefan*) 'give'	*ġeaf* (*ġæf*)	*ġēafon* (*ġēfon*)	*ġiefen* (*ġefen*)
sittan 'sit'	*sæt*	*sǣton*	*seten*
liċġan 'lie'	*læġ*	*lāgon, lǣgon*	*leġen*

VI. **Shine**-class.

496. In the infin. *ī*; pret. sing. *ā*; pret. plur. and pret. partic. *i*:—

drīfan 'drive'	*drāf*	*drifon*	*drifen*
sċīnan 'shine'	*sċān*	*sċinon*	*sċinen*
wrītan 'write'	*wrāt*	*writon*	*writen*

VII. **Choose**-class.

497. In the infin. *ēo*, *ū*; pret. sing. *ēa*; pret. plur. *u*; pret. partic. *o*:—

bēodan 'command'	*bēad*	*budon*	*boden*
ċēosan 'choose'	*ċēas*	*curon*	*coren*
frēosan 'freeze'	*frēas*	*fruron*	*froren*
būgan 'bend'	*bēag*, *bēah*	*bugon*	*bogen*

Weak Verbs.

498. The weak verbs fall under two main groups, according as the vowel of the infin. is mutated or not. The mutation-group comprises two classes, the **hear**-class (*hīeran*) and the **wean**-class (*węnian*), the unmutated verbs constituting the third or **love**-class (*lufian*).

I. **Hear**-class.

499. The following are the Early West-Saxon forms:—

		Indic.	Subj.
Pres. Sing.	1	*hīere*	*hīere*
	2	*hīerst*	*hīere*
	3	*hīerþ*	*hīere*
Plur.		*hīeraþ*	*hīeren*
Pret. Sing.	1	*hīerde*	*hīerde*
	2	*hīerdest*	*hīerde*
	3	*hīerde*	*hīerde*
Plur.		*hīerdon*	*hīerden*

Imper. Sing.	*hīer*	Infin.	*hīeran*
Plur.	*hīeraþ*	Gerund	*tō hīerenne*
Partic. Pres.	*hīerende*		
Pret.	*hīered*		

500. This class adds *-de* in the pret. and *-ed* in the pret. partic., where the *e* is liable to be dropped when an inflectional vowel is added, as in the nom. plur. *ġehīerde.* Verbs ending in *t, d, c* drop the *e* in the uninflected form also, as in *āsęnd* 'sent' (infin. *āsęndan*), where *d* is a shortening of *dd.* After the breath-consonants *t, c* the inflectional *d* is unvoiced, and *c* becomes *h*: *mētan* 'find,' 'meet' *ġemētt*, *tǣċan* 'show' *ġetǣht.* But the full forms *āsęnded, ġemēted* also occur, especially in Anglian. Similar changes take place in the pret. *-tde, -p(p)de* become *-tte, -pte,* as in *ġemētte* 'found,' *dypte* 'dipped' (infin. *dyppan*). The inflectional *d* is also unvoiced after *ss* and the other breath-consonants, as in *missan* 'miss' *miste,* compared with *rǣsde* 'rushed' from *rǣsan,* where the *s*=(z). In *dypte* the *p* is, of course, a shortening of *pp.* There are similar shortenings in *sęndan, sęnde, fyllan, fylde,* etc.

501. I b. **Seek**-class. In this subdivision of the hear-class the vowel of the infin. is unmutated in the pret. and pret. partic., the inflections being the same as in the other verbs of the hear-class:—

sęllan 'give'	*sealde (sālde)*	*ġeseald (ġesāld)*
sēċan (sǣcan) 'seek'	*sōhte, sohte*	*ġesōht, gesoht*

502. Those with *n* followed by *ċ* or *g*—*þęnċan* 'think,' *bringan* 'bring'—drop the nasal and lengthen the preceding vowel and modify it in other ways: *þęnċan, þohte, ġeþoht* = Germanic **þankjan,* **þanhta, an* before *h* having been regularly changed to nasal *ā,* which in OE as regularly became *ō*. Long vowels were shortened in OE before *ht*, so that *þōhte*, etc. became *þohte*. Seek-verbs in *-ęćć* carry the mutated vowel *ę* into the pret. and pret. partic. in Late West-Saxon: *stręććan*, 'stretch,' *sťreahte*, *streaht* (*stræhte*, *stræht*) later *stręhte*, *stręht*.

503. It will be observed that all verbs of the hear-class have long syllables in the infin.—either a long vowel, as in *hīeran*, or a vowel followed by two consonants, as in *sęndan*, *fyllan*. In the latter verb the *ll* is Germanic [cp. the adjective *full*], and is therefore kept through all the inflections of the verb, except where *l* is written for *ll* before a consonant in contracted forms: pres. indic. *fylle*, *fyllest* (*fylst*), *fylleþ* (*fylþ*), *fyllaþ*; imper. sing. *fyll*, etc. But most of the verbs of this class with double consonants in the infin., such as *sęttan* 'set,' are inflected like strong j-verbs such as *biddan* (**487**), the double consonant being also shortened in the pret. and pret. partic.: pres. indic. *sętte*, *sętst* (*sętes*), *sętt* (*sęteþ*), *sęttaþ*; subj. *sętte*(*n*); imper. *sęte*, *sęttaþ*; pres. part. *sęttende*; pret. *sętte*=**sętede*, pret. partic. *ġesęted*, *ġesętt*. Some of these verbs belong to the seek-division, such as *sęċġan* 'say': pres. indic. *sęċġe*, *sęġst* (*sęġes*), *sęġþ* (*sęġeþ*), *sęċġaþ*; imper. *sęge*, *sęċġaþ*; pres. partic. *sęċġende*; pret. *sæġde*, pret. partic. *ġesæġd*. So also *sęllan* has pres. indic. *sęlle*, *sęlþ* (*sęleþ*), *sęllaþ*, imper. *sęle*, *sęllaþ*, &c.

II. Wean-class.

504. All of these verbs have infin. *-ian* and a short root-syllable with a mutated vowel. They form their pret. in *-ede*, and their pret. partic. in *-ed*, which is never contracted. The following are the Early West-Saxon forms of *węnian* 'accustom':—

		Indic.		Subj.
Pres. Sing.	1	*węniġe*		*węniġe*
	2	*węnest*		*węniġe*
	3	*węneþ*		*węnige*
Plur.		*węniaþ*		*węniġen*
Pret. Sing.	1	*węnede*		*węnede*
	2	*węnedest*		*węnede*
	3	*węnede*		*węnede*
Plur.		*węnedon*		*węneden*
Imper. Sing.		*węne*	Infin.	*węnian*
Plur.		*węniaþ*	Gerund	*tō węniġenne*
Partic. Pres.		*weniġende*		
Pret.		*ġewęned*		

So also *fęrian* 'carry' [*faran* 'go'] *styrian* 'stir.'

III. Love-class.

505. In Germanic these verbs had infinitives *-an*, *-ōn*, of which *-ian* is a later development and therefore does not cause mutation like the *-ian* of the wean-class, which is of Germanic origin. The following are the Early West-Saxon forms:—

		Indic.		Subj.
Pres. Sing.	1	*lufiġe*		*lufiġe*
	2	*lufast*		*lufiġe*
	3	*lufaþ*		*lufiġe*
Plur.		*lufiaþ*		*lufiġen*
Pret. Sing.	1	*lufode*		*lufode*
	2	*lufodest*		*lufode*
	3	*lufode*		*lufode*
Plur.		*lufodon*		*lufoden*
Imper. Sing.		*lufa*	Infin.	*lufian*
Plur.		*lufiaþ*	Gerund	*tō lufiġenne*
Partic. Pres.		*lufiġende*		
Pret.		*ġelufod.*		

So also *āsċian* 'ask,' *macian* 'make,' and many others.

Irregular Weak Verbs.

506. Some weak verbs, such as *libban* 'live,' show a mixture of the inflections of the hear- and the love-class: pres. indic. *libbe, leofast, leofaþ, libbaþ*; subj. *libbe(n)*; imper. *leofa, libbaþ*; pres. partic. *libbende*; pret. *lifde*, pret. partic. *gelifd.*

Preterite-present Verbs.

507. These verbs have for their presents old strong preterites; thus the preterite-present verb *wāt* 'I know' was originally a strong preterite of the shine-class. The present of these verbs differs however from the strong preterites in the 2nd sing. indic., which ends in *t* or *st*, a *t* before the inflectional *t* also becoming *s*: *iċ sċeal* 'I shall,' *þū sċealt*; *iċ cann* 'I know,' *þū canst*; *iċ wāt* 'I know,' *þū wāst.*

508. From these presents new weak preterites are formed with various irregular changes: *sċeolde, cūþe, wiste.*

509. Many of these verbs are defective, the infin., imper., and participles being often wanting. The subj. is often substituted for the imper. sing. The following are the inflections of *witan* 'know':—

		Indic.	Subj.
Pres. Sing.	1	*wāt*	*wite*
	2	*wāst*	*wite*
	3	*wāt*	*wite*
Plur.		*witon*	*witen*
Pret. Sing.	1	*wiste*	*wiste*
	2	*wistest*	*wiste*
	3	*wiste*	*wiste*
Plur.		*wiston*	*wisten*

	Indic.		Subj.
Imper. Sing.	*wite*	Infin.	*witan*
Plur.	*witaþ*	Gerund	*tō witenne*
Partic. Pres.	*witende*		
Pret.	*witen.*		

Middle-English.

Early Middle English.

510. The ME levelling of weak vowels under *e* had a comparatively slight effect on the verb inflections, especially in Early Southern, where the OE verb-inflections were preserved very faithfully. But the inevitable change of *-a*, *-ast*, *-aþ*, *-ode* into *-e*, *-est*, *-eþ*, *-ede*, as in *luve*, *luvest*, *luveþ*, *luvede* =OE *lufa*, *lufast*, *lufaþ*, *lufode*, necessarily led to a complete levelling of the old wean- and love-classes of weak verbs, the ME love-class including all the OE ian-verbs whether accompanied by mutation or not.

511. The Southern tendency to drop final *n* first affected the infin. and pret. partic.: Early Southern *bīnden*, *bīnde*; *ibūnden*, *ibūnde*.

512. The tendency to shorten double consonants in weak syllables made the OE gerund *tō bindenne* into ME *tō bīndene*.

513. The tendency to drop final weak *e* after another weak syllable (**174**) led to the shortening of *tō bīndene* into *tō bīnden*, which made it liable to be confused with the infin. So also *luvie*=OE *lufiġe*, *lufian* was often shortened to *luvi*.

In the South-Thames dialects this *-i* afterwards came to be regarded as the special mark of the infin., being sometimes extended to strong verbs as well as weak verbs with OE infin. *-an*.

514. In Early Southern the pres. partic. ending is *-inde*, as in *bīndinde*, *hērinde*, which probably owes its *i* to the influence of the verbal nouns in *-inge*, *-ing*=OE *-ing*, *-ung*, such as *lerninge*=OE *leornung*.

515. Early Southern keeps the prefix *i-*=OE *ge-*: *ibūnden*, *ihēred*=OE *ġebunden*, *ġehēred*.

516. The most important change in the strong verbs is that many of them became weak. Already in OE such verbs as *slǣpan* 'sleep,' *ondrǣdan* 'fear,' had the weak preterites *slǣpte*, *ondrǣdde* by the side of the strong *slēp*, *ondrēd*; in Late West-Saxon *hębban* 'raise' has the weak pret. *hęfde* by the side of strong *hōf*, and so on. In ME this is carried much further. Thus even in the earliest ME we find the OE strong preterites *lēt* 'let,' *wēop* 'wept' represented not only by *lēt*, *wēop*, but also by the weak *lette*, *wepte*, although such forms as *wēp* still survive in Standard Late ME. Many other weak and strong forms existed side by side for a long time; and although in MnE the weak forms have nearly always prevailed, this was not always the case in ME, where, for instance, such a weak pret. as *hefde* 'raised' was in the Late ME period discarded in favour of the new-formed strong pret. *haf*, the old *hōf* being also preserved.

517. The inflections of the strong verbs that remained were modified by various levelling influences. The mutation in the contracted forms of the OE presents was got rid of by bringing in the unmutated vowel of the infin., etc., as in *berþ* 'carries,' *tret* 'treads,' *stont* 'stands,' infin. *beren*, *treden*, *stǫnden*=Early West-Saxon *bierþ* (*bireþ*), *tritt*, *stęnt*.

518. The gradation of consonants in the OE *ċēosan*, *ġecoren*, etc. was got rid of by carrying the *s* through: *chēosen*, *chēsen*, *chęs*, *ichosen*.

519. In this last verb we can also observe the extension of *ch* = OE *ċ* to the original *c* of the pret. partic., so as to make initial *ch* uniform throughout the whole verb. We can observe the opposite levelling of *ch* under *c* in such verb-forms as *kerven*, *karf*=OE *ċeorfan*, *ċearf*, which have taken their back-consonant from the OE pret. plur. *curfon* and pret. partic. *corfen*.

520. But in some verbs the old consonant-gradations were preserved, as in *forlēsen* 'lose,' *forlę̄s*, *forloren*.

521. Some of the ME changes had the contrary effect of creating new distinctions. Thus OE *ǣ*, *ǽ* was regularly shortened before consonant-groups, and the resulting *æ* was afterwards broadened to *a* (177), as in the OE pret. *tǣhte* 'showed,' which in ME passed through *tæhte* into *tahte*, whence MnE *taught*. In many preterites and pret. participles these changes gave rise only to divergence of quantity, as in *mēten*, *mette*, *imet*=OE *ġemētan*, etc., and in Northern *ledde* = Southern *ladde* from *lę̄den* 'lead' = OE *lǣdan*, *lǣdde*.

522. The following are the inflections of the strong verb *bīnden*, and of the weak verbs *hēren* 'hear' and *luvien*, as representatives of the two classes of weak verbs in Early Southern:—

Pres. Indic. Sing.	1	*bīnde*	*hēre*	*luvie*
	2	*bīndest*, *bintst*	*hēr(e)st*	*luvest*
	3	*bīndeþ*, *bint*	*hēr(e)þ*	*luveþ*
Plur.		*bīndeþ*	*hēreþ*	*luvieþ*
Pres. Subj. Sing.		*bīnde*	*hēre*	*luvie*
Plur.		*bīnden*	*hēren*	*luvien*
Pret. Indic. Sing.	1	*bǭnd*	*herde*	*luvede*
	2	*būnde*	*herdest*	*luvedest*
	3	*bǭnd*	*herde*	*luvede*
Plur.		*būnden*	*herden*	*luveden*

Pret. Subj. Sing.	1 *būnde*	*herde*	*luvede*
	2 *būnde*	*herdest*	*luvedest*
	3 *būnde*	*herde*	*luvede*
Plur.	*būnden*	*herden*	*luveden*
Imper. Sing.	*bīnd*	*hēre*	*luvie*
Plur.	*bīndeþ*	*hēreþ*	*luvieþ*
Infin.	*bīnden*	*hēren*	*luvien*
Gerund	*bīndene*	*hērene*	*luviene*
Partic. Pres.	*bīndinde*	*hērinde*	*luviinde*
Pret.	*ibūnden*	*ihēr(e)d*	*iluved.*

523. In the forms *bīnde gē, būnde gē*, *-e* is substituted for *-eþ* (**476**).

524. It will be observed that the distinction between the two classes of weak verbs is very slight, the *i* of the love-class being often dropped—*ī luve, wē luveþ*, &c.—while the imper. sing. *hēre* has taken the *e* of *luvie, luve.*

Midland.

525. In Early Midland many levellings which are only just beginning in Early Southern are fully carried out. The love-class lost their *i* entirely, and as the hear-class generally had the full Anglian endings *-est, -eþ*, there is only one set of inflections for the two classes: *hēren, lufen*= Southern *hēren, luvien.* On the other hand, the contracted forms of the hear-class are extended to the love-class, as in *birþ* 'befits,' 'becomes' pret. *birde*= OE *ġebyreþ, ġebyrede*, infin. *ġebyrian* (wean-class).

526. The characteristic feature of the Midland verb is its extension of the plur. ending *-en* of the subj. pres. and of the pret. indic. and subj.—*gif þei lufen, þei cōmen* 'came,' *gif þei cōmen, þei brohten*—to the present indic. plur.: *wē lufen, þei cumen*=Southern *wē luvieþ, heo cumeþ.* But the older *-(e)þ* is kept in the imper. plur.: *cumeþ!*, *bēþ!* 'be ye' = Southern *cumeþ*, *bēoþ*.

527. In Early Midland the gerund was completely levelled under the infin.: *tō bīnden*, *tō hēren*.

528. In Midland the pres. partic. keeps the old ending: *bīndende*, *hērende*, *lufende*. The *n* of the infin. and strong pret. partic. is never dropped as in Southern. The pret. partic. loses its prefix *ġe-*.

529. The distinction between single and double consonant forms in the old j-verbs, such as *hębban*, *hęfeþ*, *hōf*, *hafen* and *libban*, *leofaþ*, *lifde*, which was still kept up in Early Southern—*hebben*, *heveþ*; *libben*, *leveþ*, *liveþ*—began to break down in Early Midland through the extension of the single consonant forms; thus in Early Midland we find pres. plur. indic. *lifen* = Early Southern *libbeþ*, although the older infin. *libben* is still kept in Early Midland; but *hefen* is used not only as a pres. plur., but also as an infin.

Northern.

530. In the Northern dialect inflectional *þ* had been changed to *s*, and final *n* had begun to drop off already in the OE period: Old Northumbrian *bindes*, *bindas*, *binda* = Mercian *bindeþ*, *bindaþ*, *bindan*. In the Early Middle period weak final *e* was dropped, so that the infin. *bīnde* = Old Northumbrian *binda* became monosyllabic *bīnd*, under which the gerund *tō bīnd* was levelled. The subj. *bīnde* = Old North. sing. and plur. *binde* was reduced to the same monosyllable. Hence also the pret. plur. *herden* was reduced to the same form as the sing.—*herd*. The effect of these changes on a strong pret. such as that of *bīnd* was to leave only two forms —*bānd* 1st and 3rd pers. sing. indic., and *būnd* 2nd pers.

sing. and plur. and subj. generally—and the vowel-change was soon got rid of by extension of the vowel of the 1st and 3rd person sing. indic.: *ī bānd, þū bānd, wē bānd.*

531. In Late Old Northumbrian the old ending of the 2nd person pres. *-es, -as,* etc. was preserved by the influence of the new 3rd person *-es, -as* = *-eþ, -aþ.* Hence in Early Northern *-es* became the common ending of the 2nd and 3rd persons indic. pres. sing. In the pres. indic. plur *-es*=older *-as, -ias* was dropped when the verb was immediately preceded or followed by its pronoun: *wē þat bīndes, men bīndes; wē bīnd, þai bīnd.* The 'absolute' form was afterwards extended to the 1st pers. sing. as well; *ī þat bīndes.*

532. The *n* of the strong pret. partic. was not lost in Old Northumbrian because of the inflected forms *ġebundene,* etc., by whose influence the *n* was restored in the uninflected form; hence it was always kept in the ME Northern dialect as well.

533. The Northern form of the pres. partic. is *-and*: *bīndand, hērand*=Midland and OE *bīndende, hērende,* Southern *bīndinde, hērinde.* This *a* is the result of Scandinavian influence: Icel. *bindandi, heyrandi.*

534. The following are then the most distinctive verb-inflections of the three dialects in their Early Middle periods:—

		Southern.	Midland.	Northern.
Indic. Pres. Sing.	1	*bīnde*	*bīnde*	*bīnd*
	2	*bīndest, bintst*	*bīndest*	*bīndes*
	3	*bīndeþ, bint*	*bīndeþ*	*bīndes*
Plur.		*bīndeþ*	*bīnden*	*bīnd(es)*
Imper. Sing.		*bīnd*	*bīnd*	*bīnd*
Plur.		*bīndeþ*	*bīndeþ*	*bīnd(es)*
Pres. Partic.		*bīndinde*	*bīndende*	*bīndand*

Late Middle English.

535. The most important change in Standard ME and in Late South-Thames English generally is the further assimilation of the pres. partic. to the verbal nouns in *-inge* by which the earlier *bīndinde* became *bīndinge*, a change of which we see traces already in Early Southern, as in *heo riden singinge* 'they rode singing'—OE *hīe ridon singende*. But as the verbal nouns also occur without final *-e*, the distinction between *lerninge* partic. and *lerning* noun was not entirely lost.

536. Early ME *d* was changed to *t* in the weak pret. and pret. partic. of verbs in *rd*, *ld*, *nd*: *girte*, *girt*, infin. *girden*; *bilte*, *bilt* infin. *bilden*; *wente*, *went* infin. *wenden* = Early Southern *gürde*, *gürd*; *bülde*, *büld*; *wende*, *wend*. This change served to distinguish such forms as *hē sende* pres. subj. and *hē sente* pret., which in Early ME were both expressed by the first form. But it is also carried out in some words with *l*, *ll*, *n*, *nn*: *fēlen* 'feel' *felte*; *dwellen*, *dwelte*; *mēnen*, *mente*; *brennen* 'burn,' *brente*; and after *s*=(z) and *v*, where it unvoices these consonants: *losien*=OE *losian*, *loste*; *lēven*=OE *lǣfan*, *lefte*, *lafte*.

537. In Standard ME we see the same levelling and simplifying tendencies at work as in Early Midland and Northern. The old vowel-change in such preterites as *bǫnd* is still kept up, but the short form *bǫnd* is often extended throughout the pret.: *þū bǫnd*, *wē bǫnd* as well as *þū bounde*, *wē bounde(n)*.

538. In some verbs of the bear- and give-class the *ẹ̄* of the plural is sometimes extended to the sing. as in *bēr*, *sēt* by the side of *bār*, *sat*=OE *bær*, *sæt* plur. *bǣron*, *sǣton*, Anglian *bēron*, *sēton*.

539. Influence of the strong plur. pret. on the sing. is also seen in such sing. preterites as *slōw, saw*=Early Southern *slōh* plur. *slōwen*, Late OE *slōh, slōgon*, OE *seah, sāwon*.

540. In Late ME the pret. partic. begins to influence the pret. plur. As a general rule the old pret. plurals were preserved in Late ME only when they had the same vowel as the pret. partic., as in *þei bounden, þei drŏnken, þei wŏnnen* (class 3), *riden, writen* (class 6); otherwise the plur. pret. took the vowel of the pret. partic.: *þei holpen, foghten, chǭsen*.

541. The sing. of the imper. began to be extended to the plur.: *bīnd* 'bind ye' by the side of *bīndeþ*.

542. In the love-class of weak verbs the *i* was dropped entirely, and the pret. ending *-ede* was often shortened to *-ed* in accordance with the general principle of dropping weak *e* after a weak syllable: *hē lŏveþ, hē lŏved*.

543. Some of the above changes may be the result of Midland influence, of which we have an undoubted example in the substitution of *-en* (*-e*) for *-eþ* in the plur. indic. pres. *-eþ* was, of course, kept in the plur. imper., although here also the Midland ending seems to occur in its shortened form *-e*: *bīnde*.

544. The following are the Standard ME inflections of the three verbs whose Early ME inflections have been given already:—

Pres. Indic. Sing.	1	*bīnde*	*hēre*	*lŏve*
	2	*bīndest*	*hēr(e)st*	*lŏvest*
	3	*bīndeþ, bint*	*hēr(e)þ*	*lŏveþ*
Plur.		*bīnde(n)*	*hēre(n)*	*lŏve(n)*
Pres. Subj. Sing.		*bīnde*	*hēre*	*lŏve*
Plur.		*bīnde(n)*	*hēre(n)*	*lŏve(n)*
Pret. Indic. Sing.	1	*bǭnd*	*herde*	*lŏved(e)*
	2	*bounde, bǭnd*	*herdest*	*lŏvedest*
	3	*bǭnd*	*herde*	*lŏved(e)*
Plur.		*bounde(n), bǭnd*	*herde(n)*	*lŏvede(n), lŏved*

Pret. Subj. Sing. 1	*bounde*	*herde*	*lǒved(e)*
2	*bounde*	*herde(st)*	*lǒvede(st), lǒved*
3	*bounde*	*herde*	*lǒved(e)*
Plur.	*bounde(n)*	*herde(n)*	*lǒvede(n), lǒved*
Imper. Sing.	*bīnd*	*hēr(e)*	*lǒve*
Plur.	*bīnde(þ), bīnd*	*hēre(þ), hēr*	*lǒve(þ)*
Infin.	*bīnde(n)*	*hēre(n)*	*lǒve(n)*
Gerund	*bīnden(e), bīnde*	*hēren(e), hēre*	*lǒven(e), lǒve*
Partic. Pres.	*bīndinge*	*hēringe*	*lǒvinge*
Pret.	*(i)bounde(n)*	*(i)herd*	*(i)lǒv(e)d.*

The following examples will show the regular development of the different classes of strong verbs :—

I. Fall-class.

545.	*fallen*	*fell*	*fellen*	*fallen*
	hǭlden	*hēld*	*hēlden*	*hǭlden*
	grōwen	*grēw*	*grēwen*	*grōwen*
	knǭwen	*knēw*	*knēwen*	*knǭwen*

II. Shake-class.

546.	*shāken*	*shōk*	*shōken*	*shāken*
	wāken	*wōk*	*wōken*	*wāken*
	laughen	*laugh, low*	*lowen*	*laughen*
	drawen	*drough, drow*	*drowen*	*drawen*

Observe that the preterites of this class have split up into two groups, one with *ō*, the other with (uu) [**186**].

III. Bind-class.

547.	*bīnden*	*bǫnd*	*bounden*	*bounden*
	singen	*sǫng*	*sǒngen*	*sǒngen*
	drinken	*drank*	*drǒnken*	*drǒnken*
	winnen	*wan*	*wǒnnen*	*wǒnnen*
	kerven	*karf*	*korven*	*korven*
	helpen	*halp*	*holpen*	*holpen*
	fighten	*faught*	*foghten*	*foghten*

IV. Bear-class.

548.	*stę̄len*	*stal*	*stēlen, stal*	*stǭlen*
	bę̄ren	*bār, bēr*	*bēren, bār*	*bǭren*

V. Give-class.

549.	*gę̄ten*	*gat*	*gēten, gat*	*gę̄ten*
	sitten	*sat, sēt*	*sēten, sat*	*sę̄ten*

VI. Shine-class.

550.	*rīden*	*rǭd*	*riden*	*riden*
	wrīten	*wrǭt*	*writen*	*writen*

VII. Choose-class.

551.	*crēpen*	*crę̄p*	*crǭpen*	*crǭpen*
	chēsen	*chę̄s*	*chǭsen*	*chǭsen*

Modern English.

552. The main innovation in the MnE verb-inflections was the introduction of the Northern *-s* in the 3rd pers. sing. pres. indic.—*he calls*—which was introduced into Standard English through the medium of the Midland dialect. It did not entirely supplant the older *-th*—*he calleth*—which still survives in the higher literary language.

553. The MnE verb is further characterized by the development of a **gerund.** When the pres. partic. ending *-inge* lost its final vowel, the last vestige of a formal distinction between such a pres. partic. as *lerning* and the verb-noun *lerning* disappeared. In OE the number of verb-nouns in *-ung, -ing* was limited, especially in the earlier stages of the language. In ME their number increased, and when the pres. partic. in *-inge* was fully established, and became indistinguishable in form from the ing-nouns, these could be formed at pleasure from any verb; or, in other words, every pres. partic. could be used as a verb-noun. At first—in Early MnE as well as ME—these words were used entirely as nouns—taking the article *the* before them and the preposition *of* after them, etc.—as in *he thanked him for the saving of his life*, where *saving* is used exactly like the abstract noun *preservation*; but by degrees they were treated like infinitives, the article being dropped and the following noun joined on to them as to the corresponding finite verb; so that the above sentence was shortened to *he thanked him for saving his life*. In such constructions, which began in Early MnE, *saving* etc. are true noun-verbals or gerunds.

554. In MnE the dropping of weak final *e*, together with the ME tendency to drop final weak *n*, had a great effect in simplifying the verb-inflections. The monosyllabic *bind* became the representative of the following ME forms: pres. indic. 1st pers. sing. *ī bīnde*, plur. *wē bīnde(n)*, etc., pres. subj. *bīnde, bīnde(n)*. The levelling of the distinction between the pret. and pret. partic. which had begun in ME was completed in the MnE forms *herd* (*heard*), *loved* representing ME *herde, lŏved(e)* and *(i)herd, (i)lŏved*. Such weak verbs as *set* and *cast* became invariable in the pret. and pret. partic.: infin. *set*, pret. *set*, pret. partic. *set*=ME *sette(n), sette, (i)set*. Moreover in such verbs the distinction between strong and weak conjugation is effaced: compare *set* pret. *set* with *let* pret. *let*= OE *sęttan, sętte; lǣtan, lēt*.

555. The weak vowel of the endings *-est, -eth, -es, -ed* was dropped in Early MnE in the spoken language, except that full *-est, -es* was always kept after the hiss-consonants (s, z; ʃ, ʒ), being subject to exactly the same rules as the noun-inflectional *-es* (**310**), as in *missest, misses, risest, rises, wishes, singes*. Full *-ed* was preserved after the point-stops *t*, *d*, as in *hated*, *wanted*, *wedded*, *wounded* = ME *hātede*, etc. Otherwise all these endings were shortened in speech without regard to the ME forms—in *loves* (luvz), *lovest*, *loveth* (luvþ), as well as *heares*, *hears*, *hearest*, *heareth*. In this way the distinction between the two classes of weak verbs was finally done away with as far as the endings were concerned, the distinction being only partially recognizable in the sound-changes in such verbs as *hear*, *heard* (hiir, hard); *feel*, *felt*; *teach*, *taught*.

556. But in the higher language the full endings *-est*, *-eth*, *-ed* were freely used after all consonants indifferently, especially in poetry, for the sake of the metre. *-es* was not used in this way because the less familiar *-eth* could always be substituted for it. Some very common verbs were, however, used only in the short forms, such as *dost*, *doth*, *mayst*, *wouldst*, especially the contracted *hast*, *hath*, *had*=ME *havest*, *hast* etc. *-est* was generally shortened in weak preterites, as in *lovedst*, *criedst*. *-est* and *-eth* are obsolete in Present English except in the higher language, in which they naturally keep their full forms, except in *dost*, *hath* etc. The higher language also keeps full *-ed* in many forms where the spoken language contracts, as in *beloved* (bi·lɐvid) compared with *loved* (lɐvd), *blessed are the peacemakers*.

557. The vowel of the full endings is now weak (i), as in (raizist, raiziz, raiziþ, heitid), and in Early MnE as well as Late ME it was often written *i*, *y* instead of *e*, as in Early MnE *thou spekyst*, *he dwellith*, *puttyth*, *passid*, *armyd*.

558. In writing, the silent *e* of *-es* was generally omitted in Early MnE, as in *sits*, *binds*; but not after *v*, as in *loves*, nor, of course, where required to show the pronunciation of a preceding letter, as in *shines*.

559. The consonant of shortened *-es* was assimilated as

regards breath and voice to the preceding consonant in the same way as in the noun-inflections: *lets, leads* (leedz), *loves* (luvz). The same assimilations took place with shortened *-ed*: *loved* (luvd), *breathed* (breeðd), *thanked* (þaŋkt), *blessed*. *-ed* being thus used to express (t), this spelling was often extended to such preterites as *burnt, smelt*, which were written *burned, smelled*, although they come from ME *brente, smelte*. But the phonetic spellings *thank't, thankt* (*thank'd*), *dropt, crost* (*cross'd*), *accurst* also came into partial use, and some of them have become fixed, such as *past* in *half past one* compared with *the time has passed quickly*.

The above are organic changes. We have now to consider the internal changes in the verb-inflections, beginning with those of a levelling character.

560. The change of strong to weak verbs which we observe in ME went on in the transition from ME to MnE, and, in some cases, in MnE itself. Thus the Early MnE preterite *clomb* and the pret. partic. *molten* have now become *climbed, melted*. But some of the weak forms that arose in Early MnE have now been discarded, such as the Shakesperian pret. participles *comed, becomed*.

561. On the other hand, several weak verbs have been made strong by the analogy of strong verbs, such as *stick, stuck* (OE *stician, sticode*) by the analogy of *sting, stung*; *wear, wore, worn* (OE *werian, werede*) by the analogy of *swear, swore, sworn*. So also several weak verbs in *-ow* have taken pret. participles in *-own* by the analogy of *know, known*, etc., keeping the original weak pret.: *show*, pret. *showed*, pret. partic. *shown* (OE *sċēawian, sċēawode*).

562. The levelling of the short quantity of the vowels in the sing. of strong preterites under the long quantity of the pret. partic. and infin. seen in Late ME *băr* = Early ME *bęr*, *bar* is carried much further in MnE, as in *brake*, *spake* = Late ME *brak*, *spak*, pret. partic. *brǭken*, infin. *bręken* etc. When a certain number of preterites in *a* had been thus lengthened, others were lengthened without regard to the length of the other parts of the verb, such as *came*, *bade* = ME *cam*, *bad*, infin. *cŏmen*, *bidden*, although the latter had a long vowel in the pret. partic. *będen*.

563. There is also a regular process of voice-levelling in the MnE strong verb, by which final (s, f) in the pret. sing. becomes voiced as in the infin. and pret. partic., as in *rose*, *chose*, *gave*, *drove* = ME *rǭs*, *chęs*, *gaf*, *drǭf*, infin. *rīsen*, *drīven* etc., pret. partic. *driven* etc.

564. The distinction between pret. sing. and plur. was levelled, as we have seen, in the MnE weak verbs by phonetic changes. In the strong verbs it was levelled by external, analogical changes. Already in ME strong verbs the vowel of the sing. was often carried into the plur., especially when the plur. had a vowel different from that of the pret. partic., as in *þei stal* instead of *þei stēlen* (pret. partic. *stǭlen*). Hence such Early MnE preterites as *bare*, *brake*, *gave*, *sat* correspond to ME singulars.

565. In many cases, however, MnE strong preterites have the vowel of the ME pret. plur. We have seen that in Late ME there was an intimate connection between the vowel of the pret. plur. and of the pret. partic. in strong verbs, so that at last the pret. plur., when it differed from the pret. sing., almost always had the vowel of the pret. partic. Hence in MnE the vowel of the pret. plur. when thus supported by the pret. partic. was often able to supplant the original singular-vowel. This was carried out consistently in those verbs of the bind-class which had ME (uu) in the pret. plur.

and pret. partic.: *bound, found*=ME *bǭnd, fǭnd*, plur. *bounden* etc. The same change took place in other verbs of the bind-class, and in some of the shine- and choose-class, many verbs having two preterites in Early MnE, one representing the ME pret. sing., the other with the vowel of the plur.: *began, begun*; *sang, sung*; *slang, slung*; *faught, fought*=ME *bigan, sǭng, slǭng, faught—bit*; *rode, rid*; *wrote, writ*=ME *bǭt, rǭd, wrǭt*. The present forms of these preterites are *began, sang, slung, fought, bit, rode, wrote*, the tendency evidently being to favour the original sing. forms.

566. But there has been in MnE a further assimilation of the pret. to the pret. partic., which has affected nearly all verbs of the bear-class with ME *ǭ* in the pret. partic.: already in Early MnE we find the preterites *bore, broke, spoke* by the side of *bare, brake, spake*=ME *bār, brak, spak*, ME *stal* being represented by *stole* only in Early MnE. In Present English *bare* etc. survive only in the higher language.

567. When a direct association had thus been established between the pret. and pret. partic. the two parts of the verb began to be confused—a confusion which was helped by the pret. partic. in *I have seen* etc. having nearly the same meaning as the pret. *I saw* etc.—so that the pret. began to be substituted for the pret. partic. in some verbs, especially when the older form of the pret. partic. was liable to be forgotten through not being in very frequent use—as in the case of ME *shinen* from *shīnen*—or ambiguous—as in the case of ME *stǭnden*, which was both pret. partic. and infin.—or anomalous and irregular in any way, as in *sę̄ten* compared with the infin. *sitten*. Hence in MnE the original preterites *shone, stood, sat* have supplanted the older pret. participles. In Early MnE this was carried still further than in Standard Present English, as in *took, shook, arose*=*taken, shaken, arisen.*

568. In the above examples the pret. participles *shone* etc. lost their final *n* through the substitution of a form with a different vowel. Such pret. participles as *bound, begun*= ME *bounden, bigǒnnen* may be considered either as the result of extension of the MnE pret. forms *bound* etc., or of dropping the *e* of the curtailed ME forms (*i*)*bounde*, etc.

It sometimes happens that the pret. partic. ending *-en* is dropped in a verb, but preserved in an adjective formed from the pret. partic. before it had lost the *-en*, as in the adjectives *drunken, bounden*, (in *bounden duty*) compared with the pret. participles *drunk, bound.*

569. In Early MnE the ending *-est* was extended to the pret. indic. of strong verbs: *thou boundest, thou spakest*=ME *bounde, bǭnd, spak.* The rare Early MnE dropping of *-st* in weak as well as strong preterites, as in *thou saw, thou maked, thou had* is probably the result of Northern influence. But in Present English, poets often instinctively drop this harsh and heavy inflection, especially when the verb is separated from its pronoun: *where thou once formed thy paradise* (Byron). Verbs whose pret. is the same as the pres.—especially those in *-st*—frequently drop the inflectional *st*, or else add it with an intervening *-ed* for the sake of distinctness: *thou castedst* or *thou cast.*

570. The following is the Early MnE conjugation of the strong verb *see* and the weak verb *call*:—

Indic. Pres. Sing.	1	*see*	*call*
	2	*seest*	*call*(*e*)*st*
	3	*seeth, sees*	*call*(*e*)*th, calls*
Plur.		*see*	*call*
Subj. Pres.		*see*	*call*
Pret. Indic. Sing.	1	*saw*	*call*(*e*)*d*
	2	*saw*(*e*)*st*	*calledst*
	3	*saw*	*call*(*e*)*d*
Plur.		*saw*	*call*(*e*)*d*

Pret. Subj.	*saw*	*call(e)d*
Imper.	*see*	*call*
Infin.	*see*	*call*
Pres. Partic. and Gerund	*seeing*	*calling*
Pret. Partic.	*seen*	*call(e)d*

Besides the above inflections there are others which occur only as isolated archaisms. The contracted *-t*=*-eth* has left a trace in the form *list* 'wishes,' 'likes,' as in *let him do it when he list*=OE *lyst* (*lysteþ*) from the weak verb *lystan*. All three ME indic. plurals are found in the Early MnE literary language, the most frequent of which—the Midland *-en*—survives in the Shakesperian *they waxen in their mirth*. The Southern *-eth* and the Northern *-es* are much less frequent. The infin. or gerund in *-en* survives in Shakespere: *to killen*.

571. The following examples will show the regular development of the different classes of strong verbs in literary MnE. It will be observed that the best-preserved classes are the 3rd and the 6th, the others being so reduced in the number of their verbs, and there being so much divergence of form, that they retain hardly a trace of their OE characteristics:—

I. **Fall**-class.

572.	*fall*	*fell*	*fallen*
	hold	*held*	*held, beholden*
	grow	*grew*	*grown*
	know	*knew*	*known*

II. **Shake**-class.

573.	*shake*	*shook*	*shaken*
	take	*took*	*taken*

The Late ME preterites in (-uu)=OE *-ōh*, such as *drow*, *slow*, were in Early MnE levelled under the more numerous *ew*-verbs of the fall-class: *draw*, *drew*; *slay*, *slew*.

III. Bind-class.

574.	*sing*	*sang*	*sung*
	drink	*drank*	*drunk*
	sting	*stung*	*stung*
	swing	*swung*	*swung*
	bind	*bound*	*bound(e)n*
	find	*found*	*found*
	fight	*fought*	*fought*

IV. Bear-class.

575.	*bear*	*bare, bore*	*born(e)*
	steal	*stole*	*stolen*

V. Give-class.

576.	*give*	*gave*	*given*
	weave	*wove*	*woven*
	sit	*sat*	*sat*

VI. Shine-class.

577.	*drive*	*drove*	*driven*
	rise	*rose*	*risen*
	write	*wrote*	*written*
	bite	*bit*	*bitten*
	shine	*shone*	*shone*

The occasional Early MnE preterites *drave*, *strave*, etc., are probably Northern forms.

VII. Choose-class.

578.	*freeze*	*froze*	*frozen*
	choose	*chose*	*chosen*

PRESENT ENGLISH.

579. In the present Spoken English the earlier substitution of *you see*, *you saw* for *thou seest*, *thou sawest*, and of *he sees* for *he seeth* has been completely carried out, so that the older *-st* and *-th* survive only in proverbs and in phrases taken from the higher literary language, where the older forms still survive.

Having traced the English verb down to its most reduced MnE form, it will now be more instructive to regard it from a purely descriptive, unhistorical point of view.

580. If we examine the Present English verb from this point of view, the first thing that strikes us is that the traditional distinction between strong and weak verbs can no longer be maintained: without going back to ME we cannot tell whether such preterites as *sat, lit, led, held,* infinitives *sit, light, lead, hold,* are strong or weak.

581. We are therefore compelled to make a new division into **consonantal** and **vocalic.** Consonantal verbs are those which form their preterites and pret. participles by adding *d* or *t*, such as *called, looked, heard, burnt,* infinitives *call, look, hear, burn.* Vocalic verbs are those which form their preterites or pret. participles by vowel-change without the addition of any consonant, except that the pret. partic. of some of these verbs adds *-en*: *sing, sang, sung*; *bind, bound, bound*; *run, ran, run—drive, drove, driven*; *speak, spoke, spoken*; *see, saw, seen.* Under the vocalic verbs we must also include the **invariable** verbs: *let, let, let*; *cast, cast, cast.* **Mixed** verbs show a mixture of consonantal and vocalic inflection: *crow, crew, crowed*; *show, showed, shown.*

582. The great majority of verbs belong to the regular consonantal conjugation, their pret. and pret. partic. ending being—

a. (-id) after (t) and (d): *delighted, nodded.*

b. (-d) after the other voice sounds: *played, raised, saved, turned, dragged.*

c. (-t) after the other breath consonants: *hissed, pushed, looked.*

583. Compared with these verbs those of the vocalic class must be regarded as irregular, although many of them fall under more or less uniform classes. There are also irregular consonantal verbs, such as *burn, burnt,* compared with the regular *turn, turned.* There is also a small class of specially irregular or **anomalous** verbs, such as *be, was, been,* some of which—mostly comprising the old preterite-present verbs—are defective, such as *(I) can, could,* which has no infin. or participles. The irregular verbs therefore comprise all the vocalic and anomalous verbs together with some of the consonantal, all regular verbs being consonantal. All newly formed verbs are conjugated consonantally, the consonantal inflections being the only living or productive ones.

584. The following are the inflections of the consonantal verb *call* and the vocalic verb *see* in Spoken English:—

Pres. Indic. Sing. 1	*call*	*see*
2	*call*	*see*
3	*calls*	*sees*
Plur.	*call*	*see*
Pres. Subj.	*call*	*see*
Pret. (Indic. and Subj.)	*called*	*saw*
Imper.	*call*	*see*
Infin.	*call*	*see*
Pres. Partic. and Gerund	*calling*	*seeing*
Pret. Partic.	*called*	*seen*

Irregular Verbs in Modern English.

585. In the following sections the vowel-changes are arranged in the alphabetic order of the vowels of the preterites in their phonetic spelling, to which the alphabetic order of the vowels of the infinitive is subordinated, thus (ei . . . e) as in *say*, *said*, and then (ij . . e), as in *flee*, *fled*, precede (iə . . əə), and this is followed by (uw . . o), etc. Forms that occur only in the higher literary language are marked *. Obsolete forms are marked †.

Consonantal Verbs.

With Vowel-change.

Verbs which take the regular consonantal inflection (d, t), but with vowel-change:—

Vowel-change (ei . . e).

586. say, said (sei, sed). OE weak I b *sęċġan*, *sæġde*, *sæġd*. In ME the *ċġ*-forms of this verb were preserved in South-Thames English; but in the North-Thames dialects the *ġ*-forms *sęġest*, *sęġeþ*, imper. *sęġe* were extended to the original *ċġ*-forms: *ī seie*, infin. *sein*, *seien*, pres. partic. *seiende*. These became the Standard ME forms also. The OE pret. *sæġde* became *saide* in ME. In MnE *saide* became (seed), which was shortened to (sed); and the same shortening took place in *says*. All the other OE *ċġ*-verbs show a similar extension of the *ġ*-forms in ME, so that the OE infinitives *liċġan*, *lęċġan*, *byċġan* appear in MnE as *lie* (ME *līen*), *lay* (ME *leien*), *buy* (ME *bīen*), which correspond phonetically to the OE imperatives *liġe*, *lęġe*, *byġe*.

Vowel-change (ij . . e).

587. flee, fled (flij, fled). OE strong VII *flēon* (Oldest English *flēohan*), *flēah*, plur. *flugon*, pret. partic. *flogen*. There was another OE verb of the same class, some of whose forms were identical with forms of *flēon*, namely *flēogan* 'fly,' *flēag* (*flēah*), pret. plur. *flugon*, pret. partic. *flogen*. As the two verbs were similar in meaning also, they were frequently confounded in Late West-Saxon, the distinctive forms of *flēogan* being used in the sense of 'flee' as well as in that of 'fly,' and *flēon* being used in the sense of 'fly.' This confusion has lasted to the present day, in as far as many modern writers use *fly* consistently in the sense of 'run away.' In ME the confusion between the two verbs was often avoided by using the weak verb *flēden*=OE *flēdan* (*flǣdan*) 'flow,' 'be at high tide' (said of the sea) from OE *flōd* 'flood' in the sense of 'flee,' its pret. *fledde* coming gradually to be regarded as the pret. of the old strong *flēon*, *flēn*. This development was probably helped by the Scandinavian weak verb *flȳja* 'flee,' pret. *flȳþi*.

588. creep, crept (krijp, krept). OE strong VII *crēopan*, *crēap*, *cropen*. In ME *crēpen* developed a weak pret. *crepte* by the side of the strong *crēp*. **leap, lept**; **sleep, slept**; **sweep, swept**; **weep, wept** have developed in a similar way from the OE strong verbs *hlēapan*, *hlēop* I; *slǣpan*, *slēp* I; *swāpan*, *swēop* I; *wēpan*, *wēop* I. OE *swāpan* became by regular change *swǭpen* in ME; the form *sweep* is the result of confusion with other verbs of similar meaning.

Vowel-change (iə . . əə).

589. hear, heard (hiər, həəd). OE weak I *hīeran*, *hīerde*, Anglian *hēran*, *hērde*, whence ME *hēren*, *herde* with the usual shortening. In Early MnE the (e) of the pret. was regularly broadened to (a) before the (r), giving (hiiər, hard). The spelling *heard* shows the not unfrequent lengthening of ME *e* before (r)-combinations, which, of course, preserved it from the change into (a); (heerd) was then shortened to (herd), whence the Present English (həəd).

Vowel-change (uw . . o).

590. shoe, shod (ʃuw, ʃod). OE *scōian, scōde, gescōd.* ME *shōin*, pret. partic. *ishōd.* The MnE shortening is parallel to that in *rod* compared with *rood*, both=OE *rōd. shod* is now used chiefly as an adjective, *shoe* being conjugated regularly *shoed.*

Vowel-change (e . . ou).

591. sell, sold (sel, sould). OE weak I b *sęllan, sealde*, Anglian *sālde* 'give.' ME *sellen, sǭlde, isǭld.* In OE the meaning 'sell' was only occasionally implied in the more general one of 'give,' as in *sęllan wiþ weorþe* 'give for a value (price)'='sell.' So also **tell, told** from OE weak I b *tęllan.*

With t instead of d.

592. burn, burnt. In OE the intransitive 'burn' was expressed by the strong verb III *biernan*, Late West-Saxon *byrnan*, Anglian *beornan*, pret. *bǫrn, barn*, pret. plur. *burnon*, pret. partic. *geburnen*; the transitive by the weak *bærnan, bærnde.* In these two verbs the *r* had been transposed, the Germanic forms being **brinnan*, **brannjan*, with which compare the Scandinavian strong *brinna*, pret. *brann*, pret. partic. *brunninn*, and the weak *bręnna, bręndi.* In ME the originally transitive and intransitive forms came to be used indiscriminately in both senses, the weak forms gradually getting the upper hand. In Standard ME the Northern—originally Scandinavian—form *brennen, brente* was used both transitively and intransitively, the strong Northern form—also originally Scandinavian—*brinnen* occurring less frequently, generally in its original intransitive sense. The other dialects show a great variety of forms: Early Southern *beornen, bęrnen, bernen*, Early Midland *bęrnen, bernen, brennen*, Early Northern *brin* (transitive as well as intrans.), *bren*. The infin. *burnen* seems to occur first in Late Midland; the *u* is probably the result of the influence of the lip-consonant *b* on the following *eo* of Anglian *beornan*. The pret. *brent* survived for some time in Early MnE.

593. dwell, dwelt. ME *dwellen, dwelte* from Scandinavian *dvęlja* 'remain.'

594. learn, learnt. OE *leornian, leornode*; ME *lern(i)en, lernde*, later *lernte*. The adjective *learned* preserves the fuller form of the pret. partic. So also *pen, pent*; *smell, smelt*; *spell, spelt*; *spill, spilt* from the OE weak verbs *pęnnan, smęllan* 'strike,' *spellian* 'relate,' *spillan* 'destroy.'

595. spoil, spoilt. ME *spoilen, despoilen* from Old French *spolier, despoiller* [from Latin *spoliāre* 'strip,' 'plunder'] was associated with *spillen* from OE *spillan*, so that when *spillen* took the special sense 'waste liquids,' 'spill,' *spoilen* took the old meaning of *spillen*, namely 'destroy,' and formed a pret. *spoilte* on the analogy of *spilte*. *spoil* in the sense of 'plunder' is regular.

596. feel, felt from OE *fēlan* (*fǣlan*), *fēlde*. **kneel, knelt** from ME *knēlen, knelde, knelte* of Scandinavian origin.

With t instead of d and Vowel-change.

Vowel-change (ij . . e).

597. (be)reave, *bereft, bereaved. OE *(be)rēafian, rēafode*. ME *birēven, birēvde, birefte, birafte*, the last being the Standard ME form.

598. cleave, cleft 'divide,' 'adhere.' OE strong VII *clēofan, clēaf, clofen* 'divide'; ME *clēven, clǭf, clǭven*. OE weak III *cleofian, clifian* 'adhere'; ME *clęvien, clęvede*.

There was also a strong verb VI in OE *clīfan* 'adhere,' ME *clīven* pret. partic. *cliven* 'adhere,' 'climb.' In ME *clǭf*, Northern *clāf*, originally pret. of *clīven*, was used also as pret. of *clēven*, whose pret. partic. *clǭven* had in Late ME the same vowel as *clǭf*. A new weak pret. *clefte* was then formed from *clēven*. In the Earliest MnE *cleeve* 'divide' kept (ii)=ME close *ē*, but was soon confused with *cleave* (kleev) 'adhere'= Early ME *clevien*, Late ME *clęvien*, so that it was written with *ea*. The MnE pret. *clove* may be regarded either as the descendant of the OE pret. *clāf* or as the ME pret. *clęf* (from OE *clēaf*) levelled under the pret. partic. *clǭven*. The other MnE pret. *clave* is of course the Northern form of OE *clāf*. The following are the forms of the two verbs in MnE:—

cleave 'divide'; *clove*, †*clave*, *cleft*; *cloven*, *cleft*, †*cleaved*.
cleave 'adhere'; †*clave*, *cleaved*; *cleaved*.

599. deal, dealt (dijl, delt). OE *dǣlan*, *dǣlde*. **leave, left; mean, meant** from OE *lǣfan*, *lǣfde*; *mǣnan*, *mǣnde*.

600. dream, dreamt, dreamed (drijm, dremt, drijmd). OE *drīeman*, Anglian *drēman* 'modulate' [*drēam* 'melody,' 'joy']. The ME *drę̄men*, *dremde*, *drem(p)te* got the meaning 'dream' from the Scandinavian *drǫ̈yma* 'dream.' In Early MnE the verb was levelled under the noun *dream*, the ME pret. being however kept in spelling—*dremt*—as well as pronunciation by the side of the new pret. *dreamed*. The spelling *dreamt* is, of course, a blending of *dremt* and *dreamed*.

601. lean, leant, leaned (lijn, lent, lijnd). OE *hleonian* (*hlinian*), *hleonode*; ME *lęnien* (*linien*), *lęnede*. The pret. *leant* comes from another OE verb meaning 'to lean,' namely *hlǣnan*, *hlǣnde*; ME *lę̄nen*, *lende*, *lente*.

Vowel-change (ai . . ɔ).

602. buy, bought. OE *byċġan, bohte.* ME *biġġen, bīen* (**586**), pret. *bohte, bouhte.*

Vowel-change (uw . . ɔ).

603. lose, lost. OE strong VII *forlēosan, forlēas, forloren* 'destroy,' 'lose,' weak III *losian* 'go to waste,' 'get lost.' ME *lēsen, forlēsen* 'lose,' *lę̄s, forlę̄s, loren, forloren.* The dropping of the *for-* is due to the influence of *losien* = OE *losian*, whose transitive use, as in *hē losede al his folc* 'he lost all his people (army)' is due to the influence of *forlēsen.* Hence the pret. partic. *ilosed*, later *lost*, came to be used as the pret. partic. of *lēsen*, when the old pret. participles *loren, forloren* had come to be isolated from their verbs in meaning, so that MnE **lorn* in *love-lorn*, etc., *forlorn*, are now used only as adjectives. In Early MnE *lese* took (uu) from the adjective *loose* and verb *loosen* [ME *lōs, lōsnen* from Scandinavian *lǫuss* 'free,' 'loose,' *lǫusna* 'get loose'], being at first written *loose*, then *lose*, to distinguish it from the adjective *loose.*

With t instead of -ded.

604. gird, girt, girded. OE *gyrdan, gyrde.* So also **build, built, †builded; gild, gilt, gilded; bend, bent, †bended; rend, rent; send, sent; †shend, †shent; spend, spent, *wend, went** from the OE weak *byldan, gyldan, bęndan, ręndan, sęndan, sċęndan* 'put to shame,' *spęndan, węndan* 'turn.'

605. blend, †blent, blended. OE strong I *blandan* 'mix.' Weak OE *blęndan* has only the meaning 'blind.'

606. lend, lent. OE *lǣnan, lǣnde.* ME *lęnden, lenden* is a new-formation from the OE preterite-forms; from *lenden* a new pret. *lende, lente* was formed on the analogy of *senden, sente,* etc.

With Consonant-loss.

607. make, made. OE *macian, macode.* ME *makien, makede, imaked,* Late ME *mākien,* contracted *māde, (i)mād.*

With Consonant-loss and Vowel-change.

Vowel-change (ou . . æ).

608. clothe, clad, clothed. OE *clāþian, clāþode* [*clāþ* 'cloth']. Scandinavian *klǣþa, klǣþdi,* whence ME *clēþen, cladde* Northern *cledde,* as well as *clōþ(i)en, clōþede.*

Vowel-change (æ . . ɔ).

609. catch; caught. ME *cacchen, caughte* from Old French *cachier* [Low Latin *captiāre* = Latin *captāre,* a frequentative of *capere* 'seize']. *cachier* is probably a North-East French (Picard) form; the Parisian form being *chacier* (Modern French *chasser*), whence the MnE *chace, chase.* ME *cacchen* having the same meaning and the same termination as *lacchen, laughte* from OE *lǣċċan, ġelǣhte* 'seize,' 'catch' [compare MnE *latch*], naturally formed its preterite in the same way.

610. distract; †distraught, distracted. OE *strēċċan* 'stretch,' pret. *streahte, strēhte,* appears in ME in the form of *strecchen, straughte, streighte,* the pret. partic. *streight* being still kept in MnE as an adjective—*straight* literally 'stretched out.' In Late ME the Latin *distrāctus* was imported as an adj. *distract* (French *distrait*), which was made into *distraught* by the influence of *straught.* When *distract* was made into a verb in Early MnE, *distraught* was naturally regarded as its participle. Through further confusion *straught* itself was used in the sense of 'distracted,' and a new partic. †*bestraught* was formed on the analogy of *beset*.

Vowel-change (əə . . ɔ).

611. work; *wrought, worked (wəək, rɔt). OE *wyrċan*, Anglian *wircan*, the corresponding noun being *weorc*, Late West-Saxon *worc*, Anglian *werc*, which in ME influenced the verb. The ME forms are: Southern *würchen*, *wŏrchen* with the usual change of *wü-* to *wu-*, Midland *werken*, Northern *wirk*. The OE pret. *worhte* underwent the usual r-transposition in ME, becoming *wrohte*, MnE *wrought*, which in ordinary speech survives only as an adjective, as in *wrought iron*.

Vowel-change (i . . ɔ).

612. bring; brought (briŋ, brɔt). OE *bringan*, *brohte*.

613. think; thought. In OE there were two weak I a verbs of allied form and meaning: *þęnċan*, *þohte* 'think'; *þynċan*, *þuhte* 'seem,' which was impersonal, *mē þynċþ* 'it seems to me' having much the same meaning as *iċ þęnċe*. In ME *þęnċan* became regularly *þenchen* in South-Thames English, *þenken* in North-Thames English; and *þynċan* became *þünchen*, *þinchen* in South-Thames English, *þinken* in North-Thames English. The pret. *þuhte* was soon disused, *þo(u)hte* taking its place: *hē þohte* 'he thought,' *him þohte* 'it seemed to him.' In Standard ME the two verbs were still kept apart in the infin. and present tenses, which had the Midland forms *þenken, ī þenke; þinken, mē þinkeþ*, etc.; but in the compound *biþinken* 'consider'=OE *beþęnċan*, the latter had already begun to encroach. In Northern *þink* completely supplanted *þenk*, as in MnE. Hence MnE *think* is historically=OE *þynċan*, and its pret. *thought*=OE *þohte*, the pret. of the lost *þęnċan*.

Vowel-change (ij . . ɔ).

614. seek; sought; beseech; besought. OE *sēċan* (*sǣċan*), *sohte*. ME South-Thames *sēchen*, *bisēchen*, North-Thames *sēken*, *bisēken*. The MnE *seek* and *beseech* are therefore from different dialects of ME. Shakespere has the Midland form not only in *seek*, but also in *beseek*.

615. reach; †raught, reached. OE *rǣċan*, *rǣhte*. ME *rę̄chen*, *ra(u)ghte*, Northern *reghte*. So also **teach, taught** from OE weak *tǣċan* 'show.'

Invariable Verbs.

(**aa**).

616. cast. ME *casten* from Scandinavian weak *kasta*, *kastaþi*. In Early MnE there is also a regular pret. *casted*.

(**ai**).

617. *dight 'adorn' as in *storied window richly dight* (Milton). OE *dihtan* 'arrange,' 'appoint' from the Latin *dictāre*.

(**ɐ**).

618. cut. ME *kutten*.

619. shut. OE *sċyttan* 'lock,' 'bolt' [*gesċot* 'shot,' 'dart'; *sċēotan* strong VII 'shoot']. ME *schütten*, *schutten*.

620. thrust. ME *þrüsten*, *þrusten* from Scandinavian *þrȳsta*.

(**e**).

621. let. OE strong I *lǣtan*, *lēt*, *lǣten*. ME *lēten*, pret. strong *lēt*, and weak *lette* from **lētte*. In MnE the short vowel of this weak pret. was extended to the infin., etc. The obsolete verb *let* 'hinder,' still preserved in the phrase *let or* *hindrance*, is the OE weak *lęttan*, *lętte*, connected with *læt* 'slow,' *late* adv. 'late.'

622. set. OE *sęttan*, *sętte*, connected with the strong verb V *sittan*, pret. *sæt*.

623. shed. OE strong I *sćādan*, *sćēadan*, *sćēd* 'separate,' a meaning still preserved in the noun *watershed*. ME *schēden* formed a weak pret. *schadde*, *schedde*, and developed the new meaning 'separate into drops,' 'shed.' In MnE the short vowel of the pret. was extended to the pres., etc., as in *let*.

624. shred. OE *sćrēadian*, *sćrēadode*. ME *schrēden*, *schredde*, the short vowel being afterwards extended to the pres., etc. So also **spread** (spred) from weak OE *sprǣdan*.

(əə).

625. burst. OE strong III *berstan*, *bærst*, *burston*, *ġeborsten*. The *u* of *burst* is the result of the influence of the lip-consonant *b* on the *eo* of ME *beorsten*, as in *burn* (**592**), the *u* being afterwards extended to the pret. partic. *bursten*, which survived in Early MnE.

626. hurt. ME *hürten*, *hurten*.

(i).

627. hit. ME *hitten* from Scandinavian *hitta* 'find.'

628. knit. OE *cnyttan* 'tie' [*cnotta* 'knot']. The invariable pret.-form is now preserved only as an adjective in *well-knit*, etc. Otherwise the pret.-form is regular—*knitted*.

629. quit. ME *quīten* pret. *quitte* from Old French *quiter* from Latin *quiētus*. In MnE the shortened vowel of the pret. was extended to the rest of the verb. The derivative *requite* keeps its original length, having a pret. partic.

requil in Early MnE. *acquil* is invariable in Early MnE. All these verbs are now regular.

630. rid. ME *redden, rüdden, rịdden* 'rescue,' 'separate fighters' is apparently a blending of OE *hrędðan* 'rescue' and Scandinavian *ryþja* pret. *rudda* 'clear away.'

631. slit. OE strong VI *slītan, slāt, sliten.* ME has both strong *slīten*, pret. partic. *sliten*, and a weak verb *slitten*, which may have existed in OE.

632. split. ME *splatten*, of which Early MnE *splette* is probably a Northern form. *splet* seems to have been made into *split* by the influence of *slit.*

(o).

633. cost. ME *costen* from Old French *coster* (Modern French *coûter*) from Latin *cōnstāre.*

(u).

634. put. ME *putten.*

Vocalic Verbs.

Vowel-change (ai . . **au**).

635. bind; bound. OE strong III *bindan, band, bunden.* The older pret. partic. is still preserved in *bounden duty.* So also **grind, ground; wind, wound** from OE strong III *grindan, windan.*

636. find; found. OE strong III *findan, fand*—more generally weak *funde—funden.* ME pret. *fǭnd, founde.*

Vowel-change (ai . . ɐ).

637. strike; struck. OE strong VI *strīcan, strāc, stricen* 'move about,' 'touch lightly.' ME *strīken, strǭk* (Northern *strāk*), *striken*. Early MnE *strike*, pret. *stroke*, *strake*, *struck*, pret. partic. *stricken*, *strucken*, *struck*.

Vowel-change (æ . . ɐ).

✱ **638. hang; hung, hanged.** OE strong I *hōn* (from earlier **hōhan*), *hēng*, *hangen*, the *g* being a weakening of the *h* of the infin., where *ō* = Germanic *an* (**502**), so that *hōn* = Germanic **hanhan*. There was also a weak intransitive *hangian*, *hangode*, *hōn* itself being used transitively. In Early ME the consonantal variation in the strong verb was soon levelled: sometimes the infinitive form was extended to the pret. partic. which was made into (*a*)*hōn*; but afterwards the ng-forms got the upper hand, being supported by the weak verb *hangien*, and a new strong infin. *hangen* was formed, pret. *hēng*, pret. partic. *hangen*. In some dialects the pret. was shortened to *heng* with short close (e), which being an unfamiliar sound in ME was made into *i*. This new pret. *hing*, which is frequent in some Midland dialects, was made into an infin. in Northern by the analogy of the bind-class, with pret. *hang*, which afterwards made its way into the Standard dialect in the form of *hǭng* parallel to *sǭng* 'sang.' A pret. partic. *hung* was further developed on the analogy of *sing*, *sang*, *sung*, and *hung* was then extended to the pret. sing. in the same way as *clung*, etc. (**565**), the older infin. *hang* being preserved in the Standard dialect. In MnE the strong form *hung* is both transitive and intransitive, *hanged* being used only transitively, contrary to the OE usage.

Vowel-change (i . . ɐ).

639. dig; dug, †digged. ME *diggen*, *diggede*, equivalent to OE *dīcian* [*dīc* 'ditch'], of which it seems to be a modification by some analogical influence. The vocalic pret. *dug* developed itself towards the end of the Early MnE period; it is not found in the Bible.

640. cling; clung. OE strong III *clingan*, *clang*, *clungen* 'wither.' ME *clingen*, *clǭng*, *clungen* 'shrivel,' 'adhere,' 'hang.' So also **slink, slunk; spin, † span, spun; sting, stung; swing, swung; win, won; wring, wrung** from OE strong III *slincan*, *spinnan*, *stingan*, *swingan*, *ġewinnan*, *wringan*.

641. fling; flung. ME strong III *flingen* from weak Scandinavian *flęngja* [compare ME *wing* from Scandinavian *vęngr*]. *flingen* was, of course, made strong on the analogy of *sting* and the other strong verbs in *-ing*.

642. sling; slung. ME strong III *slingen* from Scandinavian *slöngva*, which passed through *slengen* into *slingen*, and then became strong in the same way as *fling*. The pret. *slang* occurs in the Bible.

643. stick; stuck, †sticked 'pierce,' 'adhere.' OE *stician* (*stiocian*), *sticode* 'pierce,' 'adhere.' ME strong V *steken*, *stak*, *steken* and *stoken* [like *spoken* = OE *specen*] 'pierce,' 'imprison,' which may represent an OE strong verb. *stuck* may owe its *u* to the influence of *stung*.

644. string; strung, stringed. This verb is a MnE formation from the ME noun *string* from Scandinavian *stręngr*, with the usual change of Scandinavian *-ęng* into *-ing*. We keep the older consonantal inflexion in *stringed instruments*.

Vowel-change (ɐ . . æ . . ɐ).

645. run; ran; run. OE strong III *irnan*, *iernan* (*eornan*), Late West-Saxon *yrnan*, pret. *ǫrn*, *arn*, pret. partic. *urnen*, with the same transposition of the *r* as in *burn*, the older forms being preserved in *gerinnan* 'coagulate,' literally 'run together,' *gerann*, *gerunnen*. The ME verb was influenced by the two Scandinavian verbs, the strong *rinna*, *rann*, *runninn* and the weak *rẹnna*, *rẹndi*, the Standard ME forms being indeed entirely Scandinavian: *rennen*, *ran*, *irunnen*. The Early Southern forms of the infin. are *irnen*, *eornen*, *urnen* probably=*ürnen* from Late West-Saxon *yrnan*. The infin. *run* appears in Northern by the side of the Scandinavian *rin*. The *u* of the infin. seems to have been originally a Southern development out of *ürnen*, perhaps by the influence of *burn*.

Vowel-change (i . . æ).

646. sit; sæt. OE strong V j-verb *sittan*, *sæt*, *seten*. ME *sitten*, *sat*, *seten* and also *siten* with the vowel of the infin. From the ME partic. *siten* is derived the obsolete MnE pret. and pret. partic. *sit*, which made the verb invariable. The obsolete MnE pret. *sate* is due to the analogy of *came*, *spake*, etc., the short *sat* being kept up at the same time by the short vowel of the infin. *sit*.

647. spit; spat. There were in OE two weak verbs of the same meaning *spittan*, *spitte* and *spǣtan*, *spǣtte*, both of which were kept in ME, where the pret. *spǣtte* became regularly *spatte*. The MnE *spit*, *spat* is, therefore, a mixture of two distinct verbs.

Vowel-change (i . . æ . . ɐ).

648. begin; began; begun. OE strong *beginnan*. So also **drink, drank, drunk(en); shrink, shrank, shrunk; sing, sang, sung; sink, sank, sunk(en); spring, sprang, sprung; stink, stank, stunk; swim, swam, swum**

from OE strong III *drincan, sċrincan, singan, sincan, springan, stincan, swimman.*

649. ring; rang; rung. OE *(h)ringan*, which is apparently weak.

Vowel-change (i . . æ . . i-n).

650. (for)bid; -bad; -bidden. OE strong V j-verb *biddan, bæd, beden* 'pray,' 'ask'; strong VII *bēodan, bēad, boden* 'offer,' 'command.' The corresponding ME forms are *bidden, bad, bę̄den* and—by the analogy of the infin.—*bidden*; *bēden, bę̄d, bǭden.* But already in Early ME the two verbs began to be confused. *bidden* in the special sense of 'ask to one's house,' 'invite' soon got confused with *bēden*, which developed the meaning 'offer an invitation,' the confusion being aided by the weak verb *bǭd(i)en*=OE *bodian* 'announce'—itself connected with *bēodan.* Hence even in Early ME we find *iboden* used in the sense of 'invited.' It was still more natural to soften down the command expressed by *bēden* by the substitution of the milder *bidden.* The pret. *bad* soon supplanted *bę̄d* by taking to itself the meaning 'commanded,' except in the emphatic *forbēden*, which in Standard ME only rarely has the pret. *forbad* instead of *forbę̄d.* The following are the Standard ME forms—

bidden, bēden ; bad ; bę̄den, bǭden.
forbēden ; forbę̄d (forbad) ; forbǭden.

In the transition to MnE the *bid*-forms were gradually extended till they entirely supplanted the others. The relation between the two forms *bad* and *bade* is the same as that between *sat* and *sate* (**562**). In Early MnE the pret. partic. was often shortened to *bid*, which was used also as a pret., so that the verb became invariable.

Vowel-change (ij . . e).

651. bleed; bled. OE weak *blēdan* (*blǣdan*), *blēdde.* [*blōd* 'blood']. So also **breed, bred; feed, fed; lead, led; meet, met; read, read** (rijd, red); **speed, sped** from the OE weak *brēdan, fēdan, lǣdan, mētan, rǣdan, spēdan.*

Vowel-change (ij . . e . . ij-n).

652. eat; ate; eaten. OE strong V, with exceptional (Germanic) lengthening in the pret. sing., *etan, ǣt*, pret. plur. *ǣton*, pret. partic. *eten.* ME *ęten, ēt, at, ęten*, the pret. *at* being of course due to the influence of the other verbs of the same class.

Vowel-change (ou . . e).

653. hold; held. OE strong I *healdan, hāldan*; *hēold*; *ġehealden, ġehālden* ME *hǭlden*; *hēld, held, hild*; *ihǭlden.* We still preserve the fuller form of the pret. partic. in *beholden.*

Vowel-change (ɔ . . e . . ɔ-n).

654. fall; fell; fallen. OE strong I *feallan, fallan*; *fēoll*; *feallen, fallen.* ME *fallen*; *fēl, fel, fil*; *fallen.*

Vowel-change (ai . . ei . . ei-n).

655. lie; lay; lain. OE strong V j-verb *liċġan, læġ, ġeleġen*, imper. sing. *liġe*, etc. The ME development of this verb is analogous to that of the other ċġ-verbs (**586**). In Early Southern the infin. *liġġen* was preserved by the side of the imper. *līe*; but in the North-Thames dialects it was levelled under the ġ-forms, becoming *līn, līen.* The Standard ME forms are *līen, lai*, pret. partic. *leien, lein.*

Vowel-change (ɐ . . ei . . ɐ).

656. come; came; come. OE strong IV, with anomalous weak vowel in the pres. and infin. and exceptional extension of the vowel of the pret. plur. to the pret. sing.: *cuman*; *cwōm, cōm*; *c(w)ōmon*; *cumen*. The pret. *cōm* was preserved in Standard ME, but was partially supplanted by the new formation *cam* on the analogy of the strong verb IV *nimen* 'take,' *nam, nŏmen*. *cam* underwent the usual lengthening into *came* in MnE.

Vowel-change (i . . ei . . i-n).

657. give; gave; given. OE *ġiefan* (*ġefan*); *ġeaf* (*ġæf*); *ġiefen* (*ġefen*).

Vowel-change (ai . . i).

658. light; lit, lighted. OE weak *lihtan, lihte* 'illuminate' and 'make light,' 'alleviate' [*leoht* adj. 'light of colour' and 'light of weight']. There was a third OE weak verb *lihtan, ālihtan* 'alight from a horse.' The MnE verb *light* in *light on* must be referred to this last. The consonantal preterite-form *lit* does not, of course, appear till *light* had become (ləit), that is, in the MnE period, when it arose from imitation of *bite, bit*, etc. The verb *alight* still keeps the older consonantal inflexion, which is also used in the other verbs.

Vowel-change (ai . . i . . i-n).

659. bite; bit; bitten. OE strong VI *bītan*. The shortened pret. partic. is still kept in the phrase *the biter bit*.

660. chide; chid; chidden. OE weak *ċīdan, ċīdde*. ME *chīden, chidde*. In Early MnE the verb was made strong

—*chide, chode, chidden*—on the analogy of *ride, rode, ridden.* The pret. partic. was then shortened to *chid,* and extended to the pret. The verb is nearly obsolete in the present spoken English. **hide, hid, hidden** is a strong verb of similar recent formation, except that it does not seem to have developed any pret. analogous to Early MnE *chode*: OE *hȳdan, hȳdde,* ME *hīden, hidde.*

Vowel-change (ij . . ij . . ij-n).

661. beat; beat; beaten. OE strong I *bēatan, bēot, bēaten.*

Vowel-change (ai . . o).

662. shine; shone. OE strong VI *sċīnan, sċān, sċinen.*

Vowel-change (e . . o . . o-n).

663. (for)get; forgot; forgotten, got. In OE the strong V verb *ġietan, ġytan* (*ġetan*); *ġeat* (*ġæt*); *ġieten, ġyten* (*ġeten*) occurs only in the compounds *beġietan* 'get,' *onġietan* 'understand,' *forġietan* 'forget' and a few others. In ME *begiten, begeten* was shortened to *giten, geten* through the influence of the Scandinavian *geta, gat, getinn* 'get,' or rather the Scandinavian word was substituted for it.

664. tread; trod; trodden. OE strong V *tredan, træd, treden.* ME *trę̄den, trad, trę̄den* and—by the analogy of *broken,* etc.—*trǭden, troden.*

Vowel-change (ij . . o . . o-n).

665. seethe; †sod, seethed; sodden, †sod, seethed. OE strong VII *sēoþan, sēaþ, soden.*

Vowel-change (uw . . o).

666. shoot; shot. OE strong VII *sċēotan, sċēat, sċoten.*

Standard ME *schēlen, schǭl, scholen.* There is also an infin. *schulen* in ME, whose *u* probably=*ū* from OE *ēo*, as in *choose* (680), which afterwards became (uu) and was written *oo* in Early MnE.

Vowel-change (ai . . ou).

667. climb; †clomb, climbed. OE strong III *climman, clamm, clummen* and also *climban, clamb, clumben,* although the latter is found only in late texts. ME *climmen, clam, clŏmmen* and *clīmben, clǭmb* (*clamb*), *clŏmben.*

Vowel-change (ai . . ou . . i-n).

668. (a)bide; †bode, †bid, bided; †biden, †bid, bided. OE strong VI *bīdan* 'wait,' *ābīdan* 'endure.' ME (*a*)*bīden, bǭd, biden,* there being also a weak pret. *abidde.*

669. drive; drove, †drave; driven. OE strong VI *drīfan.* So also **ride, rode, ridden; rise, rose, risen; shrive, †shrove, shrived, shriven; smite, smote, smitten; stride, strode, †stridden, strode; write, wrote, written** from OE strong VI *rīdan, ārīsan, scrīfan, smītan* 'smear,' *strīdan, wrītan.*

670. strive; strove; striven. ME strong VI *strīven, strǭf, striven,* which is the Old French *estriver* [from Old Low-German *strīþ* 'strife'] made into a strong verb on the analogy of *drīven.*

671. thrive; throve; thriven. ME *þrīven* from the Scandinavian strong reflexive verb *þrīfask.*

Vowel-change (ei . . ou).

* **672. wake; woke, waked.** OE strong II *wacan, wōc, wacen,* generally compounded with *on-*: *onwacan, awacan.* (*on*)*wacan* and the weak *ā*(*wæcnian*), *wacian* 'keep awake'

are intransitive. The corresponding transitive verb is *węććan, weahte, węhte.* ME has *(a)waken, wōk, waken* and *wakien, wakede; wakenen, wak(e)nede.* The (ou) instead of (uw) in the MnE *woke* is probably due to the influence of the numerous preterites of the shine-class—*rose,* etc.

673. stave; stove, staved. This verb was first formed in MnE from the noun *stave* 'piece of a cask,' itself a late formation from *staves,* plur. of *staff.* Its vocalic inflexion is of course the result of analogy.

Vowel-change (ei . . ou . . ou-n).

674. break; broke, †brake; broken, †broke. OE strong IV *brecan, bræc, brocen.*

Vowel-change (ij . . ou . . ou-n).

675. freeze; froze; frozen, †frore OE strong VII *frēosan, frēas, froren.*

676. heave; hove, heaved; †hoven, hove, heaved. OE strong j-verb II *hębban, hōf, hafen.* ME *hebben, hēven; hōf, haf; hǭven, hēven,* the last form being due to the influence of the infin., while *haf, hǭven* are due to the influence of *wēven, waf, wǭven* (679). There was also a weak ME pret. *hefde, hevede.* The MnE *hove* probably points to a ME pret. *hǭf* with the vowel of the pret. partic.

677. speak; spoke, †spake; spoken, †spoke. OE strong V *sprecan, spræc, sprecen.* In Late OE this verb began to drop its *r*—especially in the Kentish dialect. In ME the *r* disappeared entirely, and the pret. partic. took *o* on the analogy of *broken,* etc.: *spēken, spak, spēken, spǭken.*

678. steal; stole; stolen. OE strong IV *stelan, stæl, stolen.*

679. weave; wove, weaved; woven, weaved. OE strong V *wefan, wæf, wefen.* ME *węven, waf, węven, wǫven.*

Vowel-change (uw .. ou .. ou-n).

680. choose; chose; chosen. OE strong VII *ċēosan, ċēas, coren.* ME *chēsen, chęs, chosen.* There was also a West-Midland infin. *chūsen* with the regular West-Midland change of OE *ēo* into *ū.* In Early MnE (tʃiuz) became (tʃuuz), which was written phonetically *choose,* although the older spelling *chuse* survived till the end of the last century. *chese* also occurs in Early MnE.

Vowel-change (ai .. ɔ).

681. fight; fought. OE strong III *feohtan* (*fehtan*); *feaht* (*fæht*); *fohten.* ME *fighten, faught, foughten.* In the pret. Early MnE fluctuates between *au* and *ou.*

Vowel-change (eə .. ɔ .. ɔ-n).

682. bear; bore, †bare; born(e). OE strong IV *beran, bær, boren.* MnE makes a distinction between *born* in the sense of French *né* and *borne*='carried' which did not exist in OE or ME.

683. swear; swore, †sware; sworn. OE strong j-verb II *swęrian, swōr, swaren, sworen,* the *o* of the last form being due to the influence of the preceding *w.* ME *swerien, swęren; swōr, swār; swǫren.* *swār* is, of course, due to the analogy of *bęren, bār.*

684. tear; tore, †tare; torn. OE strong IV *teran.*

685. wear; wore, †ware; worn. OE weak *węrian, węrede* 'wear clothes.' The vocalic forms were first developed in Early MnE by the analogy of *bear.*

Vowel-change (ei . . ɔ).

686. freight; *fraught, freighted. The Late ME weak verb *fraughten* [imported from Dutch ?] was made into *freight* in Early MnE by the influence of the synonymous *fret*, and *fraught* itself came to be regarded as the pret. of this new verb *freight* by a vague association with *work, wrought*, etc. But *fraught* was still used as a pres. in Early MnE: *the good ship . . . and the fraughting souls within her* (Shakespere).

Vowel-change (iə . . ɔ . . ɔ-n).

687. shear; †shore, †share, sheared; shorn, †sheared. OE strong IV *sċieran* (*sċeran*); *sċear* (*sċær*); *sċoren*.

Vowel-change (ij . ɔ . . ij-n).

688. see; saw; seen. OE strong V *sēon*; *seah* (*sæh*); *sāwon* (*sēgon*); *sewen* (*seġen*). In Late Northumbrian the adjective *ġesēne* = West-Saxon *ġesīene* 'visible' was used as the pret. partic. Early ME *sēon, sēn*; *seih* (Southern), *sah, sauh* pret. plur. *sǭwen, sēien*; pret. partic. *seien, sein*. In Late ME the pret. sing. forms dropped the *h* by the influence of the pret. plur. and pret. partic., giving *sei, sai* and *saw*, the last being the usual North-Thames form, especially in Northumbrian, which also kept the Old-Northumbrian pret. partic. in the form of *sēn*. The Standard ME inflections are *sē(n)*; *seigh, sai*; (*i*)*sein*. In MnE the Northern pret. *saw* and pret. partic. *seen* were introduced into the Standard dialect.

Vowel-change (æ . . . u).

689. stand; stood. OE strong II with *n* inserted in the pres. etc.: *standan, stōd, standen*.

Vowel-change (ei . . . **u** . . . ei-n).

690. forsake; forsook; forsaken. OE strong II *forsacan* 'renounce,' 'deny.' So also **shake, shook, shaken** from OE strong II *sċacan*.

691. take; took; taken, *ta'en. ME strong II *tāken, tōk, tāken* from Scandinavian *taka, tōk, tękinn.* In Northern this verb was contracted like *make*, and the pret. partic. *ta'en* passed into Standard MnE.

Vowel-change (ai . . . **uw** . . . ou-n).

692. fly; flew; flown. OE strong VII *flēogan* (*flēgan, flīgan*); *flēag, flēah* (*flēh*); *flugon*; *flogen*. ME *flēn, flīen*; *fleigh, fley*—with the same dropping of final *h* as in *sei*=OE *ġesæh*—*flȳ*; pret. plur. *flowen, flǭwen* (influence of pret. partic.); pret. partic. *flǭwen*. The Early MnE pret. *flew* (fliu) probably arose in the same way as *drew*, etc. (**573**).

Vowel-change (ei . . . **uw** . . . ei-n).

693. slay; slew; slain. OE strong II *slēan* (from *sleahan*); *slōg, slōh*; *slagen, slæġen, slęġen*. ME Southern *slēn*, Midland *slǭn*, Northern *slā*; *slōh*, Late ME *slough, slow* =(sluu); pret. partic. *slawen, sleiҿn, slain*. In MnE, the *ai* of the pret. partic. was extended to the infin., and the *ow* of the pret. underwent the usual analogical change into *ew*. The archaic forms *slee* = *slea*, pret. *slue* still lingered in Early MnE.

Vowel-change (ou . . . **uw** . . . ou-n).

694. blow; blew; blown, blowed. OE strong I *blāwan* 'blow' (of wind), *blēow, blāwen* and *blōwan* 'bloom,' *blēow, blōwen*. ME *blǭwen, blēw, blǭwen* and *blōwen, blēw, blōwen*.

695. crow; crew, crowed; †crown, crowed. OE strong I *crāwan, crēow, crāwen.* **grow, grew, grown; know, knew, known** from OE strong I *grōwan, cnāwan.*

Vowel-change (ɔ ... uw ... ɔ-n).

696. draw; drew; drawn. OE strong II *dragan; drōg, drōh; dragen.*

Mixed Verbs.

697. There are several verbs which have a strong pret. partic. in *-en* with a regular consonantal pret. Some of these are old strong verbs which have become partially consonantal; but others are weak verbs which have taken the partic. ending *-en* by the influence of old strong verbs which they happen to resemble. In the following list the latter class are marked ‡.

698. go; went; gone. OE strong I *gān, gangan; gēong, ēode* (weak); *gegān, gegangen.* ME *gǭ(n), gange(n); yōde, wente; gǭ(n), gangen.* In ME the longer form *gang* was gradually restricted to the Northern dialect. The curtailed Southern pret. partic. *gǭ* is still preserved in the adverb *ago*=OE *āgān* 'passed' (of time).

699. grave, graved; graven, graved. OE strong II *grafan, grōf, grafen.*

700. hew; hewed; hewn, hewed. OE strong I *hēawan, hēow, hēawen.*

701. †lade, load; †laded, loaded; laden, †laded, †loaden, loaded. OE strong II *hladan, hlōd, hlæden, hladen.* The MnE change of *lade* into *load* is through the influence of the noun *load*, ME *lǭde* = OE *lād* (fem.) 'leading,' 'way,' connected with *lǣdan* 'lead,' which had also the meaning 'carry,' so that in ME *lǭde* came to mean 'load,' and was at last confused with the verb *lāden*.

702. melt; melted; molten, melted. OE strong III *meltan*. *molten* is now used only as an adjective.

703. mow; mowed; mown, mowed. OE strong I *māwan, mēow, māwen*.

704. rive; rived; riven, rived. ME strong VI *rīven, rǭf, riven* from the Scandinavian *rīfa*.

705. ‡saw; sawed; sawn, sawed. ME weak *saw(i)en*. MnE *sawn* by the analogy of *drawn*.

706. shape; shaped; shapen, shaped. OE strong II j-verb *sċieppan, sċyppan (sċęppan); sċōp; sċapen, sċæpen*. In ME this verb was influenced by the Scandinavian verb *skapa, skōp*.

707. shave; shaved; shaven, shaved. OE strong II *sċafan, sċōf, sċafen*.

708. ‡show; showed; shown, showed. OE weak *sċēawian, sċēawode* 'survey,' 'look at.' ME *schēw(i)en, schōwien*, Northern *schaw*. Early MnE *shęw* and *show*. *shown* by the analogy of *known*, etc.

709. sow; sowed; sown, sowed. OE strong I *sāwan, sēow, sāwen*.

710. ‡strew; strewed; strewn, strewed. OE weak *strēwian, streowian*. ME *strewen, strōwen, strawen*. *strewn* by the analogy of *hewn*.

711. swell; swelled; swollen, swelled. OE strong III *swellan*.

Isolated Forms.

712. Some obsolete verbs occur only in isolated forms, namely *quoth, hight, iclept, wont*.

713. quoth. OE strong V *cweþan, cwæþ, cwǣdon*,

gecweden 'say.' In ME the strong consonant of the infin. was kept throughout: *cweþen*, *cwaþ*, *icweþen*; so also *bicweþen* 'bequeath,' which in MnE is consonantal—*bequeathed*. In Late ME the simple *cweþen* was gradually disused except in the pret. sing. As *cwaþ* was often unstressed in such combinations as *cwaþ ·hē*, it developed a weak form *cwod*, *quod* through the regular rounding of unstressed *a* into *o* after a lip-consonant, as in OE *Ōswold*=earlier *Ōswald*. The explanation of the *d* is that *cwaþ hē* etc. were made into (kwaþ·ee) which became (kwað·ee, kwoð·ee); and when (kwoð) was detached and received strong stress—as it naturally would—the final (ð), being an unfamiliar sound in strong syllables, was changed into (d). The form *quoth* is a blending of strong *quath* and weak *quod*.

714. hight 'is named, called,' 'was called,' ME *highte* is a blending of the OE passive form *hātte* (**478**) and *hēht*, the active pret. of the same verb *hātan*.

715. iclept=ME *iclēped*, OE *ġecleopod* 'called' the pret. partic. of the weak verb *cleopian*, *clipian*.

716. wont 'accustomed'=OE *ġewunod*, pret. partic. of the weak verb *ġewunian* [*ġewuna* 'custom,' 'habit.']

Anomalous Verbs.

717. Most of the MnE verbs that we class as anomalous are old preterite-present verbs. Two of these preterite-present verbs—*dare* and *owe* = OE *dearr*, *āg*—have been made regular in certain meanings. The original inflections of these verbs have been much curtailed in MnE, most of them having only the inflections of the finite present and preterite. The only one which has an infin. is *dare*, which seems to have taken it from the regularly inflected verb *dare*. Two of the old preterite-present verbs—*must* and *ought*—occur now only in the OE preterite forms, which have taken the place of the OE present *mōt* and *āg*, so that these verbs are incapable of marking the distinction between pres. and pret.

718. can, canst; could, couldst. OE *cann*, *canst*, plur. *cunnon*; pret. *cūþe*; infin. *cunnan* 'know.' ME *can*, *canst*, plur. *cŏnnen*, *can*; *couþe*, *coude*; infin. *cŏnnen*. *coude* probably owes its *d* to the influence of *wolde* and *scholde* (**723, 724**). In Early MnE *coud*(*e*) it was made into *could* on the analogy of *should* and *would*=OE *sċolde*, *wolde*.

719. dare, darest, (he) **dare, †dares; durst;** infin. **dare.** OE *dearr*, *dearst*, *durron*; *dorste*; ME *dar*, *dār* (as in the pret. *bār*), *darst*; *dorste*, *durste* with the *u* of OE *durron*; infin. *durren*, *dāren*, of which the former represents the probable OE infin. *durran*, the latter being a new-formation from *dār*. In MnE *dare* in the transitive sense of 'challenge' has become quite regular: *he dared him to do it*. The intransitive pres. partic. *daring* is used only as an adjective.

720. may, mayst; might, mightst. OE *mæġ*, *þū meaht* (*mæht*), *miht*, plur. *magon*; pret. *meahte* (*mæhte*) *mihte* 'be able.' [Compare *mæġen*, *meaht*, *miht* 'power,' 'force.'] The ME forms seem to have been influenced by another OE preterite-present verb of similar meaning, namely *dēag*, *dēah* 'avail' plur. *dugon*; pret. *dohte*; infin. *dugan*. The ME forms are: *mai*, *miht*, and, very late, *mayst*, plur. *mawen*, *muwen*, *moun*; pret. *mahte*, *mihte*, *mohte*.

721. †mote (muut); **must.** OE *mōt*, *mōst*, *mōton*; *mōste* 'may.' ME *mōt*, *mōst*, *mōten*; *mōste*. The pres. survived only as an archaism in Early MnE: *as fair as fair mote be* (Spenser). Already in ME the pret. was used in the sense of the pres., and in Early MnE this usage became fixed. It began with the use of the pret. subj.—which was practically indistinguishable from the pret. indic.—to express mild command, so that *þou mōste*='you would be able,' 'you might' was understood to mean 'you will have to,' 'you must.' The vowel of *mōste* passed through (uu) into (u) in Early MnE, the shortening having probably begun in the weak form.

722. (owe); ought. OE *āg, āh, þū āht, aht*, plur. *āgon*; pret. *āhte, ahte*; infin. *āgan* 'possess.' The adjective *āgen* 'own' is an old pret. partic. of this verb. From *āgen* is formed the weak verb *āgnian*, 'appropriate,' 'possess.' In Early ME *ahte* developed regularly into *a(u)hte*, but afterwards *ǭ* was introduced from the infin. etc., giving *ǭ(u)hte*. In ME *ǭwen* in the sense of 'possess' soon took regular weak inflection—*ī ǭwe, wē ǭweþ*, etc.—still keeping the older *ǭuhte* as its pret. The meaning 'possess' gradually developed into that of 'have a debt,' 'owe,' which, again, developed the abstract meaning 'ought,' especially in the pret., which by degrees took the function of a pres. in the same way as *must* (**721**).

723. shall, shalt; should, shouldst. OE *sċeal* (*sċæl*), *sċealt* (*sċælt*), *sċulon*; *sċolde*, Northumbrian *sċalde* by the analogy of *walde* (**724**)=*wolde*. ME *schal, schalt, schulen, schullen* (by the analogy of *willen*); *scholde, schulde* (by the influence of *schulen*).

724. will, wilt; would, wouldst; imper. **will.** This verb was in OE originally a strong subjunctive preterite, with which pres. indic. forms were afterwards mixed: *wile, wille, wilt, willaþ*; *wolde, walde* (originally weak?); infin. *willan*. In OE this verb has, together with several other verbs in very frequent use, special **negative** forms, the result of contraction with a preceding *ne* 'not': *iċ nyle, þū nylt, hē nyle, wē nyllaþ*;

nolde, etc. One of these negative forms is still preserved in the phrase *willy nilly*, Early MnE *will he, nill he*=OE *wile hē, nyle hē.* The ME forms are: *wile, wŏle, wilt, wŏlt, willeþ, willen, wŏllen*; *wolde, walde, wŏlde*, whose (u) is the result of the influence of the pres. forms *wŏle*, etc., which were probably at first weak forms, in which the *w* rounded the following vowel and gradually assimilated it to itself.

725. †wot; †wist. OE *wāt, wāst, witon*; *wiste*; *witan*; *witende*. The adjective *ġewiss* 'certain' is an old pret. partic. of this verb. ME *wǭt, wǭst, witen*; infin. *witen*; pres. partic. *witinge*. In Early MnE *wot* was sometimes made the base of a regular verb: *he wotteth, wots*, pret. *wotted*, pres. partic. *wotting*. The old pres. partic. still survives in the adverb *unwittingly*, and the infin. in the adverb phrase *to wit*= viz.

The ME adjective *iwis*=OE *ġewiss* has in MnE been often wrongly divided *i wis*, as if it were the pronoun *I* with a verb equivalent to *wot*, a view which has been further supported in recent times by the chance resemblance of the Modern German equivalent of *wot*, namely *weiss*, plur. *wissen*.

726. need. This verb agrees with the preterite-present verbs in having no *s*-inflection. The loss of the *s*—which seems to have begun in the transition from ME to MnE—is apparently partly the result of similarity of meaning to that of the preterite-present verbs; but the absence of the inflectional *s* is partly due to the verb *need* 'require' being formed directly from the noun *need* through the ambiguity of such sentences as Early MnE *what need all this waste?*

We now come to the anomalous auxiliary verbs *be, have, do*.

727. The verb *be* in OE is made up of three distinct roots; that seen in (*a*) *is*, *are*, (*b*) *was*, and (*c*) *be*:—

		Indic.		Subj.
Pres. Sing.	1	*eom* (*eam*); *bēo*		*sīe*, *sȳ*; *bēo*
	2	*eart* (*earþ*); *bist*		*sīe*, *sȳ*; *bēo*
	3	*is*; *biþ*		*sīe*, *sȳ*; *bēo*
Plur.		*sind*, *sindon* (*earon*); *bēoþ*		*sīen*, *sȳn*; *bēon*
Pret. Sing.	1	*wæs*		*wǣre*
	2	*wǣre*		*wǣre*
	3	*wæs*		*wǣre*
Plur.		*wǣron*		*wǣren*
Imper. Sing.		*wes*; *bēo*	Infin.	*wesan*; *bēon*
Plur.		*wesaþ*; *bēoþ*	Gerund	*tō wesenne*; *tō bēonne*

Partic. Pres. *wesende*

728. The *ea* in *eart* and the Anglian *eam*, *earon* is a weakening of *eo* (**368**), preserved in the West-Saxon *eom* and the occasional *eort*, *eorun*. In Late Northumbrian this *ea* undergoes the usual further weakening into *a*: *am*, *arþ*, *aron*.

729. The Standard ME forms are: *am*, *art*, *is*, *bē*(*n*); subj. *bē*, *bē*(*n*); pret. *was*, *wę̄r*(*e*), *was*, *wę̄re*(*n*); pret. subj., *wę̄r*(*e*), *wę̄re*(*n*); imper. *bē*, *bēþ*; infin. *bē*(*n*); participles *bēinge*, *bē*(*n*). The ME pret. partic. is, of course, an analogical new-formation. The North-Thames plur. *ar*(*n*) is still rare in Standard ME, but is firmly established in Early MnE, which inflects: *am*, *art*, *is*, *are*; subj. *be*; pret. *was*, *wast*, *wert*, plur. *were*; subj. pret. *were*, *wert*, *were*; infin. *be*; partic. *being*, *been*. The use of *be* in the pres. indic. is still kept up in Early MnE: *I be*, *thou beest*, *they be*, etc.; the form *he bes* is, however, very rare. There is in MnE a tendency to get rid of the distinctively subjunctive inflections of this verb not only by using *thou beest* as if it were a subjunctive—*if thou beest* = *if thou be*—but also by substituting *if I was* for *if I were*, etc. *was* = *were* was frequent in the last century not only as a subjunctive, but also in the indic. *you was*. In the present Spoken English the distinction between *was* and *were* is strictly maintained, the substitution of *was* for *were* being a vulgarism. The subj. pres. is, on the other hand, extinct in the spoken language, except in a few phrases.

730. have. The OE inflections resemble those of *libban* (**506**): *hæbbe*, *hafast*, *hæfst*, *hafaþ*, *hæfþ*, plur. *habbaþ*; subj. *hæbbe*, *hæbben*; pret. *hæfde*; imper. *hafa*, *habbaþ*; infin. *habban*; partic. *hæbbende*, *ġehæfd*. In ME the old *bb* was gradually supplanted by the *v* = OE *f* of the other forms, the *v* itself being often dropped by contraction. The Standard ME forms are: *hāve*, weak *hav*, *hast*, *haþ*, plur. *hāve(n)*, *hān*, *han*; pret. *hadde*; pret. partic. *had*. In ME the weak short-vowel forms gradually supplanted the long-vowel ones; but we keep the long-vowel forms in the derivative *behave*, pret. *behaved* = ME *behāven*. The MnE literary forms are: *have*, *hast*, *hath*, *has* plur. *have*; subj. pres. *have*; pret. indic. *had*, *hadst*; pret. subj. *had*; imper. and infin. *have*; partic. *having*, *had*. Early MnE still kept the shortened infin. *ha*, *a* = ME *han*: *she might a been* (Shakespere).

731. do. OE *dō*, *dēst* (*dǣst*), *dēþ* (*dǣþ*), plur. *dōþ*; pret. weak *dyde*; imper. *dō*, *dōþ*; infin. *dōn*; partic. *dōnde*, *ġedōn*. The mutation in *dēst*, *dēþ* is common to all the dialects. In Standard ME the *ō* of the other parts of the verb supplanted the older *ē*: *dō*, *dōst*, *dōþ*, plur. *dōn*; *dide*; imper. *dō*, *dōþ*; partic. *dōinge* *dō(n)*. In MnE (uu) = ME *ǭ*.

PARTICLES.

732. All the OE particles are either **primary** or **secondary**. The secondary particles are formed from other (declinable) parts of speech; thus *hām* in *hē ēode hām* 'he went home' is formed from the masc. noun *hām* 'home,' 'homestead.' Primary particles, such as *be* 'by,' *swā* 'so' are not formed from other parts of speech. There is no strict division between the three classes of particles, most of the prepositions being used also as adverbs, some adverbs being used also as conjunctions. Thus *ǣr* is a preposition in *ǣr dæġe* 'before day(break),' an adverb in *hē eft wæs pāpa swā hē ǣr wæs* 'he was pope again as he was before,' and a conjunction in *ǣr þæt flōd cōm* 'before the flood came.'

733. Some of the particles are **simple**, some **derivative**, such as *uf-an* 'above,' some **compound** (group-compounds), such as *be-neoþan* 'beneath,' which is compounded with the preposition *be*. The above are primary adverbs. Secondary particles also admit of the same divisions, such as *hām*, *sōþlīċe* 'truly,' *ealne-weġ* 'always,' literally 'all (the) way.'

Adverb-endings.

734. In OE, adverbs are regularly formed from adjectives by adding *-e*, a preceding *æ* being generally changed to *a*: *dēope* 'deeply,' *hearde* 'strongly,' 'severely,' *nearwe* 'narrowly,' *late* 'slowly,' 'with delay' from *dēop*, *heard* 'hard,' 'strong,' 'severe,' *nearu*, *læt* 'slow.' Adjectives with a mutated vowel often have an unmutated vowel in the adverb, as in *sōfte* 'gently,' 'luxuriously,' *swōte* 'sweetly' corresponding to the adjectives *sēfte* (*sǣfte*), *swēte* (*swǣte*). The numerous adjectives in *-liċ* form their adverbs in *-līċe*, the original length of the vowel being kept, as in *ġġeslīċe* 'terribly,' *ġesǣliġlīċe* 'blessedly,' 'happily' from *ġġesliċ*, *ġesǣliġliċ* [*ġġesa* 'terror,' *sǣl* 'favourable time,' 'luck']. But *ġesǣliġliċ* occurs also in the shorter form *ġesǣliġ*; and hence in this and similar cases the adverb could be regarded as formed directly from the shorter adjective—*ġesǣliġ-līċe* from *ġesǣliġ*. In this way *-līċe* came to be regarded as an independent abverb-ending equivalent to *-e*, which, through being more distinct, it gradually supplanted in many words. Hence *-līċe* was sometimes added directly, without there being any adjective in *-liċ*.

735. In ME the two endings *-e* and *-līche* were both kept, the latter appearing as *-līke* in Early Midland, as in *dēplīke* compared with Early Southern *dēoplīche*.

736. When final *-e* was dropped in North-Thames English the distinction between the adj. *hard* and the adverb *hard*(*e*), etc. was lost. By degrees also the adverb-ending *-līke* was levelled under the adjective-ending *-li*=Southern *-lich*, and *-li* then became a regular adverb-ending. In Late ME it was introduced into the Standard dialect, where it supplanted the Early Southern *-līche*, as in *dēply*, *hardly*, *openly*. But *-ly* was also retained as an adjective-ending, as it still is in such a word as *goodly*=OE *gōdliċ*, ME *gōdlich*, *gōdli*. Some of the MnE adverbs which have the same form as adverbs, as in *pull hard*, *speak loud*, *talk like a foreigner* compared with *a hard pull*, etc. are, of course, the descendants of the OE adverbs in *-e*, such as *hearde*, *hlūde*, *ġelīce*; but others are new-formations on the analogy of these traditional ones, especially those in *-y*=OE *-iġ*, as in *pretty well*, *mighty fine*, for the OE adjectives in *-iġ* formed their adverbs in *-iġlīċe* (*mihtiġlīċe*) to avoid the ambiguity of *-iġe*, which might be mistaken for the plur. etc. inflection.

737. In Old French the uninflected forms of adjectives—originally the neut. sing.—were used as adverbs, which were introduced into ME, whence such MnE adverbs as in *just ready*, *shut close* [Old French *clos* from Latin *clausum*], *quiet* [Latin *quiētum*], *very*=ME *verrai* 'true,' 'truly,' Old French *verai* [Modern French *vrai*] from Latin *vērāx*, *vērācem*.

738. In Present English, adverbs in *-ly* are formed freely from all kinds of adjectives, as in *deeply*, *foolishly*, *willingly*, *affectedly*. The addition of *-ly* is attended by various changes of spelling, as in *merrily*, *gaily*, *fully*, *nobly* from *merry*, *gay*, *full*, *noble*. Adverbs in *-ly* are not often formed from adjectives that already end in *-ly*, these adjectives generally forming their adverbs by periphrases, such as *in a lively manner*, *in a friendly way*. Some MnE adverbs in *-ly* are formed direct from nouns, such as *namely*; but such adverbs as *daily*, *yearly*, *quarterly* in *he is paid quarterly* are old adjectives used as adverbs.

A less frequent adverb-ending in OE was *-unga*, *-inga*, by which adverbs were formed from adjectives: *eallunga* 'entirely,' *ierringa* 'angrily,' from *eall*, *ierre*. There was also in OE a class of adverbs formed from nouns—mostly names of parts of the body—by adding *-ling* and prefixing the preposition *on*, such as *on bæcling* 'backwards.' By blending these two endings a new ending *-lunga*, *-linga* was formed, as in *grundlunga* 'from the foundations,' 'completely.' In ME the ending *-linge* is frequent, the adverbial *-es* (**742**) being often added, as in *hędlinge(s)* 'headlong,' *nǫselinge(s)* 'on the nose,' 'at full length,' *sīdelinge(s)* 'sideways.' In MnE this ending has been confused with the adjective *long*. Hence in Early MnE we find *sideling*, *sidelong* 'sideways,' *flatling* and *flatlong*, as in *the blow felt flatlong*, that is, 'was given with the flat of the sword instead of the point.' In Present English *headlong* is still an adverb, *sidelong* being an adjective—*a sidelong* *glance.* The older *sidelinge* was regarded as a pres. partic., and from it was formed a verb *to sidle* (*up to*). So also the ME adverb *grŏvelinge* 'grovellingly' was made into the verb *grovel.*

739. In ME and MnE some new adverb-endings arose out of OE adverbial phrases. Thus the OE *on ōþre wīsan* 'in another way' [*wīse* weak fem. 'manner,' 'way'] was shortened and hardened into the group *ōþrewīse, ōþerwīse*; and in MnE *-wise* was used to form new adverbs, such as *likewise, nowise.* The noun *way* was used in like manner to form adverb-groups such as *midway, noway,* whence *noways* with the usual addition of *-s.* *-wise,* and *-ways* were often confused, as in *lengthwise=lengthways, endwise, coastwise.* The nouns *time* and *while*=OE weak masc. *tīma* and strong fem. *hwīl* 'time,' have also come to be used as adverb-endings in such words as *meantime, sometime(s), ofttimes, oftentimes, meanwhile, somewhile, otherwhile(s),* the last two being now obsolete.

Adverbs formed direct from Nouns and Adjectives.

740. Many OE adverbs are formed direct from nouns or adjectives, either inflected or uninflected. The following are uninflected, being formed from nouns in the acc. sing. and adjectives in the neut. sing.: *hām, norþ, sūþ, ēast, west*; *eall* 'entirely,' *nēah* 'nearly,' *genōg* 'sufficiently.'

The most important inflectional endings are *-um* and *-es*:—

741. -um: *hwīlum* 'sometimes,' *stundum* 'at intervals' [*stund* strong fem. 'period']. *-mǣlum* from the neut. noun *mǣl* 'mark,' 'point of time' is a frequent adverb-ending, as in *styċċemǣlum* 'piecemeal,' *floccmǣlum* 'in troops.' From adjectives are formed *mičlum* 'greatly,' *lȳtlum and lȳtlum* 'by little and little,' 'by degrees.' The isolated ME *whīlŏm* is still preserved in the higher language. *-mǣlum* in ME passed through *-mēlen* into *-mēle*, as in *dropmēle*, *pēcemēle*, where *styčče* was replaced by its French equivalent.

742. **-es** in OE was extended to fem. nouns as an adverb-ending: *dæġes and nihtes* 'by day and by night,' *sumeres and wintra* [*wintra* masc. gen. like *suna*], *nīedes* 'of necessity' [*nīed* fem.]; *ealles* 'entirely,' *ęlles* 'otherwise' from a lost adjective. The adverb-ending *-weardes* interchanges with the uninflected *-weard*, as in *hāmweard(es)* 'homewards.' In ME and MnE this ending was dropped in some words, as in Late ME *day and night*; but it was more often extended, especially to adverbs which in OE ended in a vowel or *n*, in order to make them more distinct, as in *always*=Early MnE *alwai*, OE *ealneweġ*, *ǭnes* 'once'=OE *ǣne*, the mutated *ǣ* being supplanted by *ǭ*=the OE *ā* in *ān*, *twīes* 'twice,' *þrīes* 'thrice'= OE *twiwa*, *þriwa*. OE *heonone* 'hence' (**747**) became *he(o)nne* in Early MnE, and by the addition of *-s*, *hennes*, OE *þanon* 'thence,' *hwanon* 'whence' becoming Late ME *þennes*, *whennes* by the influence of *hennes*. So also OE *siþþan* (**749**) 'since' passed through *siþþen*, *sin* into *siþens*, *sins*. This extension of *-s* went on in MnE also, as in *sometimes*=earlier MnE *sometime*, which is still preserved in the higher language.

Some adverbs in *-es* took final *t* in Early MnE or Late ME, as in *amidst*, *betwixt*, *whilst*, *amongst*=ME *amiddes*—a blending of OE *onmiddan* and *tōmiddes*—*betwixt(t)*, *whīles*, *amǫng*.

743. The following are examples of OE **group-adverbs**: *ealneweġ*, *ealneġ* 'always,' *ġeorstandæġ* 'yesterday,' *on weġ* 'away,' *on bæc* 'backwards,' 'back,' *ofdūne* 'down,' literally 'off the hill,' *tōdæġ* 'today,' where *tō* governs an exceptional form of the dative. All the above show isolation either of form or meaning, and therefore approximate to compounds. Such collocations, on the other hand, as *on līfe* 'alive' literally 'in life,' *on slǣpe* 'in sleep, asleep,' *on eornost* 'in earnest' show no isolation either of meaning or form. But in ME there was a tendency to shorten weak *of* and *on* to *a* whenever they were closely associated with the following word. Hence the ME forms *adūne, adūn* 'down' adv., *awai, abak, alīve, aslēpe*, the *a* having been dropped in the MnE adverbs *down, back.* The same weakening took place in ME and Early MnE combinations, as in *aclock*, now written *o'clock*=*of* (*the*) *clock*, and also in freer combinations, as in *go a fishing*=OE *gān on fisćnoþ, twice a day*=OE *twiwa on dæġe.*

In MnE this *a* was taken for the indef. article, so that in *jackanapes*=*jack-of-apes* it was made into *an* before a vowel.

Some French group-adverbs formed with the preposition *a* were introduced in ME, where they were of course put on a level with the similar native combinations: *apart, apās*=MnE *apace.*

744. In ME the OE preposition *be* became *bī* (770), but the old *be* was kept in compounds such as *beforen*=OE *beforan*, and also in some traditional collocations such as OE *be sīdan* 'by the side,' ME *besīde*, which was now completely isolated from *bī þe*(*re*) *sīde*, just as *alīve* was isolated from *in al his līf* etc. But the new preposition *bī* was sometimes introduced into these groups, being however shortened to *bi*: *bifore, bisīde.* On the analogy of the older compounds the new-formation *bī cause* 'by the cause' was made into *bicause, because.*

745. In ME and MnE the place of a lost or obscured

ending was sometimes supplied by a preposition, giving rise to new group-adverbs, such as *of a truth*=OE *sōþes*, *of right* =OE *ryhtes*, *bī pēcemēle*=OE *styċċemǣlum*, *by little and little*= OE *lȳtlum* and *lȳtlum*.

Sometimes a preposition was added even when the ending was clear, as in *at unawares*.

Pronominal Adverbs.

746. Among the OE primary adverbs there is a symmetrical group of adverbs of place, connected with the pronouns *hē*, *þæt*, *hwæt*, their endings expressing respectively rest, motion to, and motion from:—

Rest	Motion in	Motion from
hēr 'here'	*hider* 'hither'	*heonon* 'hence'
þǣr 'there'	*þider* 'thither'	*þanon* 'thence'
hwǣr 'where'	*hwider* 'whither'	*hwanon* 'whence'

The ME *th* in *hither* etc. is due to the influence of the *r* (**248**).

747. The ending *-er*, *-an*, *-on* of the other primary adverbs has no very definite meaning: *of-er* 'over,' expressing both motion and rest, *und-er*, *æft-er*; *inn-an* 'within,' *uf-an* 'above' [connected with *ofer*], *hindan* 'behind,' *foran* 'in front.' The ending *-an* was, however, extended to the noun-derived adverbs *norþ* etc., where it kept its definite meaning: *norþan* 'from the north,' *sūþan* 'from the south.' *-on*, *-an* often takes final *-e*: *heonone*, *ūtan*(*e*) 'outside.' The adverbs *þonne* 'then,' 'than,' *hwonne* 'when' are also pronominal.

748. Many OE adverbs are formed directly from pronouns. The neuter *þæt* is used as a conjunction exactly as in MnE: *hē sæġde þæt; hē sæġde þæt hē wǣre ġearu*, literally 'he said that: (namely) he was ready.' So also the pronoun *hwæþer* is used in the same way as *whether*. The indeclinable *þe* is used as a relative pronoun, both alone and in combination with *sē* (**438**), and is used also as a particle in a variety of meanings—'when,' 'because' etc. It is also added to particles to make them into conjunctions, or mark them more distinctly as such, as in *þēah-þe* 'although' conjunction, *þēah* 'though' being an adverb, *þætte* 'that' conj.=*þæt þe* (**147**). Inflected pronouns are also used as particles. *þȳ*, the instrumental of *þæt*, is used in the sense of 'therefore,' 'because,' and to express measure and proportion, as in *þȳ mā* 'the more,' correlative *þȳ . . . þȳ*=MnE *the . . . the* in *the more the merrier*. The change of *þȳ* into *the* is the result of loss of stress and confusion with the indeclinable *þe*. *hwȳ*, the instrumental of *hwæt*, is used in the sense of its MnE descendant *why*.

749. There are many group-particles in OE consisting of a preposition governing a pronoun in the dat. or instr. The combination with the preposition alone generally forms an adverb—*for þǣm, for þon, for þȳ* 'therefore'—the corresponding conjunctions being formed by the addition of *þe* —*for þǣm þe, for þon þe, for þȳ þe* 'because,' *ǣr þǣm þe* 'before,' *æfter þǣm þe* 'after'—or *þæt*: *tō þǣm þæt, tō þon þæt* 'in order that.'

siþþan, seoþþan 'since' contains an obsolete preposition **sīþ* 'since'—*siþþan*=*sīþ-þon* with shortening of the *ī*.

750. There are similar group-particles formed by combinations of pronouns with nouns and adverbs formed from adjectives, such as *þā hwīle þe* 'while,' literally 'the time when' [*þā hwīle* acc. fem. sing.], *nā þȳ lǣs* 'nevertheless,' 'notwithstanding,' literally 'not by-that less,' *þȳ lǣs þe* 'lest,' literally 'by-that less that.'

751. The group-adverbs *for-þī*, *for-þan*, *for-hwī* continued in use throughout the ME period, but became obsolete in MnE. The groups in *-þe* were modified in various ways. In the Early MnE the ambiguous *þe* was generally made into *þat*, as in *for-þī-þat*, *þe-whīle-þat*, or dropped entirely, as in *þēih*, *þouh* conj.= OE *þēah þe*. *þæt* often took the place of the inflected pronoun, as in *for-þat*, *ēr-þat*, *after-þat*, and the new-formations *til-þat*, *before-þat*. But even in the Earliest ME the pronouns were dropped, so that the bare prepositions *for*, *ēr*, *before* etc. were used as conjunctions, as in MnE, this shortening being helped by the fact that even in OE the prepositions *ǣr* 'before' and *būtan* 'without' were used also as conjunctions, the latter in the sense of 'except,' 'unless.' *þe-hwīle-þe* was shortened to *þe-hwīle* and then to *hwīle*, whence the later *whīles*, *whilst*, the older *the while*, *while* still surviving in the higher language. OE *þȳ lǣs þe* dropped the *þȳ* in Early MnE, and *sþ* was made into *st* (**147**), giving *lǣste*, shortened *leste*, *lest*.

Correlative Particles.

752. OE correlative particles are: *þȳ* . . . (**748**); *swā* . . . *swā*, as in *swā hwīt swā snāw* 'as white as snow'; *þā* . . . *þā*, *þonne* . . . *þonne* 'then . . . when' as in *þā he cōm*, *þā ēode ic* 'when he came, I went,' the second (demonstrative) *þā*, *þonne* being omitted in MnE. Indefinite adverbs are formed like indefinite pronouns (**442**) with correlative *swā—swā hwǣr swā* 'wherever.'

753. In ME the first two groups were preserved in the form of *þe* . . . *þe* and *alswǭ* . . . *ase*, *as* . . . *as*, *alswǭ* being a strong, *as*(*e*) a weak form of the OE group *eall-swā* 'entirely so.' In the other correlative groups one of the members was generally omitted in ME, as in the ME and MnE equivalents of the OE *þā . . . þā*, *þonne . . . þonne*, where the relative *when* was substituted for *þenne* = OE *þonne*, the second member being omitted.

So also *swā hwǣr swā* appears as *whęr sǫ* in ME.

Pronominal Conjunctions.

754. In OE the neuter pronouns *āuþer*, *nāuþer*, *ǣġþer* (**442, 451**) are often used adverbially in connection with the correlative conjunction-pairs *ġe . . . ġe* 'both . . . and,' *oþþe . . . oþþe* 'either . . . or,' *ne . . . ne* 'neither . . . nor,' standing in a kind of opposition to them: *hīe cūþon ǣġþer, ġe gōd ġe yfel* 'they knew each-of-the-two,' both good and evil'; *sē geswęnċed biþ āuþer, oþþe on mōde oþþe on līchaman* 'he who is afflicted either-way, either in mind or in body'; *hīe ne cūþon nān-þing yfeles, nāþer ne on sprǣċe ne on weorce* 'they knew nothing of evil, no-way, neither in speech nor in action.'

755. In Early ME the first correlative conjunction was dropped in such combinations, so that the adverbial pronoun was brought into direct correlation with the second conjunction, OE *nāþer ne . . . ne* being made into *nǫþer . . . ne*, *neiþer . . . ne* (**452**) etc.: *nǫþer on spēche ne on werke.* The original pronoun afterwards supplanted the second conjunction as well, where, being unstressed, it was liable to shortening, whence the pairs *ǭþer* (*eiþer*) . . . *or*, *nǭþer* (*neiþer*) . . . *nor*: *ęveri man schal have ǭþer gōd ǭþer üvel—eiþer gōd or üvel.* The weak *or*, *nor* were only rarely introduced into the first clause as well; but in the higher language we still use *or . . . or* instead of *either . . . or*. The new conjunctions soon came to be used without any correlative, as in the Early MnE *hē* *mihle rīden ǭþer gǭn.* The correlative *both . . . and* arose in the same way as *either . . . or* etc., the beginning of it being seen in such an OE construction as *hīe bū gesēoþ, þæt hē hīe generede, and him ēac forgeaf ēce līf,* 'they see both (neut. sing.) that he has saved them, and has also given them eternal life.'

Negation and Affirmation.

756. The negative particle in OE is *ne,* which drops its vowel in some combinations before a vowel, or *h* or *w* followed by a vowel, these consonants being also dropped, *nwi-* being made into *ny-*; thus *eom* 'am,' *hæfþ* 'has,' *hæfde* 'had,' *wāt* 'knows,' *wiste* 'knew,' *wile* 'will,' *wolde* 'would' have the negative forms *neom* 'am not,' *næfþ, næfde, nāt, nyste, nyle, nolde.* Some pronouns and adverbs have similar negative forms, such as *nān* 'none,' *nāhwæþer, nāuþer* 'neither,' *nāwiht, naht, nōwiht, noht* 'nothing,' *nā* 'not' from *ān, āhwæþer, āwiht* (*ōwiht*), *ā* 'ever.' In sentences the *ne* is prefixed to the verb, being contracted with it if possible, and to all the other words in the sentence that admit of contracted negative forms: *nān ne dorste nān þing āscian* 'no-one durst ask anything.' If the sentence does not contain any such contracted negatives in addition to the negatived verb, the stronger *nā* or *naht* is added to support the *ne* before the verb: *þæt hus nā ne fēoll* 'the house did not fall.'

757. In ME the usage is often the same as in OE: *hē nęver nadde nǭþing.* But the weak form of *nāwiht,* namely *nat, not* (**443**) from being a mere strengthening of the *ne,* began to supplant it, as in *tō mē schē wǒl nat dō þat grāce,* although *ne* is often kept, as in *Dęþ ne wǒl nat hān mī līf.*

758. In MnE *ne* disappeared entirely. At the same time the influence of Latin grammar led to the adoption of the logical principle that 'two negatives contradict each other and make an affirmative,' which is now strictly carried out in the Standard language, spoken as well as written, though the old pleonastic negatives are still kept up in vulgar speech, as in *I don't know nothing about it*=the educated *I do not know anything about it* or *I know nothing about it.*

759. Although OE *naht* was preferred to *nā* as the auxiliary negative in ME, the latter held its ground in certain collocations, especially before comparative adjectives and adverbs, and is still kept in such phrases as *he is no better*; *no more of this!* And *no* is always used as the absolute negation—in answer to questions etc.—together with *nay*, which is the Scandinavian *nei* 'no,' literally 'not-ever.' *nay* is now obsolete in speech.

760. The OE particles of affirmation are *ġēa*, Anglian *ġǣ, ġē*, ME *yę̄*, MnE *yea*, which is now obsolete; and *yes*= OE *ġise*, Anglian *ġese*, ME and Early MnE *yis, yes.* *ġise* is an old group-compound of *ġēa* and the subjunctive *sīe* 'be it'; it was therefore originally an emphatic affirmative.

Comparison of Adverbs.

761. The comparison of adverbs has already been treated of under Adjectives (**339**). In OE the regular forms of adverb-comparison were *-e, -or, -ost* and *-līċe, -licor, -liocor, -licost, -liocost*: *dēope, deoplīċe*; *dēopor*, Late OE *dēoppor* (**149**), *dēoplicor*; *dēopost, dēoplicost.* There was also a smaller class with mutation in the higher degrees, the endings being *-e*, -, *-est*, as in *lange* 'for a long time,' *lęnġ, lęnġest.* Most of the adverbs which admit of comparison are formed from adjectives; but primary adverbs also admit of direct comparison, with and without mutation: *oft* 'often,' *oftor, oftost*; *ǣr* 'before,' *ǣror, ǣrest.*

762. In MnE the comparison *-er*, *-est* is, as a general rule, applied only to those adverbs which have no special adverbial ending in the positive, especially those which have the same form as the corresponding adjectives, such as *hard*—as in *pull harder*, *pull hardest*—*loud*, *quick*, *fast*, *long*. The comparison of primary adverbs, as in *often*=OE *oft*, *oftener*, *oftenest*, has in some cases been carried further than in OE, as in *soon*, *sooner*, *soonest*, *seldomer*, the OE *sōna*, *seldon* not admitting of comparison. Adverbs in *-ly* are compared periphrastically: *fully*, *more fully*, *most fully*. But in the spoken language these adverbs often form their comparisons by inflection from the corresponding adjective: *easy*, *easier*—as in *easier said than done*—*easiest*; *cheaply*, *cheaper*, *cheapest*—as in *where it can be done cheapest*.

763. The following adverbs are compared irregularly in MnE:—

well; *better*; *best*. OE *wel*; *bet*; *betst*, which dropped its *t* in ME *best* on the analogy of *mǣst*, etc.

badly (*evilly*, *ill*); *worse*, *worst*. OE *yfle*; *wiers* (*wyrs*); *wierrest*, *wierst* (*wyrrest*, *wyrst*).

much, *more*, *most*. OE *miċle*; *mā*(*re*); *mǣst*.

little, *less*, *least*. OE *lȳtle*, *lȳt*; *lǣs*; *lǣst*.

far; *farther*, *further*; *farthest*, *furthest*. OE *feorr*; *fierr*; *fierrest*.

There are besides various isolated forms which have been treated of under the comparison of adjectives. From the comparative adverb *rather*=OE *hraþor* 'quicker,' 'sooner' a positive adjective *rathe* was formed in MnE—*the rathe primrose* (Milton)—which is now obsolete.

From some of the isolated comparatives and superlatives, whose meaning has been forgotten and which have come to be regarded as positives, adverbs have been formed by adding *-ly*: *formerly, latterly, lastly*.

PREPOSITIONS.

Old-English.

764. Of the OE prepositions some are **simple**, some **compound**. Most of the latter are made up of prepositions —especially *be*—and place-adverbs ending in *-an*, *-on*, *be-* becoming *b-* before a vowel, such contracted forms as *bufan* 'above' = **be-ufan*, being made into new compounds, such as *onbufan* 'above.' The following are the most important of these compound prepositions:—

be 'by': *beforan* 'before,' *beġeondan* 'beyond,' *behindan* 'behind,' *binnan* 'within,' *beneoþan* 'beneath,' *bufan* 'above,' *būtan* 'outside.'

on: *oninnan* 'within,' *on-būtan* 'around.'

tō: *tōforan* 'before.'

under: *underneoþan* 'beneath.'

wiþ 'towards': *wiþinnan* 'within,' *wiþūtan* 'without.'

ymb 'around': *ymb-ūtan* 'around.'

765. Other compound prepositions are formed of prepositions + nouns or adjectives in the four cases governed by OE prepositions—the acc., dat., instr., gen.: *onġemang* 'among,' literally 'into the crowd'; *onġēan*, Anglian *onġegn*, *ongēn*, 'against,' and *tōġēanes*, Anglian *tōġegnes*, *togēnes* 'towards,' 'against' contain an obsolete noun of uncertain meaning; *tōmiddes* 'amidst' is formed from the adj. *midd* 'middle'; *betwēonum*, *betwix* are formed from an obsolete adjective connected with *twiwa* 'twice.'

766. Those OE prepositions which govern both acc. and

dat., generally take the acc. to express motion, the dat. (or instr.) to express rest: *hē ēode on þæt hūs* 'he went into the house'; *hē wunode on þǣm hūse* 'he remained in the house.'

767. As we see in the last examples the preposition *on* does duty for *in*, which became extinct in Later OE.

768. The OE prepositions are closely allied to the adverbs. Most of them can be used as adverbs without any change of form. Thus *on* is an adverb in *hē dyde on his byrnan* 'he put on his corslet,' the MnE *don* and *doff* being contractions of OE *dō(n) on*, *dō of*. So also in *hē him tō cwæþ* 'he said to him' compared with *hē cwæþ tō him*. Some prepositions however, such as *for*, are not used as adverbs, while others undergo change of form. Thus the adverbs corresponding to *be* and *in* (*on*) are *bī* and *inn*: *hē stōd bī*, *hē stōd him bī*, *hē ēode inn* compared with *hē stōd be him* 'he stood by him,' *hē ēode in* (*on*) *þæt hūs*. The preposition *be* is, of course, the weak form due to want of stress, *bī* being the original strong form.

769. In such combinations as *þǣron*, *þǣrtō*, which in OE are regularly used to express *on it*, *to it*, etc. *on* and *tō* must, of course, be regarded as adverbs. *therein*, *herein* are, indeed, often expressed by *þǣrinne*, *hērinne* with the pure adverb *inne*=*innan*.

It is to be observed that the prepositions were originally all adverbs, which could modify either verbs (*he stood by*) or nouns. Adverbs were originally added to inflected nouns to express more definitely the meanings already indicated by the inflection. Thus 'motion to' was originally expressed by the acc. alone, as we see in the Latin *domum vēnit* 'he came home' and also in the adverb *home* itself, and the prepositions *on*, *in*, *through*, etc. were put before the acc.

of motion to define it more exactly. So also in *on þǣm hūse* the idea of 'rest in a place' was primarily expressed by the dative, which here represents the Arian locative.

MIDDLE AND MODERN ENGLISH.

770. In ME the adverb *bī* was extended to the function of a preposition—a change which had already begun in OE —so that *be* was preserved only in compounds and traditional groups such as *beforen, besīde.* By the change of *-an, -on* into *-e* the OE adverb *foran* and the preposition *fore* 'before' were levelled under the latter, and by the analogy of the adverbs *inne, ūte=innan, ūtan,* the preposition *mid* 'with' when used as an adverb was made into *mide,* as in *þęrmide*= OE *þǣrmid.* So also *for,* which had no corresponding adverb-form in OE, developed a ME adverb *fore,* as in *þęrfore, whęrfore.* The confusion that thus arose between OE *for* and *fore* was avoided by an extended use of the compound *before*(*n*).

771. In ME *innan* 'inside' came into general use as a preposition so as to avoid the ambiguity of OE *on*='on,' 'in.' Being generally unstressed, it was shortened first to *ine* and then to *in,* the original distinction being thus restored.

772. In ME *frǭ* from Scandinavian *frā* and *from*=OE *fram* were used both as adverbs and prepositions. We now use *fro* only as an adverb in the phrase *to and fro.*

773. In ME the preposition *mid* 'with' got confused with *wiþ* 'against'—a confusion which would easily arise in such phrases as *fight with* (OE *feohtan wiþ*), *deal with,* where the relation between the parties might be considered either from its original point of view as 'towards,' 'against,' or from that of 'participation,' 'having in common.' By degrees the more marked meaning of OE *wiþ* was expressed by *against*, and ME *wiþ* took the meanings of *mid*, which then became extinct.

For the differentiation of OE *of*, *wiþ* into MnE *of*, *off*, (wið, wiþ), see § 232.

774. In ME the rare construction of prepositions with the genitive was soon given up—except of course in isolated groups such as *tōmiddes*—and when the distinction between the other oblique cases and the nom. was lost in the nouns, and nothing was left but the distinction of nom. and objective in some of the personal pronouns, the only trace left of case-government by prepositions was that they were sometimes followed by a personal pronoun in the objective case.

775. In OE the adverbial ending *-weard* is sometimes used detached in connection with the preposition *tō* in such constructions as *wiþ hire* (dat.) *weard* 'towards her.' In ME this is often carried further, as in *tō wŏde ward*, *tō Troie wardes*=*tōward þe wŏde*, *tōwardes Troie*, *frǭ Bordeux ward* compared with *framward Teukesbūri*, where *framward* is a new formation on the analogy of *tōward*. In Early MnE the Bible still has *to God ward*.

776. In ME the *a* of *amiddes* was restored to its full form *on*, for which *in* was afterwards substituted. The body of the word was then regarded as an independent noun, so that at last *inmidst* developed into *in the midst* (*of*).

INTERJECTIONS.

777. Interjections are **primary** and **secondary**. Primary interjections are mostly imitations of sounds that accompany emotions: *ah*, *o*, *oh*, *pah*, *pooh*, *hush*. From them other parts of speech may be formed; thus *hush* is used as a verb—*to hush.* Such interjections as *what! dear me!* are secondary. There are also **mixed** interjections, made up of primary interjections combined with other parts of speech, such as *alas* from Old French *halas, alas* [Modern French *hélas*], made up of the interjection *a* and *las* = Latin *lassum* 'weary.'

778. The OE *lā! ēalā!* 'oh!' seem to be primary. *wā!* 'woe!' is the same word as the noun *wāwā, wā* 'misfortune.' *wālā! wālāwā!* 'alas!' are therefore mixed interjections.

779. Interjections may stand in various grammatical relations to other words. Hence in OE, *wā* sometimes governs a dat., as in *wā þǣm męnn!* 'woe to the man!' *wālā* governs a gen. in such phrases as *wālā þǣre iermþe!* 'alas for the misery,' on the analogy of the gen. after verbs of repenting, &c. As we see from the above examples, interjections are frequently connected with prepositions in MnE.

COMPOSITION.

Old-English.

780. The normal way of forming compounds in OE is by joining together two words—which may be themselves compound or derivative words—the former word being uninflected, the latter, if declinable, keeping its power of inflection, and, if a noun, determining the gender of the whole compound. Thus the neuter noun *gold* and the masculine noun *smiþ* can be combined to form the compound masculine noun *goldsmiþ* 'goldsmith.' So also *ǣfen-tīd* 'evening time' is feminine because its last element is a feminine noun.

These compounds of **noun + noun** are the most frequent. There are also compounds of **adjective + noun**, such as *hālig-dæġ* 'church festival' literally 'holy-day,' *cwic-seolfor* 'mercury'; of **noun + adjective**, such as *wīn-sæd* 'satiated with wine,' and of **adjective + adjective**, such as *wīd-cūþ* 'widely known.'

781. In the above examples the part of speech of the whole compound is determined by that of the last element. But there is a class of adjective + noun compounds having the function of adjectives, such as *glæd-mōd* 'having a glad mood,' *blīþ-heort* 'blithe of heart,' 'cheerful,' formed from the adjectives *glæd, blīþe* and the nouns *mōd, heorte*. As we see from the last example, the noun is sometimes shortened in such compounds. We call these compounds **conversion-compounds**, because they involve the conversion of a noun into an adjective. They are very old formations, such conversion-compounds as the Greek *dus-menḗs* 'having an evil mind,' having apparently been formed in Parent Arian.

The OE ending *-lic* is really the obscured second element of old conversion-compounds (**844**).

782. The form-isolation of compounds in OE consists in the indeclinability of the first element. It is only by this criterion that we can distinguish such compounds as *gōddǣd* 'benefit' from the word-group *gōd dǣd* 'good action,' as in the dative plural *gōddǣdum* compared with *gōdum dǣdum*.

783. Normal OE compounds take the stress on the first element; but as word-groups beginning with the genitive of a noun or an inflected adjective do the same, stress is in OE no criterion of composition as opposed to mere grouping. Hence there is in OE no formal distinction between such a word-group as *cyninges sunu* 'king's son,' in which the meaning of the whole follows from that of its elements, and one in which there is isolation of meaning, such as the plant-name *ġēaces-sūre* 'sorrel,' literally 'cuckoo's-sour.' But as most of the latter class developed into true compounds in MnE through keeping their uneven stress (786), it is convenient to regard them as 'genitive-compounds' in OE as well. The following are examples of such OE genitive compounds, many of which, it will be observed, have been obscured in MnE :—

Tīwes-dæġ 'Tuesday,' literally 'day of the war-god' (*Tīw*), the name being a translation of the Latin *diēs Mārtis* (French *Mardi*), *Ęngla-land* 'England,' literally 'land of the Anglians' [*Ęngle* plur. 'Anglians,' 'English']. These combinations are especially frequent as place-names, such as *Sēoles-īeġ* 'Selsey,' literally 'seal's island,' *Oxena-ford* 'Oxford,' literally 'ford of oxen.'

784. Verbs are very rarely compounded directly with nouns or adjectives in OE. But the frequent combinations of verbs with prefixes, such as *mis-dōn* 'act amiss,' 'do wrong,' led to combinations with certain adjectives in similar adverbial meanings, such as *full* in *fullfyllan* 'fully fill,' 'fulfil,' *full-wyrċan* 'fully work,' 'complete,' and *efen* 'even,' 'equal,' which in composition expresses the idea of community or association, as in *efen·þrowian* 'sympathize,' literally 'suffer in common with.' The want of stress in the first elements of these compounds shows that they are felt as mere prefixes.

Modern English.

785. In MnE some compounds are formed by adding to the first element the Latin and Greek connecting-vowel *o*, but only when the first element is in a Latin or latinized form, as in *Anglosaxon*, *Anglo-Indian*, *Franco-German*, *a concavo-convex lens*.

The connecting vowel *o* is very frequent in Greek compounds, such as *hippo-dámos* 'horse-taming,' *philo-sophía* 'philosophy,' literally 'loving wisdom.' In such forms as *hippo-*, *philo-* is preserved one of the most frequent forms of uninflected nouns and adjectives in a primitive stage of Parent Arian. When inflections were fully developed, these old uninflected forms survived only as the first elements of compounds.

The *ng* in the MnE *nightingale* may be due to the influence of *evening*. In MnE *handiwork* the *i* is the OE prefix *ġe-*, preserved in *enough*=OE *ġenōg*, the OE form of the compound being *hand-ġeweorc*. The *i-* was preserved in MnE probably through association with the adjective *handy*. *handicraft*=OE *handcræft* probably owes its *i* to the influence of *handiwork* and *handy*.

786. One of the formal tests of composition in MnE as well as in OE is the inseparability and indeclinability of the first element. But owing to the scantiness of the inflections in MnE and its more rigid word-order, these tests are not so decisive in it as in OE, especially when an adjective is the first element. The only certain test by which we can distinguish between compounds and mere word-groups in MnE is stress, the former throwing the stress on to one of the elements, while in the latter the stress is equal. This is how we distinguish between the compound ·*blackbird* and the group ·*black* ·*bird*.

787. One result of this further development of stress-distinctions in MnE is that we are able to recognize a special class of MnE genitive-compounds, distinguished from mere genitive-groups in the same way as compounds beginning with an adjective are distinguished from the corresponding word-groups, namely by having uneven instead of even stress, as in the compound *crow's-foot* (a plant) compared with the group *a crow's foot.*

788. Hence also the OE compounds *goldfæt, gōddǣd* have in MnE been separated into the groups ·*gold* ·*vessel, good deed,* such OE compounds as *goldsmiþ, cwicseolfor* being preserved as compounds in the form of *goldsmith, quicksilver* by their uneven stress; while the OE groups *dōmes dæġ, blæc bęriġe* have been made into the compounds *doomsday, blackberry.*

789. Some compounds of MnE formation have a noun in the plural as their first element, but only when this noun in the plural has developed a meaning of its own different from that of the singular, so that it is isolated from its singular, the connection between them being sometimes forgotten. Such compounds are *clothesbrush, clothes-basket,* etc., *newsboy, newspaper.*

790. As regards the use of the different parts of speech in composition, the most noticeable difference between OE and MnE is the greater freedom with which in MnE verbs enter into composition with nouns and adjectives, the result of the combination being sometimes a noun, as in *break-water, clasp-knife,* sometimes a verb, as in *browbeat, whitewash,* according as the last element is a noun or a verb. But such compounds are still comparatively rare, the main combination of verbs being with particles, as in OE.

Meaning of Compounds.

791. The general rule of English—as also of Parent Arian—composition is to put the adjunct-word before the head-word, on the same principle of putting the modifier before the modified word as we follow in the group adjective

+noun. Hence the order in the compound *blackbird* is the same as in the group *black bird.*

In such groups as *man-of-war, bread-and-butter,* on the contrary, the modifying element follows, instead of preceding, and accordingly the stress is thrown on to the second element.

792. In many cases the logical relation between the elements of a compound may be defined with certainty and accuracy. Thus it is perfectly clear that in *goldfish* the first element defines the second one by stating something that the second element resembles, the compound being equivalent to 'gold-resembling fish,' or more definitely 'gold-coloured fish.' So also it is evident that *sight* in *sightseer* stands in the same relation to *seer* as it does to the verb *see* in *he saw the sights,* and that the elements of *churchgoer* stand to one another in the same relation as *church* and *go* do in *he goes to church.*

793. But in many cases these logical relations are less definite. Thus a *water-plant* might mean a plant growing in the water, or a plant growing near the water, or, on the analogy of *water-melon,* we might suppose it to mean a plant containing a great deal of moisture, and perhaps growing in a comparatively dry place. The logical relations between the elements of causal and phenomenon-compounds are often difficult to define accurately, even when the meaning of the compound itself is definite, as in *sundial,* which might be explained either as a 'dial *for* showing the position of the sun,' or as a 'dial worked—as it were—*by* the sun instead of by clockwork, etc.'

794. It must, indeed, be borne in mind that this very vagueness is the chief reason why composition is resorted to: it is only by leaving open the logical relations between the elements of compounds that we are able to form them as we want them without stopping to analyze exactly the logical or grammatical relations between the words we join together, as we might have to do if we connected them together by more definite means, such as prepositions or inflections.

795. An important general distinction between compounds as regards their meaning is the **closeness** of the logical connection between them. We may from this point of view distinguish between **coordination-** and **subordination-compounds.** Thus in a causal compound the relation between the two elements is an intimate one, like that between the clauses of a causal complex sentence. There are hardly any pure coordination-compounds in English, such a combination as *deaf-mute*='a person who is deaf and dumb' being an even-stress group-compound and not a pure compound.

DERIVATION.

Native Elements.

Prefixes.

796. Some of the OE prefixes are **strong** (strong-stressed), some **weak** (weak-stressed). Noun- and adjective-prefixes—that is, prefixes added to nouns and adjectives respectively—are generally strong, as in *·mis-dǣd* 'misdeed,' *·un-cūþ* 'unknown'; while verb-prefixes are generally weak, as in *for·giefan* 'forgive.' When the same prefix is used both with nouns (and adjectives) and with verbs, it generally takes a shortened and weakened form in the latter combination, which is the natural result of its weak stress. The following are examples of such pairs of originally identical prefixes:—

·and-ġiet 'intelligence'	*on·ġietan* 'understand'
·æf-þunca 'grudge'	*of·þynċan* 'to grudge'
·or-þanc 'device'	*ā·þęnċan* 'devise'
·bī-gang 'circuit'	*be·gān* 'practise'

797. When a verb is formed direct from a noun or adjective, the strong form of the prefix is preserved unchanged, as in *·andswarian* (*andswęrian*) 'to answer' from the noun *·and-swaru* 'answer.'

798. Conversely, in a noun formed from a verb the verb-prefix is preserved unchanged, as in *ā·līesednes* 'redemption,' literally 'loosenedness,' from *ā·līesan* 'release,' 'redeem.'

It sometimes happens that a noun which originally had a strong prefix takes the corresponding weak one by the influence of a verb of similar meaning. Thus *bīgang* is often made into *be·gang* by the influence of *be·gān*.

799. In some cases older distinctions between the strong and weak forms of prefixes have been levelled. Thus the weak *for-* in *for·dōn* 'destroy,' *forweorþan* 'perish' appears in the earliest OE as *fer-*, *for-* being then used only as the corresponding strong form in such nouns as *·forwyrd* 'destruction,' from which it was gradually extended to verb-forms. So also *tō-* in *tō·brecan* 'break to pieces' is represented by *te-* in earlier OE.

800. In the case of these two prefixes the weak stress was kept in the originally weak forms in spite of the adoption of the strong forms. But in some cases the prefix not only kept its strong form when transferred to a verb, but also its strong stress; thus the prefix *mis-* has strong stress in *·misdōn* as well as in *misdǣd*.

801. The prefix *ġe-*, on the other hand, always has weak stress, not only before verbs, as in *ġe·sēon* 'to see,' but also in nouns, such as *ġesihþ* 'sight,' where it has supplanted an older strong form.

802. Prefixes to pronouns and particles are sometimes weak, sometimes strong.

The following are the most important of the OE prefixes, the strong being marked (·).

803. ā- (strong form *or-*). The original meaning of this prefix was 'out,' 'from,' 'forth,' which may still be traced in such verbs as *ārīsan* 'arise,' while in many cases it is practically unmeaning—or, at most, emphatic—as in *āberan* 'carry,' 'endure.'

804. ·ā- is a shorter form of *āwa* 'always.' It is a strong prefix which is used only with pronouns and particles to give them an indefinite meaning, as in *·āhwæþer* 'either of two,' *āhwǣr* 'anywhere,' from *hwæþer* 'which of the two?' and *hwǣr* 'where?'

805. ·ǣġ- was originally *ā* 'always' followed by the prefix *ġe-* in its older form *ġi-* (**808**), whose *i* mutated the preceding *ā* into *ǣ*, and was then dropped, giving *ǣġ-*. The *ā* in this prefix served merely to emphasize and generalize the collective meaning of the *ġe-*, so that *ǣġ-* is equivalent to 'all' or 'every,' as in *·ǣġhwæþer* 'each of two,' *ǣġhwǣr* 'everywhere.'

806. be- has *bī-* for its strong form. It was originally the same word as the preposition *be* 'by,' whose strong form is the adverb *bī* 'by.' *be-* and *bī-* preserve the meaning 'around,' kept also in Greek *amphi-*, which represents the fuller Arian form of which *bī* is a shortening. This primitive meaning is seen in *bīgang*, *begān*, in which 'going round' developed into the meanings 'worship,' 'cultivate.' The most general function of *be-* is to specialize the meaning of transitive verbs, as in *behōn* 'hang with,' *besęttan* 'beset,' and to make an intransitive verb transitive, as in *bewēpan* 'bewail,' *beþęnċan* 'consider' from *wēpan* 'weep,' *þęnċan* 'think.' In some cases it is privative, as in *beniman* 'deprive' [*niman* 'take'], *behēafdian* 'behead.'

807. for- is quite distinct from the preposition *for*; it expresses destruction, loss, etc., as in *fordōn* 'destroy,' *forweorþan* 'perish' from *dōn* 'do,' *weorþan* 'become,' originally 'turn' [compare Latin *vertere*], being sometimes only intensitive, as in *forbærnan* 'burn up.'

808. ġe-, which is prefixed equally to verbs, nouns, adjectives, pronouns, and particles, has primarily a collective meaning, as in *ġefēra* 'companion,' originally 'fellow traveller,' from *fōr* 'journey' [*faran*, 'go,' 'travel'], *ġebrōþru* 'brothers' [*brōþor*, 'brother'], *ġehwā* 'each one' from *hwā* 'who?' It is often only intensitive, and often practically unmeaning, as in *ġemynd* 'memory,' 'mind.' As a prefix to the preterite participle of verbs, as in *ġebunden* 'bound,' it is really a grammatical inflection.

809. mis- is a prefix both to verbs and nouns, as in *mislīcian* 'displease,' *misdǣd* 'misdeed.'

810. of- is cognate with the preposition and adverb *of* 'off, of.' The strong form *æf-* has been supplanted by the weak form in such words as *ofspring* 'progeny.' In this word the original meaning of the prefix has been preserved, but in most cases it is only intensitive, as in *ofslēan* 'kill' [*slēan* 'strike'], or unmeaning, as in the preterite participle *ofþyrsted* 'thirsty.'

811. on-, strong *and-*, as in *and-wyrde* 'answer,' literally 'against-wording,' where it still preserves its original meaning of 'against,' being cognate with the Greek *anti* 'against.' In some words it expresses 'separation,' 'change,' as in *on-*

bindan 'unbind,' *onlūcan* 'unlock,' 'open,' *onwęndan* 'overturn,' 'change to the worse.' In many words it is unmeaning, as in *ondrǣdan* 'dread.'

on-derivatives such as the above must be carefully distinguished from compounds with the preposition or adverb *on* 'on,' such as ·*on-winnan* 'make war on,' 'assail,' *onġēan* 'against.'

812. tō-: as in *tōbrecan* 'break to pieces,' *tōdǣlan* 'distribute' [*dǣl* 'portion,' 'share']. This prefix always keeps its original meaning of 'separation,' 'destruction,' and is thus easily distinguished from compounds with the preposition *tō* 'to,' such as ·*tōcyme* 'arrival' [*cyme* 'coming'], *tō·gædre* 'together.'

813. ·un- 'un-' is a prefix to nouns, adjectives, and secondary adverbs, and is generally purely negative, though sometimes intensitive in the sense of 'bad': *undǣd* 'wicked deed,' 'crime,' *uncūþ* 'unknown,' *unsōfte* 'ungently,' 'severely.'

814. In ME *ge*- was weakened to *i*-, as in *ivēre, ibūnde(n)*. It soon began to be dropped in the North-Thames dialects, as in *līc* 'like'=South-Thames *ilīch*, OE *ġelīc*. In Standard ME it seems to have been preserved in poetry for the sake of the metre after it had become extinct in the spoken language. But it has been kept to the present day in *enough*=ME *inōh*, OE *genōg*, *handiwork* (785. 2), *ywis*=OE *ġewiss* 'certain,' and in the preterite participles *yclept*=OE *ġeclèopod* 'called,' *yclad*. Also through confusion with *every* in *everywhere* from OE **ǣfre ġehwǣr*.

alike must be referred to the OE *onlīc*, which had the same meaning as *ġelīc*.

815. In ME the prepositions *of* and *on* were liable to be weakened into *a* (743). The same change took place with the prefixes *of-* and *on-*, and as OE *ā-* was shortened to *a-*, all three prefixes were often levelled under one form. This levelling was helped by the fact that already in OE there was a certain confusion between these endings through the vagueness of their meanings in many words. Thus we find in OE *ābīdan, onbīdan* 'await,' *onwacan* and *āwacan* 'awake,' *ondrǽdan* 'fear,' *ofdrǽdd* pret. partic. 'afraid.' *of-* was preserved in *ofspring* through its strong stress. So also *and-* in *andsware, answare.* Towards the end of the ME period the prefix *a-* was dropped in many words, partly through its vagueness of meaning, partly through its indistinctness of sound. It is now preserved only in a few words, such as *arise, awake, awaken*=OE *ārīsan, āwacan, āwæcnian, acknowledge*=ME *aknǭulęchen*, to which corresponds OE *oncnāwan, ashamed*=OE *ofsċeamod, abide*=OE *onbīdan* 'wait,' and the obsolete *athirst*=OE *ofþyrsted.*

816. But those verbs in *on-* which expressed a definite reversal of the meaning of the verbs they were formed from, such as *onbindan*, saved their prefixes from being weakened into the ambiguous *a-* by identifying it with the almost synonymous noun- and adjective-prefix *un-*, whence the MnE *unbind, unlock*, and many new-formations, such as *unhook, unchain.*

817. *tō-* was preserved in ME, as in *tōbreken, tōrenden*, but has become obsolete in MnE, though the Bible still has *all tobrake his skull*, where *all* is adverbial.

818. *for-* is still preserved in MnE, as in *forbid, forswear, forlorn*=OE *forloren*, preterite participle of *forlēosan* 'lose'; but many of the ME derivatives have become obsolete, and *for-* is no longer a living prefix.

In *forego*=OE *forgān* 'go without,' 'forego' the prefix has been confused with the separable prefix or adverb *fore*= OE *fore* 'before.'

819. The mainly noun- and adjective-prefixes *mis-* and *un-* are still living prefixes, being freely used to form new derivatives, such as *misadventure*, *misrepresent*, *unrest*, *unlimited*.

820. The only old verb-prefix that can be regarded as still living is *be-*, with which an immense number of new verbs have been formed in MnE as well as ME. Many of these have been formed directly from nouns—French as well as English—such as *befriend*, *benighted*, *besiege*. The noun *byword* still keeps the strong form, being formed on the analogy of ME *bīspel*=OE *bīspell* 'parable'; but such nouns as *bystreet*, *bystander*, may be regarded rather as compounds with the adverb *bī*. Some nouns have taken *be-* from the corresponding verbs, such as *belief*=OE *ġelēafa*, the corresponding verb being *believe*=OE *ġelīefan*, Late OE *belīefan*.

Suffixes.

821. Of the OE endings some, which contained *i* or *j* in Germanic, cause mutation of the preceding vowel, as in *gylden* 'golden.' When the same ending sometimes mutates, sometimes not, the mutated forms are generally the original ones, the unmutated forms being the result of later influence of the unmutated word from which the derivative was formed. Thus *beren* 'belonging to a bear'=earlier *biren* owes its *e* to the influence of the noun *bera* 'bear.'

Noun-forming.

(*a*) *Concrete.*

822. -end '-er' is the noun-form of the present participle ending *-ende*, and forms nouns denoting agents from verbs, such as *hǣlend* 'healer,' 'Saviour,' *sċēotend* 'shooter,' 'warrior.' It became extinct in ME, its place being supplied by the ending *-ere*. But it still survives disguised in *friend*= OE *frēond* literally 'lover,' and *fiend*= OE *fēond* 'enemy,' literally 'hater.'

823. -ere, -ǣre, masc. '-er' forms agent-denoting nouns from verbs: *fisċere* 'fisher,' *leornere* 'learner,' from *fisċian* 'fish,' *leornian* 'learn,' *fisċian* itself being formed from the noun *fisċ*. *bōcere* 'scribe' seems to be formed directly from *bōc* on the model of the Latin *librārius*. In ME the *ǣ* in the form *-ǣre* was shortened, and underwent the regular change into *a*, so that in Early ME we find such forms as *fischare* by the side of *fischere*. In Late ME there was a good deal of confusion between these endings and the French and Latin endings *-er*, *-ier*, *-eer*, *-our*, *-or*, which often had the same meanings as the native ending (**915**). This confusion was increased in Early MnE by the levelling of *-er*, *-ar*, *-or*, etc. under (ər) [**230**]. Hence such forms as *liar*=OE *lēogere*, *sailor* compared with *a fast sailer* [OE *seġlan* 'sail'].

824. -estre fem. '-ess': *bæcestre* 'female baker' [*bæcere* 'baker'], *tæppestre* 'female tapster.' In ME this ending, being unstrest, soon lost its final *e*, and the resulting *-ster* came to be regarded as an emphatic form of *-er*, and consequently was applied to men as well as women, so that the Early ME feminines *bakstere*, *tappistere* developed into the Late ME masculines *baxter*, *tapster*. Many of these trade-names in *-ster* survive only as proper names, such as *Baxter*, *Brewster*, *Webster*. In MnE this ending is also used to express 'one who does a thing habitually,' generally with an implication of contempt, as in *punster*, *trickster*. The only noun in *-ster* which is still distinctly feminine is *spinster*, which has, however, lost its meaning of 'female spinner,' being now used only in that of 'unmarried woman.'

825. -ing masc.: *earming* 'poor wretch' [*earm* 'poor'] *lȳtling* 'little one' [*lȳtel* 'little']. This ending is specially used to form patronymics, such as *æþeling* 'son of a noble,' 'prince' from *æþele* 'noble,' 'aristocratic,' *cyning* 'king,' literally 'son of a king,' the underived *cyne* being preserved only in compounds such as *cynehelm* 'crown,' literally 'king-helm.' These patronymics are formed freely from personal names: *Scielding*, *Æþelwulfing*, *Elising* 'son of Elisha.' Many of them are preserved as proper names, such as *Manning*, *Harding*, especially in place-names, such as *Billingsgate*, *Islington*, *Reading*, so called from the clans of the *Billingas* 'sons of Bill' etc.

This ending is also found in names of animals, as in *hæring* 'herring,' and in names of things, especially coins, such as *scilling*, *pęning*, *fēorþing* (*fēorþung*, *fēorþling*) 'farthing,' literally 'fourth part (of a *pęning*)' from *fēorþa* 'fourth.'

826. -ling masc. in OE generally expresses affection, familiarity, or contempt: *dēorling* 'favourite,' from *dēore* 'dear,' 'precious,' ME *derling*, MnE *darling*, *hȳrling* 'hireling,' *underling*. There are many others in MnE, most of which are new-formations, such as *starveling*, *worldling*, *changeling*. This suffix is frequent in names of animals, generally expressing youth or smallness, as in *youngling* 'young animal,' also used in the sense of 'young human being,' *nestling*, *gosling*. Some of these may be of OE origin.

827. **-en** fem. with mutation: *gyden* 'goddess,' *fyxen* 'vixen' from *god*, *fox*.

(*b*) *Abstract.*

828. **-nis(s)**, **-nes(s)** fem. is the regular ending for forming abstract nouns from adjectives: *gōdnis* 'goodness,' *ġelīcnis* 'likeness,' *beorhtnis* 'brightness.' This ending is still in living use in MnE, being added to foreign as well as native adjectives, as in *closeness*, *graciousness*.

Words in *-ness* only rarely take concrete meanings, as in *witness*, *wilderness*.

829. **-u** fem. with mutation forms abstract nouns from adjectives: *lęngu* 'length,' *brǣdu* 'breadth,' *hǣtu* 'heat,' *ieldu* 'old age,' archaic MnE *eld*, *wrǣþ(þ)u* 'anger,' ME *wraþþe*, MnE *wrath*, from the adjectives *lang*, *brād*, *hāt*, *eald*, *wrāþ*.

830. **-uþ**, **-þ** fem. with and without mutation: *trēowþ* 'fidelity,' *þīefþ* 'theft,' ME *þēfþe*, *þefte*, from *trēowe* 'faithful,' *þēof* 'thief,' *slǣwþ* 'sloth,' which in ME became *slǭuþe* by the influence of the adjective from which it was formed, namely OE *slāw*, ME *slǭw* 'indolent.' To *ġeoguþ* 'youth' corresponds the adjective *ġeong* 'young.' In ME the ending *-þe*=OE *-þ* was substituted for the equivalent *-e*=OE *-u*, as being more distinct, whence the MnE *length*, *breadth*=ME *lengþe*, OE *lęngu*, etc. Similarly OE *dīepe* from *dēop* 'deep' has become *depth*. So also ME *wele*, MnE *weal*=OE *wela* 'prosperity,' 'wealth,' has developed a secondary form *wealth* on the analogy of *health* from OE *hǣlu*. In ME and MnE some new derivatives in *-th* have been formed, not only from adjectives, as in *warmth*, *dearth*, but also directly from verbs, as in *growth, stealth*, the latter on the analogy of ME *þēfþe* 'theft.'

831. **-ung, -ing**, fem. forms abstract nouns from verbs: *bletsung* 'blessing,' *leornung*, *leorning* 'learning,' *rǣding* 'reading,' from the verbs *bletsian*, *leornian*, *rǣdan*. In OE this ending is restricted in its use, and is very rarely used to form derivatives from strong verbs because these are generally provided with other derivatives, such as *cyme* 'coming,' *gang* 'going' corresponding to the strong verbs *cuman*, *gān*. In ME the use of *-inge*, *-ing* was so much extended that at last abstract nouns could be formed with it from any verb, till it finally developed into a purely grammatical form—the gerund (**553**). In MnE many words in *-ing* have assumed concrete meanings, such as *being* = 'creature.' In most cases these concrete words in *-ing* express either the result of the action expressed by the verb, as in *building* 'what is built,' 'edifice,' *dripping*, *leavings*, or the instrument of the action of the verb, as in *clothing*, *covering*, *footing* 'ground to put the foot on.' In some words *-ing* has a collective meaning, as in *paling*, *shipping*. Some of these words, such as *shipping*, seem to be formed directly from nouns.

The following endings were originally independent words in OE itself:—

832. **-dōm** masc. is from the noun *dōm* 'judgment,' 'authority,' and expresses first 'rank,' and then condition generally: *cynedōm* 'royal authority,' 'kingdom,' *king* having been substituted for the less familiar *cyne* (**825**) in ME, *martyrdōm*, *crīstendōm*, *wīsdōm*. In MnE there are a few new-formations, such as *dukedom*. *christendom* and *heathendom* have now become concrete. In OE itself *lǣcedōm* 'medicine' from *lǣce* 'leech,' 'physician' had a concrete meaning.

833. -hād masc. from the noun *hād* 'rank,' 'condition,' 'character,' 'nature': *bisċophād* 'rank of bishop,' 'episcopacy,' *prēosthād* 'priesthood,' *ċildhād*, *mæġþhād* 'virginity,' the more familiar *mæġden* being substituted for *mæġþ* 'virgin,' 'maid' in the ME *maidenhōd*. *widwan-hād* 'widowhood' is really a group-compound of *hād* and the genitive of the weak noun *widwe*. In ME this ending became *-hōd* with close *ō* instead of *ǭ*, whence the MnE *-hood*. The frequent ME form *-hēde*, *-hēd* is the result of the influence of another ending of similar meaning, namely *-rēde* from OE *-rǣden* (**834**), the form *-hōde* being another result of these blendings. In OE *-hād* is used only with nouns, but its ME and MnE representatives form derivatives from adjectives also, such as *hardihood*, *likelihood*, *falsehood*. Many of the derivatives from nouns have taken concrete—mostly collective—meanings, as in *priesthood* and the new-formations *brotherhood*, *neighbourhood*. The ME form *-hēde* is now almost extinct, surviving only in *maidenhead* and *Godhead*.

834. -rǣden fem., gen. *-rǣdenne*, from the noun *rǣden* 'regulation,' 'agreement' [connected with *ġerǣdan* 'put in order,' 'arrange' and the MnE *ready*]: *ġeferrǣden* 'fellowship,' 'agreement,' *frēondrǣden* 'relationship,' 'friendship.' In OE this ending was applied only to nouns. ME keeps many of the OE derivatives, *frēndrēde*, *sibrēde* 'relationship' = OE *sibbrǣden*, and on the analogy of these forms the new derivative *haterēde*, *hatrēde* 'hatred' [ME *hate* is a blending of the OE noun *hete* 'violence,' 'hostility' and the corresponding verb *hatian*]. The analogy of *sibrēde*, etc. also led to the ME change of OE *cynren* 'line of descendants,' 'family' [*-ren* = *ryne*, 'course,' connected with *iernan* 'run'] —into *kinrēde*, whence, by the usual insertion of *d* (**200**), the MnE *kindred*.

835. -sċipe masc. '-ship,' from a lost noun connected with the verb *sċieppan* 'shape,' 'create': *hlāfordsċipe* 'lordship,' 'authority,' *frēondsċipe, weorþsċipe* 'honour' [*weorþ* noun and adjective 'worth,' 'worthy']. This ending is frequently used in MnE to form new derivatives, especially from personal words, as in *ownership, consulship, relationship.* In OE it is used to form derivatives almost exclusively from nouns, but in MnE we have such derivatives as *hardship, courtship* from the adjective *hard* and the verb *to court.*

Adjective-forming.

836. -ede forms compound adjectives from names of parts of the body preceded by a modifying word: *sūrēagede* 'blear-eyed,' literally 'sour-eyed,' *þrihēafdede* 'three-headed.' In MnE this ending has been necessarily shortened to *-ed,* and so has become indistinguishable from the preterite participle inflection.

837. -en with mutation generally denotes material, being also used in the more general sense of 'belonging to': *ǣċen* 'of oak' [*āc* 'oak'], *gylden* 'golden,' *wyllen* 'woollen' [*wulle* 'wool'], *hǣþen* 'heathen' [*hǣþ* 'heath']. In *beren* from *bera* 'bear,' as in *beren fell* 'a bear's skin,' earlier *biren,* the *e* has been brought in from the noun; so also in *lēaden* 'leaden' [*lēad* 'lead']. In MnE these adjectives restore the unmutated vowel everywhere, as in *golden, woollen,* on the analogy of which new derivatives had been formed, such as *wooden, hempen.* The similarity of meaning between material nouns and adjectives has in some cases led to the conversion of adjectives in *-en* into nouns, as in *linen* = OE *līnen* 'flaxen' from *līn* 'flax,' and the tree names *aspen* = OE *æspe, linden* = OE *lind* fem.

Some adjectives in *-en* with mutation were originally preterite participles of strong verbs: ***druncen*** 'intoxicated,' ***āgen*** 'own,' ***fægen*** 'glad,' whence MnE *fain*, from ***drincan***, ***āgan*** 'possess,' ***ġefēon*** 'rejoice.'

838. -iġ '-y' corresponds sometimes to Germanic *-ig*, *-īg*, sometimes to Germanic *-ag*, etc., causing mutation in the former case, but not in the latter: ***hāliġ*** 'holy' [***hāl*** 'entire,' 'sound'], ***mōdiġ*** 'proud,' ***īsiġ*** 'icy'; ***hęfiġ*** 'heavy' [connected with ***hębban***, preterite participle ***hafen***, 'lift'], ***bysiġ*** 'busy,' ***dysiġ*** 'foolish,' whence MnE *dizzy*. In MnE this ending has been widely extended, and in many words it has taken the place of the material *-en*, as in *fiery*=OE ***fȳren*** [***fȳr*** 'fire'], *clayey*, *gluey*, where the Early MnE spelling *-ey* is preserved, as it regularly is after vowels.

-iġ is also a noun-ending, as in ***bodiġ*** 'body,' ***īfiġ*** 'ivy,' ***huniġ*** 'honey.'

839. -isc '-ish' with mutation—which is sometimes got rid of by the influence of the underived word—is most frequently used to form names of nations, but also in derivatives from common nouns: ***Ęngliśc***, ***Fręnċiśc*** 'French' [***Francland*** 'land of the Franks,' 'France'], ***Śćyttiśc*** 'Scotch' [***Śćottland***, 'Ireland,' afterwards 'Scotland'], ***Węliśc*** 'Welsh'; ***ċierliśċe męnn*** 'serfs' [***ċeorl*** 'serf'], ***folciśc*** 'popular,' 'vulgar.' In ME some of the names of nations were contracted by omission of the vowel of the ending, whence the MnE *French*, *Scotch* by the side of the fuller *Scottish*, in both of which the unmutated vowel has been restored by the influence of *Scot*, *Scotland*. In the other words formed from nouns *-ish* generally expresses contempt, as in *mannish*, *womanish* compared with *manly*, *womanly*, *childish* compared with *childlike*, *brutish*. *-ish* added to an adjective expresses simple diminution, as in *oldish, longish,* especially with names of colours, such as *reddish, yellowish.*

840. -sum '-some' forms adjectives from nouns, adjectives, and verbs; *wynsum* 'pleasant' [*wynn* 'joy']; *langsum* 'tedious'; *hīersum* 'obedient' [*hīeran* 'hear,' 'obey']. There are many ME and MnE new formations: *handsome, troublesome; wholesome, wearisome.*

The following endings were independent words in Germanic:—

841. -feald '-fold' [compare the verb *fealdan* 'fold'] forms adjectives from adjective-words, especially numerals: *maniġfeald* 'manifold,' 'various,' *seofonfeald, hundfeald,* 'hundredfold.'

842. -full '-ful,' from the adjective *full* 'full,' forms adjectives from abstract nouns: *carfull* 'careful,' *sorgfull* 'sorrowful,' *synnfull* 'sinful.' There are numerous new-formations in ME and MnE—some from concrete nouns: *artful, powerful, masterful.*

843. -lēas '-less' from the adjective *lēas* 'deprived of,' 'without' [compare *forlēosan* 'lose'] forms adjectives from nouns and verbs: *ġelēaflēas* 'unbelieving,' *slǣplēas* 'sleepless'; *reċċelēas* 'careless,' from *reċċan* 'reck.' In ME this ending appears both as *-lēs* and as *-les* with the vowel shortened, which may be due to the influence of *lesse* 'less,' It is frequently used in new-formations, such as *fearless, useless.*

844. -liċ '-ly': *eorþliċ* 'earthly,' *frēondliċ* 'friendly,' *ġēarliċ* 'annual.' These derivatives were originally conversion-compounds with *līc* 'body,' the weak vowel being afterwards shortened, so that *wīfliċ* 'feminine,' for instance, meant originally 'having the body or form of a woman'

(**781**). Derivatives in *-līc* from adjectives and adverbs are less frequent: *lāþlīc* 'hateful,' *ūplīc*, *upplīc* 'sublime.' This ending is freely used in new-formations in ME and MnE, as in *princely*, *quarterly*, *sickly*.

845. -weard, '-ward,' from an obsolete adjective connected with *weorþan*=Latin *vertere* (**807**), forms adjectives from nouns, adjectives, and adverbs: *hāmweard*, *inneweard* from *hām* 'home,' *inne* 'within.'

Verb-forming.

846. -na is a Scandinavian suffix forming weak intransitive verbs, mostly inchoative and from adjectives, as in Icelandic *hvītna* 'become white,' *harþna* 'become hard.' Many of these verbs were imported in ME, such as *harþna*, which became *hardnen* by the influence of the ME adjective *hard*. There have been many new-formations in ME and MnE, some from adjectives, such as *gladden*, *redden*, some from nouns, such as *lengthen*.

The native verbs *awaken*, *fasten* are not formed direct from *wake* and *fast*, but the OE weak verbs *āwæcnian*, *fæstnian* were formed from the nouns *wæcen* 'watching,' *fæsten* 'fastness,' 'fort,' which are, of course, derivatives of *wacan* 'wake' and *fæst* 'fast,' 'firm.'

847. -sian with mutation: *clǣnsian* 'cleanse,' *blœdsian*, *bletsian* 'bless,' from *blōd* 'blood,' with shortening of the *ǣ*, the original meaning being 'to sprinkle (the altar) with blood.' In Scandinavian this ending appears as *-sa*, as in *hreinsa* 'purify' [*hreinn* 'pure'], whence our *rinse*.

848. -lǣċan from the noun-ending *-lāc*, preserved in MnE only in *wedlock*=OE *węddlāc* [*wędd* 'pledge,' 'contract']: *ġenēalǣċan* 'approach' from *nēah* 'near,' *ġeryhtlǣċan* 'correct.' In ME a new verb *cnǭulę̄chen* was formed with this ending from OE *cnāwan* 'know,' whence in Late ME a noun *cnǭulę̄che* was formed which, by the change of weak *ch* into (dʒ) gave MnE *knowledge.*

Foreign elements.

849. The foreign derivative elements in English are mainly of French, Latin, and Greek origin. Many which were at first introduced into English in their popular French forms were afterwards latinized, at first in spelling only, but afterwards, in many cases, in pronunciation also. In some cases they were wholly or partially latinized in French itself, though sometimes—in Late Old French—in spelling only. In some cases false etymological spellings of derivative elements of Latin origin were introduced either in French or English, some of which have corrupted the pronunciation.

850. Although foreign derivatives are often so disguised as no longer to be recognizable as derivatives, yet many foreign derivative elements have remained as distinct as the native ones. Many of them are freely used to form new derivatives from words of native as well as foreign origin. Some of them are even detached and used as independent words, such as *extra.*

Prefixes.

851. In Latin many of the prefixes are liable to various changes according to the nature of the initial consonants of the word they modify, the full form of a prefix ending in consonants being generally preserved before a vowel, while before consonants the final consonants of the prefix are liable to assimilation and loss; and these variations have generally been preserved when the words containing them were imported into French and English.

852. The foreign prefixes will now be treated of in their alphabetical order. Specially French prefixes are marked *, Greek prefixes are marked †, Latin prefixes being left unmarked.

853. ab-, abs-, a-, 'from, away': *ab-erration, ab-rupt*; *abs-tinent*; *a-vert*. The above are formed from verb-roots. *abnōrmis*, which in English was made into *abnormal* on the analogy of the Latin adj. *nōrmālis*, is an example of an *ab*-derivative from a noun—Latin *nōrma* 'pattern.' All the above words were taken directly from Latin or from learned French. In popular French *ab-* became *av-*, but the Latin form was generally restored, as in *abus* from *abūsum*, whence MnE *abuse*.

854. ad-, a-, also in the assimilated forms *ag-*, *af-* etc., according to the consonant that follows, 'to.' In Old French this prefix was shortened to *a-*, as in *aventure* 'adventure' from Latin *rēs adventūra* 'a thing about to happen.' The double consonants in such Latin words as *aggravāre*, *assentāre*=*adgravāre*, *adsentāre* were shortened both in pronunciation and writing in Old French—*agrever*, *asenter*—double *s* being, however, often kept (*assenter*) to show that the *s* was pronounced (s) and not (z). But in Late Old French the *d* was often introduced again by the influence of the Latin orthography, whence the spellings *adventure*, etc. Hence many of these words appear in ME in a variety of forms, one, of early introduction, pure Old French, the other or others more or less latinized, while in some cases the latinized form does not appear till after the ME period. Thus in ME we have *aventure* and a contracted form *aunter*, in Early MnE *adventer*, which in the Present English has been further latinized into *adventure*. The double consonants were restored in the same way, sometimes in ME, but generally nŏt till later; thus we have ME *agrēven*, *asenten* (also *assenten*)=MnE *aggrieve*, *assent*. Sometimes the prefix *a-* was made into *ad-* from a mistaken etymology, as in *advance*, *advantage*=ME *avancen*, *avantāġe*, Old French *avancer* being a verb formed from the particle *avant* = Latin **ab-ante*.

855. amb-, -am, an-, 'around': *amb-ition*; *per-ambulate*; *an-cipital* 'two-headed,' 'doubtful.'

856. †amphi- 'around': *amphi-bious*, *amphi-theatre*.

857. †an- before vowels and *h* + vowel, **a-** before other consonants, 'un-': *an-archy* [compare *mon-archy*], *an-hydrous* 'without water'; *a-theist*.

858. †ana- 'up,' 'again,' 'apart,' 'according to,' 'reversal,' etc.: *ana-thema*, originally 'thing put up or dedicated,' *ana-baptist*, 're-baptist,' *ana-logy* 'according to proportion,' *ana-gram* 'transposition of letters,' *ana-chronism*.

859. ante-, anti- 'before': *ante-cedent*; *anti-cipate*. Freely used in new-formations, such as *anteroom*, *antedate*.

860. †anti- 'against': *Anti-christ*, *anti-pathy*, *anti-podes*. Freely used in new-formations, such as *anti-radical*, *anti-spasmodic*.

861. †apo-, before vowels **ap-**, before *h* **aph-**, the *h* itself being dropped: 'from,' 'away,' 'forth,' etc.: *apo-cope* literally 'cutting away,' *apo-stasy*; *aph-orism*.

862. bi- 'half,' 'twice': *bi-ennial* [compare *annual*], *bi-sect*. *bi-cycle* is a newly formed hybrid from Greek *kúklos* 'circle.'

863. †cata-, cat-, cath-, 'down,' 'through,' etc.: *cata-ract*, *catastrophe*, *catalogue*; *cat-echize*; *catholic*.

864. circum-, circu- 'round': *circum-navigate, circumstance, circumspect, circumvent*; *circu-itous.*

865. cis- 'on this side of': *Cisalpine.*

866. com-, con-, co- 'with,' 'together,' being another form of the preposition *cum* 'with'; often merely intensive. In Old French the vowel of this prefix was made into *ŏ* through the influence of *cum*, which was often lengthened in ME words taken from French, whence the MnE (ɐ, au) in *comfort, council, counsel* etc., the (o) in such words as *conduit*, earlier MnE (kɐndit) being due to the spelling. In Old French—as also occasionally in Latin itself—the final consonant of this prefix was often dropped before consonants, whence the MnE *covent=convent* in *Covent Garden* [Latin *cōnventiō*], *covenant.* The following are further examples of this prefix: *commit, comprehend, comfort* [Old French *cŏmforter, cŏnforter*]; *convince, conclude, concern, conduct*; *coincide, cohere*; *col-league, connect, corrupt.* This prefix is used in new-formations, such as *com-mingle, compatriot*, especially in the form of *co-*: *co-exist, co-tenant.* The predominance of the latter ending has led to the change of *contemporary* into *cotemporary*; but the former is now preferred, as being nearer the Latin form.

867. contra-, contro-, *counter- 'against,' originally used only to form verbs. The Old-French form is *cuntre-*, *cŏntre-* with the *o* made into *ŏ* on the analogy of Old French *cŏm-*, *cŏn-*, out of which English *counter-* has developed in the same way as in *counsel* etc. But in Old French *cŏntre-* was often made into *contre-* by the influence of the Latin spelling. The Latin forms are less frequent than the French: *contradict, contravene*; *controversy, controvert.* The form *counter-* is used not only in French words, such as *counterfeit, counterpart, counterpoise*, but also in new-formations, such as *counter-attraction, counterbalance, counter-revolution. counter* is also used as an independent adverb, as in *to run counter to*, being partly the Old French adverb and preposition *cŏntre*, partly the detached prefix.

868. de- is partly the Latin (and French) *dē* 'from,' 'away,' also expressing 'difference,' 'negation,' 'completion,' being often only intensitive, which is both a preposition and a prefix; partly French *des-, dé-* from Latin *dis-* 'asunder,' 'apart,' which often develops the same negative meaning. *de-*=Latin *dē-*: *degrade, devious*, literally 'out of the path,' *dethrone. de*=Latin *dis-* (also *dī-*, and assimilated *dif-*): *defeat* [Latin **disfacere, disfactum*], *depart, detach.*

869. *demi- 'half' from Latin *dimidium*: *demigod, demi-semibreve. demy* (di·mai) is used as an independent word.

870. †di- 'twice': *digraph, di-phthong, diploma.* The double *ss* in *dissyllable* was introduced in French through confusion with the Latin prefix *dis-*.

871. †dia-, di- 'through': *diadem, diameter; diocese, diorama.*

872. dis-, di-, assimilated **dif-** 'asunder,' 'apart,' 'privation,' 'negation.' The Old French form *des-* [Modern French *dés-, dé-*] is still preserved in *descant* 'tune with modulations.' In the other derivatives taken from Old French the Latin *dis-* has been restored, as in *disarm*=Old French *desarmer, disdain* [compare Modern French *dédaigner*], *dishonest, disease.* The following are of direct Latin origin: *discreet, dissolve, distant; different, difficult.* The form *di-* is rare in words of French introduction, such as *diminish*, and not very frequent in words of Latin form, such as *divide, dilate, divert. dis-* is freely used in new-formations, such as *disconnect, disburden, disheartened.* In *dislike*=ME *misliken* it has been substituted for a similar-sounding native prefix; so also perhaps in *disbelieve, distrust.*

***en-, *em-** 'in': see **in-, im-.**

873. **†en-, em-,** assimilated **el-,** 'in': *encyclopedia, energy; emblem, emphasis; ellipse.*

874. **†endo-** 'within': *endogamous* 'marrying within the tribe,' *endogenous* 'growing from within.'

***enter-** 'between'; see **inter-.**

875. **†epi-, ep-, eph-** 'upon': *epigram, epidemic; ephemeral.*

876. **ex-, e-,** assimilated **ef-** 'out of.' The Old French form is *es-*, Modern French *é-*. *es-* has been preserved in English only in a few obscured words, such as *essay, escape.* Wherever the meaning of the prefix has been kept clear it has been restored to its Latin form in English: *exchange* from Old French *eschangier, extend, extinguish.* The other Latin forms are seen in *elegant, evade; effect.* As x=(ks), an initial *s* is often dropped after *ex-*, as in *ex-pect* [compare *re-spect*], *exude, extirpate* [from Latin *sūdāre* 'sweat,' *stirps* 'stem']. *ex-* is frequently used in new-formations to express 'one out of office' etc., as in *ex-president, ex-secretary*; so also in the adjective *ex-official.*

877. **†ex-, ec-** 'out of': *exodus; ec-stasy.*

878. **†exo-** 'outside': *exogamous* 'marrying outside the tribe,' *exoteric* 'suitable for outer world, for people in general.'

879. **extra-** 'beyond' is used in Latin chiefly with adjectives: *extraordinary, extravagant*; so also in the new-formations *extra-official, extra-parochial.* *extra* by itself is used in English as an adjective and adverb, being either the Latin adverb and preposition *extrā* 'beyond,' or else the detached prefix. Hence such combinations as *extra work,* *extra careful*, *extra-superfine* are not derivatives, but word-groups or compounds.

880. †hyper- 'over,' 'beyond': *hyperbole*, *hyperborean*, *hypercritical*.

881. †hypo-, hyp-, hyph- 'under': *hypodermic* 'belonging to the parts under the skin,' *hypothesis*; *hyphen*.

882. in-, im-, in-, i-, assimilated **il-** etc. 'un-'—with which it is cognate as well as with Greek *an-*—is joined to adjectives and occasionally to nouns. The following are examples of words which had this prefix in Latin itself: *insane*, *insipid*, *injury*; *impious*, *ignorant*; *illiberal*, *immortal*. In English this prefix is applied only to foreign words of some length, as in *inequality*, *injustice* compared with *unequal*, *unjust*. If new words are formed from foreign words by means of English endings, *un-* is prefixed, as in *ungrateful*, *undecided*, compared with *ingratitude*, *indecisive*. But *un-* is also prefixed to some words with exceptionally familiar Latin endings such as *-able*, as in *uneatable*, *unconquerable* compared with *intolerable*, *invincible*.

883. in-, im-, il-, etc. 'in,' 'into' is mainly a verb-former. The French form of this prefix is *en-*, *em-*, preserved in English in such words as *endure*, *engage*, *envoy*; *embellish*, *employ*. But in many words of French introduction the Latin form has been restored, as in *indite*, ME *endīten*, *inquire*, *imprint*. As the spelling makes no difference in the present pronunciation—*en-*, *em-*=(-in, -im)—it fluctuates in some words between the Latin and French forms, the latter being now preferred in such cases of doubt, as in *encage*, *enjoin*, *entitle*, *embark*, formerly written also *incage* etc., although *impeach* now follows the Latin spelling. The following are examples of purely Latin words with this prefix: *inaugurate*, *invade*; *impel*; *illuminate*, *immerse*, *ir-*

ruption 'breaking in.' There are many new-formations with the French form of the prefix: *enlarge*; *embody*, *enliven*. In *impoverish* and *improve* the Latin form of the prefix has taken the place of the less distinct *a-* from Latin *ad-*, the former word being the Old French *apovrir* [Latin **appauperīre*], while the latter is a variation of *approve*=*aprove*. In a few words, such as *inborn*, *income* the prefix is of English origin.

884. inter-, *enter- 'between.' The French form is preserved only in *enterprise*, *entertain*, the Latin form having been substituted in all other words of French introduction: *intercede*, *interpret*, *interval*. In *intellect*, *intelligent* and their derivatives the Latin assimilation before *l* is kept, which is disregarded in other words, such as *interlude*. This prefix is frequently used in new-formations, such as *international*, *intertwist*.

885. intro- 'within,' 'into': *introduce*, *introspection*.

886. †meta-, met-, meth- 'with,' 'after,' 'change': *metaphysics* 'the study that comes after physics,' *metamorphosis*; *method*.

887. ne- 'not': *nefarious*, *ne-uter*, *neutral*,

888. non- 'not.' The adverb *nōn* 'not' is not used as a derivative in Latin, occurring only as the first element of a few group-compounds such as *nōn-nūllī* 'some,' literally 'not-none.' In Modern French and English it is used as a prefix in such words as *nonsense*, *nonentity*, as it already was in Late Latin in *nōn-entitās*, It is freely used in new-formations, such as *non-conductor*, *non-intervention*.

889. ob-, o(b)s-, o-, assimilated **occ-** etc., 'towards,' 'against': *ob-stacle*, *obviate*; *os-tensible*; *omit*; *occur*, *offend*, *opposite*. In some cases the full *ob-* has taken the place of an assimilated form, as in *obfuscate*.

*par- see per-.

890. †**para-, par-, parh-** 'beside,' 'against': *paradox, paragraph*; *parenthesis, parody*; *parhelion.*

891. per- 'through,' occurring also as a preposition. The assimilated *pel-* is preserved in English only in *pellucid.* The French form both of the prefix and of the preposition is *par*, preserved in English only in *pardon* [Late Latin *perdonāre*] and *parboil.* In other words the Latin form has been restored, as in *perfidy, permit, pervade.* ME *parfit* from Latin *perfectus* through French *parfait* was latinized in ME first into *perfil*, then into *perfect.*

***por-**, see **pro-**.

892. post- 'after': *posthumous, postpone, postscript.*

893. pre- Latin *prae-* 'before,' French *pre-*: *precept, precede, prefer, prescribe, present, pretend.* It is freely used in new-formations in the sense of 'before in time,' as in *preconceive, pre-engage, presuppose.*

894. preter- Latin *praeter-* 'beyond': *preter-ite, pretermit, preternatural.*

895. pro-, prod- 'before,' 'forth,' 'away from,' 'deprivation,' as in *profane* literally 'away from the temple,' *prohibit* 'acting as substitute,' as in *proconsul*, 'relation,' as in *proportion.* *prō* 'before,' 'for' etc. is also an independent preposition. There was in Latin an allied prefix *por-*, as in *portendere* 'portend.' The popular Old French form of *prō-* and the preposition *prō* was *pur, pŏr* [modern French *pour*], which was probably a blending of *prō* and *per.* This form is preserved in such words as *purchase* [Latin **prōcaptiāre*], *pursue*; *portrait*; *poursuivant, pursuivant* 'state messenger or attendant.' The following are examples of the Latin form: *pro-duce, progress, provide*; *prod-igy, prodigal.*

896. †**pro-** 'before': *problem, programme, prologue.*

897. †**pros-** 'towards': *pros-elyte* literally 'coming towards,' *prosody*.

***pur-**, see **pro-**.

898. **re-**, **red-**, 'back,' 'repetition,' as in *repeat*, 'opposition,' as in *resist*, having often only an intensitive force, as in *rejoice*. In French *re-* often became *r-* before a vowel, but the full form was restored in English, as in *reenter* from French *rentrer*. The fuller form *red-* is preserved in *redeem*, *redolent*, *redintegrate*. *re-* is freely used in new-formations, such as *reconsider*, *reintroduce*, *recover an umbrella* distinct from the traditional *recover*.

899. **retro-** 'backwards': *retrograde*, *retrospection*.

900. **se-**, **sed-** 'apart,' 'away': *secede*, *select*, *separate*; *sedition*.

901. **semi-** 'half': *semicircle*, *semicolon*. Also in new-formations, such as *semi-detached*.

902. **sine-** 'without': *sinecure*.

903. **sub-**, assimilated **suc-** etc. 'under,' whence a great variety of secondary meanings—'near,' 'behind,' 'following,' 'inferiority,' 'diminution,' 'approaching,' 'help,' 'completion,' the primary meaning also developing into that of 'stealth,' 'secrecy': *subscribe*, *suburb*, *subsequent*, *subordinate*, *subdivide*, *subvention*, *suborn*; *succumb*, *support*, *suffice*, *supply*, *succour*, *surreptitious*. *sub-* is freely used in new-formations, such as *subcutaneous*, *subway*, especially to express subordination etc., as in *sub-committee*, *sub-editor*, *sublet*, and diminution, as in the adjectives *sub-transparent*, *sub-tropical*.

904. **subter-** 'under': *subterfuge*.

905. **super-** 'above,' 'beyond' became *sur-* in Old French, which is frequently preserved in English, as in *surmount*, *surpass*, *surface* by the side of its Latin original *superficies*. It expresses 'beyond in time' in *survive*, *super-*

annuated. Its most frequent metaphorical meanings are 'addition,' 'excess,' 'superiority,' as in *surname* [which is an Anglicised form of French *surnom*]; *surfeit, supernatural, superfluous*; *surpass, supereminent.* The Latin form of the prefix is freely used in new-formations, generally to express 'excess': *super-sensual* 'beyond the reach of the senses,' *super-phosphate.*

906. supra- 'above,' 'beyond': *supramundane.*

***sur-**, see **super-**.

907. sus- has the same meaning as *sub-*, being a contraction of *subtus*: *susceptible, suspend, sustain* [Latin *sustinere* through French]. Shortened to *su-* in *su-spect, suspicion.*

908. †syn-, sy-, assimilated **syl-** etc. 'with,' 'together': *synagogue, syntax*; *sy-stem*; *syl-lable, symmetry.*

909. trans-, tra- 'across,' 'through,' 'beyond.' The Old French form is *tres-*, preserved in English only in *trespass*, compared with the Latin form of the prefix in *transgress. transs-* is shortened to *trans-* as in *transcend.* Various shades of the primary meaning are seen in such words as *transient, transitory, transpire, tra-duce. trans-* often expresses 'change,' both of place as in *transplant, transpose*, and of quality as in *transform, translate, travesty.* It is used in new-formations, as in *Transatlantic, tranship.*

***tres-**, see **trans-**.

910. ultra- 'beyond,' both of place and of quantity and superiority: *ultramontane* 'beyond the mountains,' that is, 'belonging to the Italian party in the Church of Rome,' *ultramarine* 'a colour brought from beyond the sea,' *ultramundane.* Freely used in new-formations to express excess: *ultra-radical, ultra-clerical*, whence the detached *ultra* has come to be used as an independent adjective in the sense of 'extreme,' as in *ultra measures*, whence the derivatives *ultraist, ultraism*.

Suffixes.

911. The foreign suffixes will now be treated of under the general heads of 'noun-forming' etc., and the subdivisions 'personal,' 'abstract,' the suffixes under each section being arranged so that those which consist entirely of vowels come first, and are followed by those that contain consonants in the alphabetic order of those consonants.

Noun-forming.

Personal.

912. ***-ee** is the strong form of French *-é* from Latin *-ātus*, and denotes the person who takes a passive share in an action or agreement, the corresponding active agent being denoted by *-or, -er*. Thus *lessee* is the person to whom a house is let on lease, as opposed to the lessor; so also *grantee, legatee, mortgagee*. Some of these derivatives have no special active word corresponding to them, such as *patentee, referee, trustee*. In these words the passive meaning is less prominent, and *patentee*, for instance, may be taken to mean either 'one to whom a patent is granted,' or 'one who takes out a patent'; and in some cases *-ee* is a purely active suffix as in *absentee, devotee, refugee*.

The weak form of this suffix is *-y, -ey*, as in *attorney*=Old French *atŏrné* **924**).

-iff, see **-ive** under 'Adjective-forming.'

-an, -ean, -ian, -ine, -nt, see under 'Adjective-forming.'

913. **-ar, -er, -eer, -ier** from Latin *-ārius, -āris*, Low Latin

-erius, whence the Old French *-ier*, which in ME became *-ēr*. In ME *-ēr* was shortened to *-er* when weak, whence such MnE derivatives as *officer*, *prisoner*, *stranger*. In ME it was often levelled under the English suffix *-ere*, as in *scolere*, *templere*. Many words took the ending *-ar* through the influence of the original Latin forms, some already in ME, such as *vicar*, others later, such as *scholar*, *Templar*. The MnE *-eer*, *-ier* comes from the strong form of the French suffix, both forms being freely used in new-formations, especially *-eer*: *cavalier*, *cuirassier*, *muleteer*, *pamphleteer*, *volunteer*.

914. **-or** from Latin *-or*, ***-our** from Latin *-ōrem*, through Old French *-ŏr*. In Latin this ending is preceded by derivative *t*, which under certain conditions becomes *s*: *imperātor*, *professor*. In Old French the *t* was weakened and then dropped, leaving a hiatus, as in *empereŏr*, *sauveŏr* (Latin *salvātōrem*). The *t* was of course kept in learned words of later importation into French, and was reintroduced into popular words when they were latinized, whence the MnE forms *autour*, *author* (**210**), *creditor*, *orator*. In Early MnE the spelling *-our* was still preserved, but we now write the Latin *-or* even in words that have not been otherwise latinized, such as *emperor*, *tailor*, *conqueror* = earlier *emperour* etc., though we still write *saviour*.

915. *-or* has in many words taken the place of French *-er* (as also in some English words, § **823**): *bachelor* [Early MnE *bacheler*], *chancellor*, *warrior* = OE *bacheler*, Modern French *bachelier* etc. This is partly the result of *-or* and *-er* having the same sound (ər) even in Early MnE (**230**). In some words the opposite change has taken place, as in *miner*, *robber* = ME *minour*, *robbour*.

-ary, see under 'Adjective-forming.'

916. -ard, -art. Although introduced into English from French, this suffix is of Germanic origin. In the Germanic languages *-hard* 'hard' in the sense of 'strong,' 'brave,' was a frequent termination of proper names of men, many of which were introduced into Old French, whence they passed into English, such as *Richard, Reynard*; *Renard* was originally a man's name—Old High German *Reginhart*—which was given to the fox in the story of 'Renard the fox,' which was introduced into France in the twelfth century from Flanders. In Flemish the name of the fox is *Reinaert*, which in French became *Renart*; and the story became so popular in France that *renard* is now the only French word for fox, the Old French *goupil* 'fox' surviving only as a proper name. The name-suffix *-ard, -art* was soon used in Old French and the other Romance languages to form personal nouns, which were at first nicknames, and had a depreciatory sense. Thus from the Romance forms of Latin *cauda* 'tail' was formed Italian *codardo*, Old French *cöart* 'coward.' Other examples are *bastard, wizard*, which were imported from French, and English formations such as *braggart, drunkard, sluggard.* This suffix is used to express nationality in *Spaniard, Savoyard*, probably at first with an idea of ridicule. It was also used to form names of animals, as in *buzzard, mallard* 'wild drake' [formed in French from the adjective *male*]; rarely to form names of things, as in *petard, poniard* [Old French *poing* 'fist'].

-ese, see under 'Adjective-forming.'

917. *-ess, French *-esse* from Latin *-issa* denotes female persons and—more rarely—female animals: *goddess, priestess, countess, shepherdess, patroness lioness, tigress.* Exceptional formations in point of meaning are *Jewess, negress*; *mayoress* ='wife of mayor.' Final weak and silent vowels are omitted before this suffix, as in *princess, negress, votaress* from *prince, negro, votary*. Nouns in *-er, -or* often throw out the vowel when *-ess* is added, as in *tigress, actress* from *tiger, actor*. Nouns in *-erer, -eror*, and some in *-urer* drop the second of these two weak syllables before *-ess*, as in *sorceress, conqueress* from *sorcerer, conqueror*. Similarly in *governess* from *governor*. Some words show further changes: *abbess, anchoress* from *abbot, anchorite*; *duchess* (*duke*), *marchioness* (*marquis*), *mistress* (*master*).

918. †**-ist**, Latin *-ista* from Greek *-istḗs*, generally expresses 'trade,' 'pursuit,' or adherence to a party, dogma etc.: *artist, florist, chemist, communist, royalist, deist*. It is used in a more general sense in such derivatives as *bigamist, copyist, provincialist*. In *tobacconist* from *tobacco* an *n* is inserted on the analogy of *botanist, mechanist* etc., in *egotist* by the side of *egoist* a *t* on that of *dramatist*, both insertions being prompted by the desire to avoid hiatus.

The parallel †**-ast** in *phantast, enthusiast*.

919. †**-ite**, Latin *-īta* from Greek *-ī́tēs*, is used to form names of nations, sects etc: *Canaanite, Israelite, Carmelite*; *jacobite*.

920. **-trix** is the Latin fem. of *-tor*: *executrix, testatrix* from *executor, testator*.

Diminutive.

921. **-ule**, **-cule**: *capsule, globule*; *animalcule*—also in the fuller Latin form *animalculum*—*corpuscule*. The latter ending was shortened to *-cle* in French in most words where the diminutive meaning was not prominent, whence the English *article, miracle, spectacle* etc. But several of them retain the diminutive meaning, especially where *i* precedes: *cuticle* 'outer thin skin,' *particle*.

922. -et, -let. *-et* forms diminutive nouns and adjectives: *circlet, islet, cygnet*; *dulcet, russet.* On the analogy of *circlet* from *circle* etc., where the *l* came to be regarded as part of the suffix, a new diminutive *-let* has developed itself, which is freely used in new-formations, such as *leaflet, streamlet, troutlet.* In many words these suffixes have lost their diminutive meaning.

Abstract.

923. *-y, -ey. *-y* represents Early MnE, ME and Old French *-ie* from Latin *-ia*, and is chiefly used to form abstract nouns, as in *fury, modesty, perfidy*, and in more popular French words, such as *company, courtesy, fancy.* Some of these words have more special and concrete meanings, such as *comedy, family, navy.*

-y = Latin *-ia* is frequent in names of countries, as in *Italy, Germany, Normandy*, although in most cases the full Latin ending has been restored, as in *Asia, India, Austria.* *-y* also corresponds to the Latin neuter ending *-ium*, as in *monastery, remedy, study*, forming concrete as well as abstract words.

924. *-y* is also the MnE representative of weak ME *-ē*, which when strong becomes *-ee* in MnE (**912**). *-y*=ME *-ē* from French *-é* = Latin *-ātus* (**945**), is sometimes abstract, but generally concrete in a collective sense or in names of districts: *treaty*; *clergy*; *county, duchy.*

925. It often answers to Old French *-ée* from Latin (generally Late Latin) *-āta* with the same meaning as *-ātus*: *destiny, entry*; *army, jury*; *country.*

926. The spelling *-ey* is a mere variety of *-y*, as in *Turkey* (ME *Turkīe*), *attorney* (French *-é*), *journey* (French *-ée*).

-y and *-ey* represent a variety of other French vowels in isolated words.

927. -ice, *-ess, *-ise from Latin *-itia, -itiēs*, Late Latin *-icia*, which in Latin were used chiefly to form abstract nouns from adjectives: *avarice, malice, notice.* The popular Old French form was *-esse*, kept in ME words such as *largesse* 'largess' [*large* 'liberal'], *richesse* 'riches' (**311.** 1). These suffixes were also used in Old French to form derivatives from nouns, whence the MnE *cowardice, merchandise*, which has a concrete meaning. There are some English new-formations in *-ice, -ise*: *practice, practise, treatise.*

928. -cy, -sy. These suffixes were first developed from the Latin combinations *-t-ia, -c-ia* in such words as *constancy, fallacy* from Latin *cōnstantia* (Late Latin *constancia*), *fallācia*, themselves formed from the derivative adjectives *cōnstāns* (*cōnstantem*), *fallāx* (*fallācem*). In MnE they are still associated with derivative *t* and *c*, often taking the place of other endings of Latin origin, especially *-tion*, as in *conspiracy* [compare *conspirator*], *degeneracy* [*degenerate*], *obstinacy* = Latin *cōnspīrātiō* etc. They have the same abstract meaning in many other new-formations, such as *intricacy, intimacy, lunacy* from *intricate, intimate, lunatic*, where the second suffix *-ic* is disregarded. In these words the *c* is still felt to be a modification of the derivative *t*, but in the still more recent formations *idiotcy* [also *idiocy*], *bankruptcy* the *t* is kept before it, so that the *-cy* has developed into an independent, primary suffix. A special use of these suffixes is to denote rank and office: *curacy, magistracy, ensigncy*; *minstrelsy.* Some of the above have also a collective sense. *legacy* has a concrete meaning.

929. †-ad, -id were used to form titles of epic poems, as in *Iliad* 'the tale of Ilium or Troy,' *Aeneid* 'the adventures of Aeneas,' whence many new-formations in modern times, such as *Lusiad*, *Columbiad*, the suffix *-ad* being often used to form titles of satirical poems, such as *The Dunciad* 'epic of dunces.'

930. The Greek *-ad* occurs also in other functions, being used especially to form abstract nouns from numbers, as in *monad*, *triad*, *myriad*, and *decade* with the French form of the suffix.

931. ***-ade** is a French adaptation of Italian *-ada* from Latin *-āta*, of which *-ée* is the regular French form, as in *armée*, whence the English *army* [compare the Spanish *armada*]. *-ade* generally forms collective nouns from other nouns: *balustrade*, *barricade*, *colonnade*; sometimes from verbs, as in *cavalcade* [Italian *cavalcare* 'ride']. It also forms abstract nouns from nouns and verbs: *blockade*, *promenade*, *serenade*.

932. ***-age** from Latin *-āticum* forms nouns from various parts of speech with a great variety of meanings, the most marked of which are (*a*) collectiveness, as in *baggage*, *bandage*, *plumage*; (*b*) profit or charge in relation to the root-word, as in *mileage* 'payment or allowance for travelling per mile,' also collectively 'aggregate of miles,' *postage*; (*c*) action or state (rank, quality): *coinage*, *tillage*, *voyage*: *bondage*, *courage*, *peerage*.

-al, see under 'Adjective-forming.'

933. **-ment**, Latin *-mentum*, forms nouns from verbs. It forms abstract nouns expressing action, state, or result, as in *argument*, *emolument*, which in Latin means both 'labour,' and 'gain.' So also in many new-formations: *agreement*, *employment*, *treatment*, which are formed from French verbs, and *bereavement*, *fulfilment*, which are formed from English verbs. In concrete words *-ment* expresses sometimes the means of an action, as in *instrument, ornament,* sometimes its result, as in *fragment, segment.*

934. From *-ment* is formed the adjective-suffix **-mental** (**958**), as in *experimental, instrumental,* whence again is formed the abstract noun-suffix **-mentality** (**947**), as in *instrumentality.*

-in, -ine, see 'Adjective-forming.'

935. -ion (**-sion, -tion**) from Latin *-iō* (*-iōnem*), which forms abstract nouns from verbs: *opinion, rebellion; compulsion, passion; education, action.* Some have developed concrete meanings, such as *nation, legion.* The popular Old French form of this suffix was *-ŏn,* the *i* being absorbed into the preceding sound in various ways, whence MnE *reason* [compare the more learned *ration*], *treason.* In less familiar words the Latin *i* was restored, whence the ME forms *opiniūn, condicioun* etc.

936. -ana is used in new-formations from names of persons to signify literary gossip about them, as in *Johnsoniana* 'sayings of, or anecdotes about Dr. Johnson,' *Walpoliana*; also publications bearing on them and their literary works, as in *Shakesperiana.* This suffix is the Latin neut. plur. of adjectives in *-ānus* (**963**), as used in such phrases as *dicta Vergiliāna* 'sayings of Virgil' (*Vergilius*). The detached *ana* has come to be used as a noun to signify 'collection of anecdotes of celebrities' etc.

937. -ance, -ence from Latin *-antia* (*-ancia*), *-entia* (*-encia*), which form abstract nouns from the present participle endings *-āns, -ēns,* acc. *-antem, -entem* (**970**), as in *arrogance, ignorance; experience, penitence.* The above words preserve their Latin roots, but most of the derivatives in *-ance* are of French formation: *entrance, grievance.*

938. These endings often take on the suffix *-y* (**923**), giving **-ancy, -ency**, as in *brilliancy, consistency* by the side of *brilliance, consistence*. In the case of *excellence, excellency* there is a difference of meaning. Some occur only in the longer form, such as *infancy, agency*.

939. -or, *-our from Latin *-or, -ōrem* forms abstract nouns, chiefly from verbs. In MnE the French spelling *-our* is preferred to the Latin *-or*, especially in more popular words, the usage being the contrary of that which prevails with the personal ending *-or* (**914**); but in America the shorter *-or* is consistently extended to the abstract *or*-derivatives as well, as in *honor*=British English *honour*, parallel with *author*. The following are examples of this suffix: *colour, honour*; *liquor, splendor*. There are some new-formations: *demeanour, behaviour*.

940. The lengthened ending **-ory**=Latin *-ōrius, -ōria*, forms adjectives and abstract nouns—in which *t*, (*s*) precede the ending—such as *obligatory, compulsory*; *history, victory*.

941. *-ry, Old French *-rie*, arose from the addition of the abstract suffix *-ie* (**923**) to the French ending *-(i)er* (**913**), as in *chevalerie, chivalerie* 'body of knights,' 'chivalry' from *chevalier* 'rider,' 'knight' [Late Latin *caballārius*]. In English also it was associated with the personal suffix *-er* through such derivatives as *fisher-y*. In MnE this suffix is mainly used in derivatives from nouns, and occasionally from adjectives, expressing (*a*) actions or qualities, as in *bigotry, drudgery, pleasantry*; (*b*) condition, as in *outlawry, slavery*; (*c*) occupation, trade, art etc., as in *casuistry, chemistry, heraldry*; (*d*) the place of actions, occupations etc., as in *nunnery, nursery*; (*e*) the result or product of action etc., as in *poetry, tapestry*; (*f*) collectivity, as in *peasantry, yeomanry*.

942. -ure from Latin *-ūra*, which is generally preceded by derivative *t*, (*s*). In popular Old French forms the *t* disappeared, in the same way as in *-ée* (**912**); thus Latin *armātūra* becomes in Old French *armeure*, which in MnE has become *armour* by the influence of the suffix *-our*. The *t* is of course preserved in learned words, such as *nature*. The chief function of this suffix is to form abstract nouns, generally from verb-roots: *figure*; *departure*; *composure*. It also forms concrete nouns, such as *furniture*, *picture*. In some words it has taken the place of *-ir*, *-or*, as in *pleasure*, *treasure*=Old French *leisir*, *pleisir*, *tresor*.

-ese, see under 'Adjective-forming.'

943. **†-ism**, Latin *-ismus*, from Greek *-ismós* is freely used to form abstract nouns expressing action, habit—especially habits of language or pronunciation—as attachment to some creed, party etc.: *Anglicism*, *archaism*; *despotism*, *patriotism*; *Calvinism*, *conservatism*. *egotism* by the side of *egoism* owes its *t* to *egotist* (**918**).

944. In Greek this suffix is added to adjectives in *-ikós* forming the compound suffix *-ikismós*, Latin *-icismus*, whence English **-icism**, as in *Atticism*, *fanaticism*, *Scotticism*, *witticism*. In the last two *-icism* must be regarded as a simple derivative, there being no corresponding adjective in *-ic*.

945. **-ate** from Latin *-ātus*, gen. *-ātūs* expresses office, function, as in *consulate*, *episcopate* and the new-formations *professorate*, being sometimes used to express the holder of the office, as in *magistrate*, and also in a collective sense, as in *syndicate*, *electorate* 'body of electors' (also 'dignity of Elector').

946. **-itude** from Latin *-itūdō* forms abstract nouns from adjectives: *fortitude*, *sollicitude*. In *multitude* it has developed a concrete meaning.

947. ***-ty** Latin *-tās*, *-tātem*, Old French *-te*, ME *-tē*- forms abstract nouns from adjectives: *liberty*; *variety*; *antiquity*, *vanity*. *-ity* is often added in this way to adjective-suffixes, so that, for instance, **-city** corresponds to *-cious*, as in *capacity* (*capacious*), **-idity** to *-id*, as in *timidity*, **-ality** to *-al*, as in *reality*, **-ility** to *-il* and *-ile*, as in *civility*, *fertility*, **-arity** to *-ar*, as in *regularity*, the most regular and frequent correspondence being that between *-ble* (**948**) and **-bility**, as in *nobility*, *durability*. The above are all of direct Latin origin. Others have passed through French changes, such as *certainty*, *plenty*, *pity*, *property*. In some words this suffix has a concrete meaning, as in *city*, *university*.

Adjective-forming.

948. ***-ble** from Latin *-bilis*, as in *nōbilis* 'noble,' *tolerābilis* 'tolerable,' *terribilis* 'terrible.' In English *-ble* is generally preceded by *a* or *i*—these being the vowels that most frequently precede it in Latin—only exceptionally by other vowels, as in *soluble*. In Latin it has no very definite meaning, and is used both in an active and passive sense; but in English the passive meaning prevails, *-ble* being associated with the adjective *able* from Latin *habilis*, *navigable*, for instance, being regarded as equivalent to 'able to be navigated.' So also in *admirable*, *legible*, *soluble*. In some however the suffix has an active meaning, as in *durable*, *favorable*; *forcible*, *sensible*. There are many new formations in *-able*, such as *unbearable*; *reliable* formed from *rely on*.

949. There is another suffix **-ble** of French origin, from Latin *-plex* (*-plicem*) '-fold,' which we have in the English word *double*, *treble*, the *p* of the Latin form being restored in *triple* and in formations from the higher numbers, such as *quadruple*, and in *multiple*.

950. **-bund**, ***-bond**: *moribund*, *rubicund*; *vagabond*, which is also a noun.

951. **-ic**, French *-ic*, *-ique* from Latin *-icus* and Greek *-ikós*, forms adjectives, generally from nouns, many of these derivations being also used as nouns, some exclusively so. Thus we have the Latin *domestic*, *public*, the Greek *catholic*, *tonic*. This suffix also forms part of the Latin compound suffix *-atic*, as in *aquatic*, *lunatic*. There is also a Greek ending *-tic* preceded by different vowels, in which the *t* is part of the body of the word: *emphat-ic*, *despotic*.

952. *-ic* is also used to form names of races and languages, as in *Celtic* (*Keltic*), *Germanic*, and new-formations such as *Finnic*, *Hanseatic*, formed from *Hansa*, *Hanse-towns* on the analogy of *Asiatic* from *Asia*.

953. Of the nouns in *-ic* some denote persons, such as *catholic*, *rustic* and the collective *public*, all of which are also adjectives, and *lunatic*, which is now used chiefly as a noun; while others denote things, such as *tonic*, others language, such as *Celtic*, *Gaelic*, which however is generally expressed by *-ish* (**985**). There are also many which denote arts and sciences, such as *arithmetic*, *logic*, *music*, especially in the plur.: *mathematics*, *optics*. In Greek *logic* was called *hē logikḗ tékhnē* 'the reason science,' where the adjective *logikós* is in the fem., agreeing with *tékhnē*; afterwards *logikḗ* by itself was used as a fem. noun, which was adopted into Latin, either unchanged—*logicē*—or with the Latin fem. ending—*logica*; and from Latin this and the other words of the same kind passed through French into English. In Greek these adjectives were also used as nouns in the neut. plur., as in *tà mathēmatiká*, literally 'the mathematical (things).' The MnE use of the plur. *mathematics* is an imitation of this usage, aided by the English habit of making adjectives into nouns by adding the plur. *-s*, as in *greens, news*.

954. Derivations in *-ic* often take on the adjective suffix *-al*, the new **-ical** and the shorter *-ic* being often used almost indifferently, as in *generic(al), mythic(al), poetic(al)*, while in other cases the addition of *-al* is accompanied by a marked divergence of meaning, as in *politic(al), comic(al)*. When a word in *ic(s)* is used exclusively as a noun, the corresponding adjective always takes *-al* for the sake of distinction, as in *music(al), mathematical*.

955. **†-iac** forms adjectives—which are sometimes also used as nouns—from nouns, the ending *-al* being often added, as in the case of *-ic* (**954**): *maniac, demoniac(al), Syriac*.

956. **-id** forms adjectives from adjectives, verbs, and nouns: *acid, fluid, intrepid, morbid, splendid*. Some of these, such as *acid* and *fluid*, are also used as nouns.

957. **†-oid.** Greek *-eidēs* from *eîdos* 'form' makes nouns into adjectives, such as *anthrōpoeidḗs* 'having the form of a man.' In Latin Greek *ei* is written *ī*, and as the ending was generally preceded by *o*, *-oid* has come to be regarded as an independent suffix in such words as *anthropoid* 'resembling man,' *rhomboid*; on the analogy of which there are numerous new-formations, such as *alkaloid, aneroid*, most of which are nouns.

958. **-al.** Latin *-ālis* is a very frequent adjective-ending, as in *equal, natural, royal*, which is the French form corresponding to the learned *regal*, both from Latin *rēgālis*. So also **-ial**: *essential, pestilential*.

959. *-al* is often added to the adjective-suffix *-ic* (**951**), the resulting **-ical** being often regarded as an independent suffix, whence such new-formations as *whimsical*.

960. *-al* also forms nouns with a great variety of meanings, such as *individual*, *general*; *animal*; *mineral*, *journal*, *capital*, all of which were originally adjectives, many of them being still used as such.

961. *-al* is especially used in MnE to form abstract nouns, mostly from verbs, such as *arrival*, *funeral*, *trial*. Some of these—such as *funeral*—had the same ending in ME, while others had the ending *-aille*, which is the old French form of the Latin adjective neut. plur. *-ālia* from *-ālis*. Thus *victuals* appears in ME in the form of *vitaille*, which is also the Old French form, from Latin *vīctuālia*, which afterwards influenced the spelling of the word.

962. **-il**, **-ile**, Latin *-ilis*, *-īlis*, the former being mainly from verb-roots, the latter from nouns. From *-ilis*: *fertile*, *fragile*. From *-īlis*: *civil*, *hostile*. In *gentle* we have an English shortening of French *gentil*, which was re-introduced into MnE in the form of *genteel*, *gentile* being a third doublet which represents the original Latin form *gentīlis* 'belonging to a *gēns* or family.' The shortening is French in *humble*, *subtle*, also written in the more learned form *subtile*.

963. **-an**, **-ane** from Latin *-ānus* forms adjectives denoting persons, such as *human*, *republican*, *veteran*, many of which are also used as nouns. Others, such as *publican* and the French *artisan*, are used only as nouns. This suffix is used especially to form adjectives and nouns denoting religious sects etc., such as *Anglican*, *Mahometan*, and nations, as in *Roman*, *American*; it has a similar function in *Elizabethan*.

964. The popular French form of this suffix was *-ain*, which is preserved in a few English words, such as *captain*, *villain*.

965. *-ane*, as in *humane*, *mundane* was in Early MnE a mere orthographic variant of *-an*, *human* and *humane* being written at random without any distinction of meaning.

966. -ean, French *-een*, which has the same meaning as *-an*(*e*), is a lengthened form of Latin *-aeus*, *-eus*, the lengthening *-aeānus* occurring in Latin itself in some words. By the influence of the English pronunciation of Latin the ending is in most words pronounced (·iən), but the older pronunciation, in which the suffix is short and weak, is still kept up in such words as *Mediterranean*, *herculean*. Strong *-ean* in *Pythagorean*; *Chaldean*, *European*.

967. -ian=Latin *-iānus* also has the same meaning as *-an*, being especially frequent in adjectives and nouns expressing occupation, rank etc.: *historian*, *musician*, *tragedian*; *patrician*, *plebeian*; *Christian*, *presbyterian*; *barbarian*, *Italian*.

968. -ine, **-in** from Latin *-inus*, *-īnus* forms numerous adjectives, some of which are also used as nouns: *Alpine*, *crystalline*, *elephantine*; *divine*, *feminine*; *Philistine*; *clandestine—Latin*. The pronunciation (·ijn) in *marine*, *machine* is an imitation of modern French.

969. There are many original nouns in Latin *-in*(*e*), such as *libertine*, *medicine*; *dolphin*, *resin*. There is a large number of chemical words in *-ine*, *-in*, such as *casein*(*e*), *iodine*. When such words become familiar they are generally written *-ine* and pronounced with the French (-ijn), as in *gelatine*, *glycerine*. So also in numerous newly formed trade-words, such as *brillantine*, *butterine*.

970. -ant, **-ent** from the Latin pres. partic. endings *-āns* (*-antem*), *-ēns* (*entem*), form adjectives and nouns from verbs. Adjectives: *arrogant*, *ignorant*; *eminent*, *innocent*. Nouns: *dependant* [adjective *dependent*], *inhabitant*, *student*; *torrent*; *instant*, *accident*. Many words in *-ant* are French formations:

brilliant, Early MnE, Old French *brillant*; *pleasant*; *merchant*, *servant*.

971. -lent, from Latin *-lentus* and *-lēns* (*-lentem*); *opulent*; *pestilent*, *violent*.

From these must be distinguished adjectives formed from present participles (969), such as *benevol-ent*, *insol-ent*.

-ple, see **-ble**.

972. -ar from Latin *-āris*: *familiar*, *regular*, *similar*. The popular Old French form of this suffix was *-er*, and some of the above words were introduced in ME English with it, such as *singuler*, but the ending was latinized in MnE.

973. -ary from Latin *-ārius* forms adjectives and personal nouns: *extraordinary*, *necessary*; *dignitary*, *incendiary*.

974. -ior. In Latin *-ior* (*-iōrem*) is the comparative ending of adjectives, which are also used as nouns: *inferior*, *superior*, *junior*, *senior*.

975. -ese from Latin *-ēnsis*, *-ēsis* forms adjectives and nouns from names of countries: *Chinese*, *Maltese*, *Portuguese*.

976. -ose, ***-ous** from Latin *-ōnsus*, *-ōsus*, which was used to form adjectives from nouns: *bellicose*, *verbose*; *fabulous*, *furious*, *glorious*. So also in the new-formations *mischievous*, *murderous*.

977. In MnE many Latin words were imported into the written language in the nom. masc. sing. inflection, because that was the one that came first in the dictionaries and grammars, *-us*—which is the most frequent form of this case in Latin—being written *-ous* on the analogy of *-ous*=Latin *-ōsus*; thus in MnE we have *barbarous* from Latin *barbarus* (fem. sing. nom. *barbara* etc.), the popular Old French *barbar* being also the ME form; so also in *credulous, obvious.* The less frequent nom. sing. masc. ending *-is* is made into *-ious*, as in *illustrious, scurrilous.*

978. ***-esque** from Italian *-esco*, Latin *-iscus*, forms adjectives and nouns: *arabesque, picturesque, statuesque.* The noun *burlesque* is also used as a verb.

979. -t, -te, -ate, -ite, -ute. *-t* often represents the ending of the Latin pret. passive partic., preceded sometimes by a consonant, but generally by the vowel *ā*, and occasionally by other vowels. Thus the following English adjectives come from Latin passive participles in *-t: content* [generally made into *contented*], *abrupt; accurate, private; complete; definite; absolute.* Others come from Latin passive participles with the Latin change of *t* into *s* in certain combinations: *dense, diverse.* Some of these—such as *content*—existed as popular words in Old French, the others being afterwards—in English as well as French—formed directly from the Latin passive participles on the analogy of the popular forms. In Latin, adjective-participles in *-ātus* were sometimes formed directly from nouns, as in the Latin words corresponding to *caudate* 'tailed,' *insensate*; and in MnE many more adjectives of this kind have been formed directly from Latin nouns, even where there are no such formations in Latin itself; thus we have *lunulate* 'shaped like a little moon,' 'crescent-shaped' [Latin *lūnula* 'little moon'], *angustifoliate* 'with narrow leaves.' *-ate* was also substituted for the French ending of the passive partic., as in *affectionate.*

980. Many of these adjectives naturally developed into nouns. In Latin itself we have personal (masc.) nouns such as *lēgātus* 'one deputed,' 'legate'; and in Late Latin *cūrātus*, which in Classical Latin is used only as an adjective 'careful,' has developed the meaning 'curate.' In Latin we have also neuter nouns in *-um* formed from these participle-adjectives, such as *mandātum* 'what is commanded,' 'mandate,' and Late Latin *manūscrīptum* 'hand-written,' 'manuscript.' Many others have been formed in modern times, some of which are used only as nouns, some also as adjectives: *delegate, favourite; extract, duplicate.* Some of these nouns are formed from the Latin pret. partic. of deponent verbs, which have an active meaning, such as *adept* 'one who has attained proficiency,' from the deponent verb *adipīscor* 'obtain.'

981. The chemical noun-suffix *-ate* arose from the Latin technical terms of the older chemists, who called the result of the action of vinegar (Latin *acētum*) on lead (Latin *plumbum*) *plumbum acētātum* 'vinegared lead,' or simply *acētātum*, which was regarded as a noun, whence we now say *acetate of lead, nitrate of soda*, shortened into *nitrate.* To express a less degree of chemical action the ending **-ite** has been arbitrarily formed from *-ate—nitrite of soda.*

982. In accordance with the general tendencies of English, many of these adjectives were made into verbs; thus, as the adjectives *dry* and *clear* (OE *drȳge*, Old French *cler*) had become indistinguishable from the verbs *to dry, to clear* (OE *ādrȳgan*, Old French *clairier*) so that the verbs seemed to be formed directly from the adjectives, so also such adjective-participles as *content, corrupt, separate* came to be used as verbs. At first the ending *-t(e)* did duty for the passive partic. of these new verbs, as in *he was contract to Lady Lucy* (Shakespere), *they have degenerate*, but they soon began to take the English inflection *-ed*, so that a distinction was made between *the land was desolate* (adj.) and *the land was desolated* (earlier *desolate*) *by war.* By degrees some of the new participles came themselves to be used as adjectives, such as *contented, situated* = the older *content, situate.* The ending *-ate* having now the function of a verb, it became usual to adopt Latin verbs into English in the form of their passive participles, especially when these were formed in *-ātus*; hence such verbs as *asseverate*, *venerate* were formed direct from the Latin verbs *assevērāre* etc. without the intervention of an adjective-partic. in *-ate*, although, of course, it is not always certain in individual cases whether there was such an intervening form or not. This verb-forming *-ate* was extended to verbs imported from French, as in *isolate* [French *isoler* from Latin *īnsulāre*, whence the more learned form *insulate*], *felicitate*. Lastly *-ate* has been used to form verbs from Latin words where there was no corresponding Latin verb in *-āre*, as in *incapacitate*, formed from Latin *capācitās*, *incapāx*, *substantiate*. *-ate* is also used to form verbs from words of non-Latin origin, such as *assassinate*.

983. **-ive** from Latin *-īvus* forms adjectives and nouns: *active*, *furtive*, *primitive*; *captive*, *native*; *alternative*, *motive*. The popular Old French form of this suffix was *-if*, preserved in MnE *caitiff*—of which *captive* is the learned doublet—*plaintiff*. In some of these the ending was afterwards Latinized as in *plaintive* from *plaintif*.

Verb-forming.

984. ***-fy**, French *-fier* from Latin *-ficāre*, a weakening of *facere* 'do,' 'make,' forms causative verbs from nouns and adjectives (pronouns): *deify*, *modify*; *fortify*, *purify*.

985. ***-ish**. Many French verbs in *-ir* conjugate partly with *-iss* before the inflections, which is taken from the Latin ending *-scō* (*-ēsco*, *-īscō* etc.) of inchoative verbs. In Old French this *ss*=Latin *sc* had nearly the sound (ʃ), and in ME it was extended to the infin. and all the other parts of the verbs that had it, as in *finisshen* 'finish,' *flŏrisshen* 'flourish'=

Old French *fenir* [Modern French *finir*], *flŏrir*, 1st pers. plur. pres. indic. *fenissons*, *flŏrissons* from Latin *finīre*, **finiscere*, *flōrēre*, *flōrēscere*. So also in *abolish*, *nourish*, *punish*. From such as these it was extended in ME to many French verbs which never had any iss-forms, as in *astonish* from Old French *estoner*, *distinguish*, *publish*. It was also used in purely English verb-formations, such as *famish* from *famine*.

The original Latin inchoative *-scere* occurs only in words taken directly from Latin or which were Latinized in French: *acquiesce*, *effervesce*, *effloresce(nt)*.

-ate, see under 'Adjective-forming.'

986. †**-ize**, **-ise**, French *iser*, Latin *-isāre*, *issāre* from Greek *-ízein*, is used to form verbs from nouns and adjectives. It occurs in Greek formations, such as *agonize*, *crystallize*, *theorize*; forms derivatives from Latin words, such as *civilize*, *patronize*, *realize*; from French words, as in *authorize*; and is freely employed in new-formations, such as *galvanize*, *hypnotize*. The spelling *-ize* in imitation of the Greek form of the suffix has now supplanted the older *-ise*.

INDEX

(The references are to the paragraphs.)

THE END.